**Integrated Motivational
Interviewing and Cognitive Behavioral Therapy (ICBT)**

Integrated Motivational Interviewing and Cognitive Behavioral Therapy (ICBT)

A Practitioners Guide

Joseph Hyde
JBS International
North Bethesda, Maryland
US

Maria Torres
School of Social Welfare, Stony Brook University
Stony Brook, New York US

Win Turner
Center for Behavioral Health Integration
School of Social Welfare, Stony Brook University
Montpelier, Vermont
US

R. Lyle Cooper
Meharry Medical College
Nashville, TN US

Copyright © 2024 by John Wiley & Sons, Inc. All rights reserved, including rights for text and data mining and training of artificial technologies or similar technologies.

Published by John Wiley & Sons, Inc., Hoboken, New Jersey.
Published simultaneously in Canada.

No part of this publication may be reproduced, stored in a retrieval system, or transmitted in any form or by any means, electronic, mechanical, photocopying, recording, scanning, or otherwise, except as permitted under Section 107 or 108 of the 1976 United States Copyright Act, without either the prior written permission of the Publisher, or authorization through payment of the appropriate per-copy fee to the Copyright Clearance Center, Inc., 222 Rosewood Drive, Danvers, MA 01923, (978) 750-8400, fax (978) 750-4470, or on the web at www.copyright.com. Requests to the Publisher for permission should be addressed to the Permissions Department, John Wiley & Sons, Inc., 111 River Street, Hoboken, NJ 07030, (201) 748-6011, fax (201) 748-6008, or online at http://www.wiley.com/go/permission.

Trademarks: Wiley and the Wiley logo are trademarks or registered trademarks of John Wiley & Sons, Inc. and/or its affiliates in the United States and other countries and may not be used without written permission. All other trademarks are the property of their respective owners. John Wiley & Sons, Inc. is not associated with any product or vendor mentioned in this book.

Limit of Liability/Disclaimer of Warranty: While the publisher and author have used their best efforts in preparing this book, they make no representations or warranties with respect to the accuracy or completeness of the contents of this book and specifically disclaim any implied warranties of merchantability or fitness for a particular purpose. No warranty may be created or extended by sales representatives or written sales materials. The advice and strategies contained herein may not be suitable for your situation. You should consult with a professional where appropriate. Further, readers should be aware that websites listed in this work may have changed or disappeared between when this work was written and when it is read. Neither the publisher nor authors shall be liable for any loss of profit or any other commercial damages, including but not limited to special, incidental, consequential, or other damages.

For general information on our other products and services or for technical support, please contact our Customer Care Department within the United States at (800) 762-2974, outside the United States at (317) 572-3993 or fax (317) 572-4002.

Wiley also publishes its books in a variety of electronic formats. Some content that appears in print may not be available in electronic formats. For more information about Wiley products, visit our web site at www.wiley.com.

Library of Congress Cataloging-in-Publication Data
Names: Hyde, Joseph, author. | Turner, Win, author. | John Wiley & Sons, publisher.
Title: Integrated motivational interviewing and cognitive behavioral therapy (ICBT) : a practitioners guide / Joseph Hyde, Win Turner.
Description: Hoboken, New Jersey : Wiley, [2024] | Includes index.
Identifiers: LCCN 2024006953 (print) | LCCN 2024006954 (ebook) | ISBN 9781394241927 (paperback) | ISBN 9781394241941 (adobe pdf) | ISBN 9781394241934 (epub)
Subjects: LCSH: Cognitive therapy. | Motivational interviewing.
Classification: LCC RC489.C63 H93 2024 (print) | LCC RC489.C63 (ebook) | DDC 616.89/1425–dc23/eng/20240403
LC record available at https://lccn.loc.gov/2024006953
LC ebook record available at https://lccn.loc.gov/2024006954

Cover Design: Wiley
Cover Image(s): © SDI Productions/Getty Images

Set in 9.5/12.5pt STIXTwoText by Straive, Pondicherry, India

SKY10076862_060524

Contents

Figures and Tables *vii*
Acknowledgements *viii*

Introduction *1*
To Students and Fellow Practitioners *1*
Key References Include *1*
The Following Features Help Make this Guide Practical *2*
The Guide is Organized Into Three Main Sections *2*

1 **An Overview of Proven Tools and Techniques for Motivational Interviewing/Motivational Enhancement Theory, and Cognitive Behavioral Therapy Treatment** *3*
Motivational Interviewing and Motivational Enhancement Therapy *3*
Motivational Interviewing and the Process of Change *5*
The Two Phases of Motivational Interviewing *6*
Cognitive Behavioral Therapy *14*
Treating Co-occurring Disorders *18*
Recovery Supports *20*
Patient Activation Within the Context of ICBT *20*
On Spirituality *20*
Enhancing Cultural Relevance in Clinical Practice *22*

2 **Clinician Guidance for 16 Sessions of Integrated Cognitive Behavioral Therapy** *28*
Introduction *28*
Law of Thirds *29*
Review of Progress and Between-session Challenges *33*
Session 1. Eliciting The Life Movie *36*
Session 2. Enhancing Situational Awareness *55*
Session 3. Learning Assertiveness *69*
Session 4. Supporting Recovery Through Enhanced Social Supports *85*
Session 5. Supporting Recovery Through Healthy Replacement Activities *97*
Session 6. Problem Solving *107*
Session 7. Handling Urges, Cravings, and Discomfort *120*
Session 8. Working with Thoughts: Part 1 *139*
Session 9. Working with Emotions *154*
Session 10. Making Important Life Decisions *172*

Session 11. Enhancing Self-awareness of Substance Use *191*
Session 12. Using Mindfulness, Meditation, and Stepping Back *208*
Session 13. Addressing Suicidality *220*
Session 14. Using Medication in Support of Treatment and Recovery *229*
Session 15. Engaging with Self-help *244*
Session 16. Using an MI/CBT Approach for Traumatic Stress and Substance Use *252*

3 Techniques and Tools Supporting Fidelity of Implementation and Clinical Supervision *279*
Introduction *279*
Acronyms *280*
Adherence Tools and Techniques: Checklists *281*
Clinical Supervision Techniques to Improve Adherence *282*
ICBT Clinician Checklist Protocol *283*

References *290*
Index *297*

Figures and Tables

Figures

Figure 1   The Three Types of Helping Interactions   *4*
Figure 2   Three Elements of Change   *5*
Figure 3   How a Patient Might Experience Ambivalence Toward Change   *6*
Figure 4   Personalized Reflective Discussions, Phase 1, Enhancing Motivation and Commitment to Treatment   *13*
Figure 5   Phase 2, Using Functional Analysis to Raise Awareness, Identify Treatment Priorities, and Individualize Treatment   *14*
Figure 6   Sample Therapy Sessions According to the Law of Thirds   *29*
Figure 7   New Roads Worksheet   *198*

Tables

Table 1   Clinical Interventions Addressing Substance Use and Mental Disorders   *19*
Table 2   Domains and Sample Questions from the Cultural Formulation Interview   *26*
Table 3   Common Predictors and Levels of Suicide Risk   *222*

Acknowledgements

Integrated Motivational Interviewing and Cognitive Behavioral Therapy for Adults: A Practitioners' Guide (ICBT) incorporates and revises previous works developed by JBS International, Inc., first published in 2013. Authors of this revised 2024 guide are Joe Hyde, LMHC, CAS; Maria Torres, PhD; Win Turner, PhD; and Lyle Cooper, PhD.

Thanks are extended to all who contributed content to and critically reviewed this guide. The following experts provided important input and generously shared their knowledge and expertise: Amber Murray, BSN, MA; Angie McKinney Jones, MSW; Patty Ferssizidis, PhD; Jody Kamon, PhD; and Andrea Coleman, MS.

A special thanks is extended to Jeannie Newman MLIS, MSW Managing Editor and to the JBS Editors for their support, careful review, and feedback in preparing this document.

We chose to write this guide for practitioners, using "plain English" and a practical approach. In developing the original manuscript, we sought to make it portable across settings. We came to later know that not only are these clinical interventions portable across settings, but also across most diagnoses. We looked at the work of Chorpita et al. (2005), who stated that across the majority of evidence-based practices, a common set of strategies and interventions addresses substance use disorder, depression, and anxiety. Portability is a value that informs our thought. This is more recently reflected in contemporary scholarship regarding process-based cognitive behavioral therapy that is transdiagnostic (Hayes & Hoffman, 2018).

Introduction

To Students and Fellow Practitioners

The treatment approach for mental disorders described in this guide follows a clinical method that draws on innovations and essential elements influenced by motivational interviewing (MI), motivational enhancement therapy (MET), mindfulness, values-based clinical practices, functional analysis, and cognitive behavioral therapy (CBT). Since the original guide was completed in 2013, we have continuously updated content to reflect (1) emerging science on behavioral health treatment and interventions, (2) recognition of gaps in what we have written, based on instructor and student feedback, and (3) a desire to incorporate our evolving social context reflecting social justice issues and lessons learned from the COVID-19 pandemic.

Key References Include

Beck, J., & Aaron, A. T. (2011). *Cognitive behavior therapy: Basics and beyond* 2nd ed. Guilford Press.

Carroll, K. M. (1998). A cognitive-behavioral approach: Treating cocaine addiction. *Manual 1: Therapy manuals for drug addiction series*. NIH Publication No. 94-4308. National Institute on Drug Abuse. https://archives.drugabuse.gov/sites/default/files/cbt.pdf.

Hayes, S. C., & Hofmann, S. G. (Eds.) (2018). *Process-based CBT: The science and core clinical competencies of cognitive behavioral therapy*. New Harbinger Publications, Inc.

Marlatt, G. A., Barrett, K., & Daley, D. C. (1999). Relapse prevention. In Galanter, M., & Kleber, H. D. (Eds.), *The American Psychiatric Press textbook of substance abuse treatment* 2nd ed. American Psychiatric Press.

Miller, W. R., & Rollnick, S. (2012). *Motivational interviewing: Helping people change* 3rd ed. Guilford Press.

Sampl, S., & Kadden, R. (2001). Motivational enhancement therapy and cognitive behavioral therapy for adolescent cannabis users: Five sessions. *Cannabis Youth Treatment Series*, Vol. 1. Substance Abuse and Mental Health Services Administration (SAMHSA). https://eric.ed.gov/?id=ED478681.

Steinberg, K. L., Roffman, R. A., Carroll, K. M., McRee, B., Babor, T. F., Miller, M., & Stephens, R. (2005). *Brief counseling for marijuana dependence: A manual for treating adults*. HHS Publication No. (SMA) 05-4022. Center for Substance Abuse Treatment, SAMHSA. https://store.samhsa.gov/sites/default/files/d7/priv/sma15-4211.pdf.

Integrated Motivational Interviewing and Cognitive Behavioral Therapy (ICBT): A Practitioners Guide, First Edition. Joseph Hyde, Maria Torres, Win Turner, and R. Lyle Cooper.
© 2024 John Wiley & Sons, Inc. Published 2024 by John Wiley & Sons, Inc.

The Following Features Help Make this Guide Practical

a) Across many evidence-based practices (EBPs) for a variety of behavioral health conditions, clinical researchers have identified a common set of practice elements (Chorpita et al., 2005; Chorpita & Regan, 2009). This guide is informed by the call to focus on training and to disseminate these essential skills across the health care system and to promote the use of these universal clinical interventions (Barlow, 2008).
b) The guide's 16 core interventions are designed to fit within conventional models of service and can span diverse practice settings (e.g., general outpatient services embedded within primary care settings, including federally qualified health centers and general outpatient substance use disorder [SUD] or mental health settings).
c) The evidence-based clinical skills and interventions presented in this guide are easily transferable from one setting to another.
d) The clinical sessions are clearly laid out without being overly prescriptive or restrictive. The interventions are flexible enough to be integrated into clinicians' personal styles and creativity (i.e., they do not have to be followed in a particular order).

The Guide is Organized Into Three Main Sections

- **Section 1** reviews MI, MET, CBT, the personal reflective summary as a treatment tool and some of the newest thinking on the processes of therapy.
- **Section 2** provides guidance for the implementation of 16 distinct clinical strategies. Sessions focus on engaging, building motivation, clarifying treatment priorities for the patient, and developing a patient–clinician agreement. Other sessions address skills training, effective and healthy replacement activities, building personal awareness and mindfulness, developing specific skills to manage cravings and urges to use substances, and managing distressing thoughts and emotions. Two sessions cover known beneficial strategies equally useful with all treatment approaches: (1) use of medications in support of treatment and recovery and (2) engagement with self-help. The format of each session facilitates delivery of sessions according to a common framework, while, at the same time, tailoring delivery of selected sessions to a patient's individual needs. Session tools will help clinicians learn and understand delivery of each session, facilitate specific session feedback, and reduce paperwork burdens. *Session handouts and forms, other supporting materials, and references appear at the end of the guide, along with a list of acronyms used throughout.*
- **Section 3** discusses techniques and tools that support adoption and sustained implementation of interventions, with a focus on enhancing fidelity. The techniques include a discussion of proven strategies for enhancing clinical supervision to increase competency in essential clinical skills.

We encourage users of this guide to first read it through and then to use the session outlines and fidelity tools to support delivery of the interventions with their clients based on their goals and needs. Worksheets, handouts, and other materials appear in corresponding sections at the end of the guide and may be copied and used as needed in sessions.

Earlier editions of this guide focused principally on addressing SUDs and co-occurring disorders. This edition reflects that these clinical strategies are trans-diagnostic.

Section 1

An Overview of Proven Tools and Techniques for Motivational Interviewing/Motivational Enhancement Theory, and Cognitive Behavioral Therapy Treatment

Current approaches to understanding the treatment of substance use, mental illness, and COD are driven by empirical advances in neuroscience and behavioral research rather than by theories alone. Good evidence now exists that biological factors, psychosocial experiences, and environmental factors influence the development, continuation, and severity of disorders. Contributing experiences may occur at home, at work, or in the community, and a stressor or risk factor may have a small or profound effect, depending on individual and environmental differences. The following review of motivational interviewing (MI), motivational enhancement therapy (MET), personalized reflective summary (PRS), and cognitive behavior therapy (CBT) informed by this evidence provides context for the treatment sessions in this guide.

Motivational Interviewing and Motivational Enhancement Therapy

MI is an effective, evidence-based method for helping patients with a variety of health and behavioral concerns. Motivational approaches, as developed by Miller and Rollnick (2012), seek to foster the intrinsic drive people have for healing, positive change, and self-development. Since Miller and Rollnick's original work was published in 1983, more than 25,000 articles citing MI and 200 randomized clinical trials of MI have appeared in print. MI's efficacy has been substantiated by several MI training research projects (Miller et al., 2004).

Integrating Motivational Enhancement and Cognitive Behavioral Skills Building to Elicit Change—How It Works

- Motivational enhancement is achieved by building rapport through reflective discussions, helping patients understand the pros and cons of use, and establishing collaborative goals based on the patient's needs and values.
- Motivational enhancement strategies assess and increase the patient's readiness, willingness, and ability to change.
- The clinician's first and primary task is to engage and collaborate with the patient to build internal motivation.

Integrated Motivational Interviewing and Cognitive Behavioral Therapy (ICBT): A Practitioners Guide, First Edition. Joseph Hyde, Maria Torres, Win Turner, and R. Lyle Cooper.
© 2024 John Wiley & Sons, Inc. Published 2024 by John Wiley & Sons, Inc.

- In CBT, behavioral health issues are viewed as interrelated intra- and interpersonal issues, recurring and habitual disorders that can be successfully treated.
- Through treatment, the patient learns to become aware of situations and emotions and of how to cope, solve problems, and build healthy replacement actions to achieve wellness.

Figure 1 The Three Types of Helping Interactions

MET is a structured intervention approach that uses MI techniques. MET interventions typically involve specific feedback and a reflective discussion with the client following screening or assessment and a goal-setting interaction (planning). The descriptions of MET sessions in this guide include scripts illustrating the effective use of MI techniques.

MET, a short-term technique originally used in the treatment of alcohol and SUDs, was later included in the treatment of anxiety and depression. This approach to treatment focuses on helping people feel more motivated to change their harmful behavior. It integrates aspects of MI and the transtheoretical model of change.

MI categorizes helping interactions according to the following three styles: directing, guiding, and following (see Figure 1). With a directing style, the helper provides information, instruction, and advice. This contrasts with the following style, which is defined by listening, understanding, and not influencing another's choice. In the middle of these styles is the guiding approach, which emphasizes listening and offers expertise and direction when requested or needed.

MI research has demonstrated that the clinician's choice of interaction style (i.e., directing, guiding, or following) directly affects the process for the patient's readiness for change. Intrinsic desires for change and accompanying "change talk" increase when the clinician helps the patient explore the discrepancies between current behaviors, values, and goals. Change talk refers to a patient's discussion of their desire, ability, reason, and need to change a behavior, as well as a commitment to changing. If the clinician mistakenly offers too much unsolicited advice, the patient's arguments against change increase and become "sustain talk," the opposite of the desired effect (Miller & Rollnick, 2012). Sustain talk is usually characterized by talking about why change cannot happen.

It is most helpful when the clinician seeks a collaborative partnership with patients. This partnership is characterized by a respectful evoking of their own motivation, wisdom, values, and goals and of the knowledge that whether or not change happens comes down to each person's choice, an autonomy that cannot be taken away no matter how much one might wish that at times. This approach is often referred to as encompassing the MI spirit. Buber (1971) describes such interactions as an "I–thou" manner of interacting that values the opinions of others and does not objectify them to manipulate ("I–it") (Miller & Rollnick, 2012). MI spirit respects that both clinicians and patients bring expertise to the session. Clinicians bring expertise in processes that support and facilitate change. Patients are experts in their lives. MI spirit invites clinicians to bring their true selves to the encounter. The authentic self goes beyond what you do for a living or who you are to someone else (e.g., mom, brother, and girlfriend). It is who you are at your core—your kindness, values, compassion, and empathy. Evidence suggests that as we bring and practice compassion, our patients begin to experience more self-compassion.

Several excellent clinician workbooks and easy-to-use competence scales can assist in learning and practicing the techniques described here. For those with limited exposure to MI, it would be helpful to read about MI and to participate in MI skills training. See http://www.motivationalinterviewing.org/mi-resources for more information. The first two sessions in Chapter 2 of this guide are based on MI and MET techniques.

Motivational Interviewing and the Process of Change

Change occurs all the time as a natural and self-directed event. Examples of natural changes that might take place over our lifetimes include moving to a new home, ending or beginning a significant relationship, or changing jobs. Many times, addressing a change in one domain affects another. For example, if a person is working to address depression, taking care of their physical body could be part of the treatment plan. Similarly, if a person just received a concerning diagnosis, the decision to work with a social worker or therapist to address the impact of the diagnosis on their mental health could be part of the treatment plan.

Three elements of any change are readiness, motivation, and ambivalence (see Figure 2). Miller and Rollnick (2012) break down readiness to change into three components: (1) an awareness of the problem, (2) a commitment to doing something, and (3) the action of making a change. This model is based on the theory of change developed by Prochaska and DiClemente (1998). The theory proposes a "stages of change" model consisting of precontemplation, contemplation, preparation, action, and maintenance. The model is viewed as cyclical rather than linear, with relapse occurring, so the individual may cycle back through the stages several times.

Traditional views of motivation held that it was static; therefore, clinicians had little or no influence over a patient's motivation. Patients were viewed as either motivated or not. If a patient was not motivated, this was considered the patient's problem or a sign of resistance to treatment, and sometimes the individual was blamed for not being motivated. Individuals who were motivated agreed to follow all instructions and accepted the labels (e.g., alcoholic) given to them. Individuals who were not motivated resisted the idea of having a problem and refused to follow treatment protocol.

It has since been discovered that motivation is fluid and changing rather than fixed. It is influenced by internal life and life circumstances and, in the case of therapy, by the style of the clinician (Miller et al., 1993), clinician's expectations (Leake & King, 1977), and patient's expectations. Motivation is influenced positively by clinicians who listen empathetically and negatively by

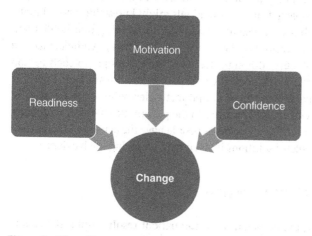

Figure 2 Three Elements of Change

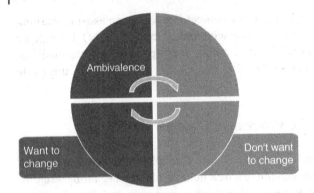

Figure 3 How a Patient Might Experience Ambivalence Toward Change

clinicians who are confrontational. A clinician's bias about a patient can also have an adverse effect on the patient's motivation.

Characterizing a patient as resistant, unmotivated, lazy, manipulative, or difficult often becomes a self-fulfilling prophecy that leads to more self-defeating attitudes (e.g., fear of failure, reluctance to being dependent on others, and hypersensitivity to feeling controlled by someone else). The MI approach suggests that if the clinician changes the way of interacting with a patient, the patient will interact differently with the clinician. Change is more likely when the clinician maintains a perspective of hope, optimism, and possibility and views the patient as capable of evolving and engaging meaningfully in a transformation process.

Others can elicit and reinforce motivation. Understanding motivation as interactional leads to clinicians viewing lack of motivation as a strategy to protect against fear of failure, loss, unwanted dependence on others, or having others in control. This understanding, in turn, increases the clinician's acceptance of the individual and decreases the need to control and confront the individual.

Ambivalence, the third element of change, is the result of simultaneous, competing motivations that lead in different directions (see Figure 3). Examples include the following:

- Desire to gain medication benefits and avoid side effects
- Desire to be strong and healthy and to relax and eat enjoyable foods
- Hope for change and fear of failure

MI is based on the idea that people generally are not unmotivated but, rather, have multiple, competing motivations. This is where people get stuck. Individuals might know they should make a change or that things could be better, but they also are attached to something that holds them back (e.g., drugs, friends, a relationship, convenience, familiarity, and security). Ambivalence is a normal component of psychological problems, although the specifics are unique to each person and sometimes to each situation. Ambivalence protects the side that does not want to change.

While a clinician's natural tendency might be to support or protect a viewpoint, it is wise to avoid "taking a side" prematurely because this will invoke reactance in the patient. Reactance is reluctance on the patient if they perceive a loss of autonomy. MI assumes people have the capacity to solve their own problems and to come up with resourceful solutions if given help removing the barriers.

The Two Phases of Motivational Interviewing

There are two phases of MI. In phase 1, the clinician helps the patient resolve ambivalence and build motivation. In phase 2, the clinician helps to strengthen commitment and to create a plan for change. Phase 1 generally demonstrates the patient-centered aspect of MI, with more directive interactions taking place in phase 2. In some cases, it is first necessary to raise the awareness of ambivalence or conflicting motivations before resolving the ambivalence.

Phase 1 of Motivational Interviewing: Engaging, Resolving Ambivalence, and Building Motivation

The work of phase 1 is based on the MI spirit, applying specific principles using identified strategies.

Spirit. The MI spirit is the underlying assumption that individuals can develop in the direction of health and adaptive behavior, given the tools and opportunity to do so. This belief is essential for the full and effective use of MI, along with a willingness to entertain the possibility of:

- **Collaboration.** Work in partnership with the patient.
- **Empowerment.** Listen, elicit, and affirm from the patient.
- **Autonomy.** Accept the patient's ability to choose.
- **Compassion.** Nourish another's well-being and growth.

Steps. The four steps generally considered essential to MI include:

1) Developing discrepancy
2) Reducing discord
3) Expressing empathy
4) Supporting autonomy

The purpose of **developing discrepancy** is to create a disconnection between where the person has been or currently is and where the person wants to be. The goal is to resolve the discrepancy by changing behavior. Resistance is seen as a behavior and, as such, is a state and not a permanent trait of an individual.

The principle of **reducing discord** implies it takes two to resist. It is interpersonal. Fortunately, discord is highly responsive to the clinician's style. Specific suggestions for reducing discord are described below.

Expressing empathy is one of the most important elements of MI. High levels of empathy during treatment have been associated with positive treatment outcomes across different types of psychotherapy. The key to expressing empathy is reflective listening, a specific and learnable skill. By listening in a supportive, reflective manner, the clinician demonstrates understanding of the patient's concerns and feelings. An empathetic style will:

- Communicate respect for and acceptance of the patient and their feelings
- Encourage a nonjudgmental, collaborative relationship
- Establish a safe and open environment for the patient that is conducive to examining sensitive issues and to eliciting personal reasons and methods for change
- Allow the clinician to be a supportive and knowledgeable consultant
- Compliment rather than denigrate
- Gently persuade, with the understanding that change is the patient's choice

When a clinician **supports autonomy**, the patient's ability to make decisions and choices is recognized and respected. This implies that responsibility for the patient's behavior resides with the patient. The clinician also supports the patient as the only one who can make choices about changing behavior.

Motivational Interviewing Strategies

The first and core MI strategy is described using the mnemonic OARS, which consists of:

- **Open-ended questions**
- **Affirmations**
- **Reflections**
- **Summaries**

Open-ended questions cannot be answered with a *yes* or *no* response or with brief, specific information (e.g., "I'm from Jefferson City"). Rhetorical questions are not open-ended and avoid socially desirable responses. Open-ended questions enable the clinician to explore widely for information and help uncover the patient's priorities and values. Open-ended questions engage and draw out the patient.

Examples of Open-Ended Questions

- *Where did you grow up?*
- *Tell me a bit about your work.*
- *What brings you here today?*

Affirmations affirm a person's struggles, achievements, values, and feelings. They emphasize the individual's strength or notice and appreciate a positive action. Affirmations should always be genuine and express positive regard and caring.

Examples of Affirmations

- *It takes courage to face such difficult problems. This is hard work you are doing.*
- *You really care a lot about your family. Your anger is understandable.*

Reflections are statements made after a patient's communications. They provide a way for the listener to confirm understanding of what was said or meant. A reflection can be a guess or hypothesis about what was really meant. Reflections are made as statements where the inflexion goes down at the end of the statement. They are the primary way to respond to patients. As a guess, the statement may not be accurate, and the patient will respond and clarify what was meant.

There are two types of reflections, simple and complex. Simple reflections express exactly what was heard. They rephrase (repeat with new words) the patient's comments.

Example of Simple Reflection

Patient: I did not want to come in.
Clinician: I hear you do not want to be here today

Complex reflections paraphrase (make a guess about unspoken meaning) or reflect the feeling or both. Generally, simple reflections are more common at the beginning of the relationship, and complex (deeper) reflections occur more frequently as understanding increases. There are several types of complex reflections:

- Double-sided reflection presents both sides of what the patient is saying, which is extremely useful in pointing out ambivalence.
- Amplified reflection amplifies or heightens the resistance that is heard.
- Reframing or "getting a new pair of glasses" suggests a new way of looking at something that is more consistent with behavior change or change talk of the patient.

Examples of Complex Reflection

Patient (P): I do not want to be here today.
Clinician (C): I hear that. So, how come you decided to show up?
P: I'm on probation for possessing weed, and, if I do not show up, I could end up in jail.
C: So, your freedom and calling your own shots in your life is really important to you.

Summaries are statements that pull together the comments made and transition to the next topic. They are helpful for moving the conversation along. Summaries should only be used after a minimum of three reflections.

Example of a Summary

You mentioned a number of things about your current lifestyle, such as cutbacks at work and the stress you feel. You spoke of having little energy for doing some of the things you used to like to do and did to relax. What do you think might help you get back to doing some of the things you once enjoyed?

Giving Advice

Clinicians frequently ask when they may give advice or provide information during MI. Giving advice or information at the wrong time or with the wrong approach is one way to encourage resistance from patients. There are three situations where giving advice is appropriate:

- The patient asks for advice or information.
- The clinician asks permission to give advice.
  - "May I make a suggestion?"
  - "Would you be interested in some resources?"
  - "Would you like to know what has worked for some other people?"
- The clinician qualifies the advice to emphasize autonomy.
  - "A lot of people find that [____] works well, but I don't know if that's something that interests you."

Example of Giving Advice

You know, that's certainly something I can do, but I'm wondering if I really have enough information about the problem to give you good advice right now. Would you mind telling me a little bit more about the situation?

When a patient asks for advice, it is important that the clinician not jump in if the patient does not seem ready or sincere. In these situations, it is more appropriate to ask permission to get more information before giving advice.

Too often in treatment settings, patients are labeled "resistant" if they do not want to change and/or argue against recommendations to do so. Miller and Rollnick (2012) intentionally have moved away from using the term "resistant," as it is negative, inaccurate in its implications, and not useful in training MI skills to help patients with change. Instead, MI theory considers these interactions as composed of two elements: ambivalence residing in the patient and the skill level of the provider. When arguments or sustain talk are present, it is predictive of no change. These types of patient expressions are a signal of cognitive dissonance and often are reactions to the provider's counseling style.

In simple terms, cognitive dissonance is an uncomfortable feeling caused by contradictory ideas (e.g., when beliefs and values contradict one's behavior). People are motivated to reduce the dissonance by changing attitudes, beliefs, and behaviors or by justifying or rationalizing attitudes, beliefs, and behaviors. When encountering discord and/or expressions of sustain talk, it is important to avoid arguments with the individual. Do not push back, as this puts the individual in the position of defending the opposite side. The old term "rolling with resistance" implied that to help elicit change, the clinician would go with the direction of the conversation rather than confronting, preaching, or trying to control the conversation. The use of reflections, particularly complex reflections, is one way a clinician can help reduce sustain talk. It is also helpful to remind the patient (and for the clinician to remind themself) about autonomy and to let the patient know that change is ultimately their choice.

Phase 2 of Motivational Interviewing: Building Change Talk, Strengthening Commitment, and Building Confidence

Change talk can flow naturally by simply using OARS. The application of OARS is primarily a patient-centered mode and explores the patient's ambivalence about behavior change. Often through empathic, reflective listening, the patient's ambivalence shifts toward the "change" side and away from the "status quo" side of the ambivalence. During this phase, trust and rapport have been established to the extent that the patient is ready to collaborate in resolving the ambivalence.

Recognizing Change Talk Versus Sustain Talk

Change talk and sustain talk are opposites. Sustain talk supports keeping things the same. Change talk expresses movement in the direction of change.

> **Examples of Change Talk and Sustain Talk**
>
> *Sustain talk:* "Marijuana has never affected me."
> *Change talk:* "It isn't worth it to be landing in jail."

There are seven types of change and commitment talk, represented by the mnemonic DARN-CAT:

- Desire to change ("want, like, wish ...")
- Ability to change ("can, could ...")
- Reasons to change ("if ... then ...")
- Need for change ("got to, have to, need to ...")

- Commitment ("I will")
- Activation ("making a plan, starting action")
- Taking steps ("I did, I started doing")

The MI goal in phase 2 is to increase the change talk and decrease the sustain talk.

Change Talk Discussion

When change talk does not occur naturally, tools can be used to elicit it. When trust is developed, questions that would earlier have been classified as roadblocks that engendered resistance are now classified as techniques for eliciting change talk. Thus, it is important to not introduce the change talk discussion too early (i.e., not before the patient has sufficiently explored the ambivalence about the behavior and is now ready to explore and resolve ambivalence about change). It is only at this point that the more directive techniques can be employed. The following are strategies for eliciting change talk:

- Ask evocative questions.
- Explore the decisional balance (weighing costs and benefits).
- Ask for elaboration or examples.
- Use a looking-back question (to a time when things were OK).
- Use a looking-forward question (how does the patient want life to be different?).
- Query the extremes (the worst that could happen if the patient quits and the best that could happen if the patient quits).
- Use the change/readiness rulers.
- Explore goals and values.

Commitment Talk

Commitment is the language that confirms something different will happen. The difference between change talk and commitment talk lies in the strength of the statement. During change talk, the idea of change is explored; with commitment talk, the intention to make the changes is expressed. Good questions to use for eliciting commitment talk are: "Will you do it?" If so, "Where, when, and with whom?" The more specific the answer generated, the more likely the action will take place. Being accountable to oneself and others is often part of the lesson learned in the treatment process. Clinicians are encouraged to elicit commitment talk and subsequent follow-through at the end of each session to affirm patient engagement and skills practice and to gradually shape commitment for dramatic behavior change.

Examples of Change Talk and Commitment Talk
Change talk: "I know my kids want me to." *Commitment talk:* "I'll definitely give it a go."

Bridging Screening and Assessment to Treatment: The Personalized Reflective Discussion

The MI and MET approach to building initial collaborations from the "get go" uses screening and assessment results to generate a specific type of reflective discussion, which results in this PRD. This discussion aims to increase the following: (1) awareness for areas of strength and risks, (2) readiness and the desire to change, (3) reasons and most needed targets of change, and (4) plans to work together to develop the most helpful path toward wellness. Although individuals may be aware that they are using a particular substance or are depressed (or both), they may not realize they are at significant risk for negative health and other consequences. Simply hearing information reflected back—summarized to include the pros and cons/risks they themselves have shared—can be a powerful motivator.

Clinicians in clinic settings conduct evaluations or review results from assessments with patients in treatment. Earlier work using personalized feedback reports (e.g., Sampl & Kadden, 2001) often gathered the following information during the assessment sessions(s):

Personal Reflective Summary (Substance Use)
- Alcohol and/or substances used by the patient
- Perceived benefits of use
- Levels of use (e.g., frequency and quantity)
- Problems associated with using alcohol or other substances (e.g., physical/emotional health, relationships, work, and role functioning)
- Current and past misuse or dependence symptoms
- Reasons to quit or to make a change
- Current motivational level regarding substance use and change
- Feelings of confidence or efficacy in being able to accomplish desired changes
- Other co-occurring concerns

Personal Reflective Summary (Behavioral Health Issues)
- Symptoms (e.g., depression, anxiety, and trauma)
- Findings from validated screenings (e.g., Patient Health Questionnaire-9 [PHQ-9] and Generalized Anxiety Disorder 7-item Scale [GAD-7])
- Problems associated with behavioral health concerns (e.g., affect and self-limiting thoughts, physical/emotional health, relationships, work, role functioning, alcohol, or other substance misuse)
- Life stressors
- Current duration and history of symptoms
- Helpful/nonhelpful medications taken
- Reasons for seeking help or making a change
- Current motivational level regarding capacity to make a change
- Feelings of confidence or efficacy in being able to accomplish desired changes

The examples listed above represent themes for substance use and for mental health concerns, helping to develop a collaborative understanding, as well as themes for treatment goals and the most appropriate session skills to deliver.

MI/MET sessions make use of the PRS as an enhancement of previous reflective summary approaches, which focus on motivation only. The first clinical session, "the Life Movie," is an MET session.

The following describes the PRS process:

- Following the intake process and after the assessment meeting with the patient, the clinician should be aware of the following:
- A working hypothesis on the focus of treatment and that those services can be provided in this setting. The focus of treatment can include the primary areas of concern and examine the domains listed above, including severity (which includes history, benefits of use, problems caused by use, and reasons for considering change) and current motivation to change
- Client readiness (reasons for change)

- Client priorities for treatment
- Use of medications (if any) and medication adherence
- Resources for social support
- Additional life domains (e.g., passions or strengths, including hobbies or interests, spirituality, and employment)
- The clinician delivers "Clinical Session 1: The Life Movie" with the goals of better understanding the person's life and building a working collaboration to support the client on their path toward wellness. The session helps build a bridge from the intake assessment to the integrated motivational interviewing and cognitive behavioral therapy (ICBT) sessions by helping to clarify client priorities and to better understand the internal and external context for patient issues. Sessions 1 and 2 describe details.
- In Sessions 1 and 2, the clinician uses MI/MET reflective discussions and applies functional analysis strategies to help identify and plan treatment sessions (Carroll, 1998; Leahy, 1996; Longabaugh et al., 2005; Agostinelli et al., 1995; Davis et al., 2003; Juarez et al., 2006). This strategy helps patients and clinicians identify issues within a broader contextual framework and set treatment priorities that will help patients engage in specific treatment sessions that address those needs. Session 2 further details this process.

For the important Session 2, the primary objective is to identify functional relationships between patient intrapersonal and interpersonal processes that are linked and that can trigger substance use or emotional disruptions, traumatic responses, or other mental illness symptoms. Too often, such "functional analysis conversations" have occurred in a somewhat mechanistic fashion. Clinicians are encouraged to use a more dynamic approach that emphasizes rapport between the clinician and patient, stronger collaboration, and increasing awareness of the pros and cons of behaviors. The discussion can begin to shift toward a more specific identification of the patterns of behavior. Importantly, this process also facilitates a clearer understanding and builds personal awareness, a core CBT goal.

Functional analysis is a core skill and strategy for patient awareness raising. This awareness raising is the building block for nearly all behavioral therapies and helps the patient create the space between stimulus and response, where the patient has the opportunity to make a conscious decision.

Figures 4 and 5 illustrate personalized reflective discussions with the two interrelated processes.

The types of dialogue the two figures illustrate help build patient self-awareness and facilitate readiness for change. This allows the patient to focus on what needs to be done as preparation for

Figure 4 Personalized Reflective Discussions, Phase 1, Enhancing Motivation and Commitment to Treatment

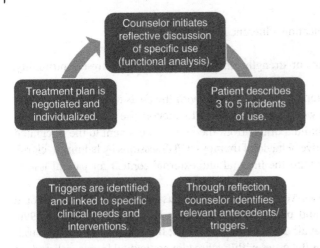

Figure 5 Phase 2, Using Functional Analysis to Raise Awareness, Identify Treatment Priorities, and Individualize Treatment

that change. The discussion following routine engagement conversations focuses on having the patient describe three to five previous incidents when they used substances or another target behavior of concern. The clinician elicits the antecedents, patient's internal experience, interpersonal or situational factors, perceived benefits, and consequences of the behavior.

Through this dynamic conversation, the clinician listens for and reflects on what the patient identifies as skills deficits and other needs that may be addressed within the treatment process. Following this discussion, the clinician summarizes the identified needs and seeks concurrence from the patient to address them within the proceeding treatment sessions. Through this process, every treatment experience is individualized and tailored to the unique needs of the person seeking services. The clinician gains insight into which specific skills-oriented and/or recovery-support sessions to cover in treatment.

Clinicians are encouraged to use the sample forms provided with the session descriptions in Chapter 2 or to develop their own format based on their particular style or the information collected at their clinics. Creating and sharing the PRS gives a focus to critical information in the screening and assessment process.

As a patient expresses increasing interest in modifying behaviors, the clinician carefully supports the efforts to change without directly prescribing the change. When the patient expresses a commitment to change, the clinician asks the patient about the steps that they will take to make the change. The clinician may provide a menu of self-change and clinician-assisted change options, depending on the patient's interests and experience in making personal changes. Self-change advice may be in the form of a brief handout about behavioral changes. The clinician-assisted change takes place through the agreed-upon treatment sessions.

Cognitive Behavioral Therapy

Models of CBT are the most extensively evaluated interventions for the treatment of both mental health conditions, including depression, anxiety, and trauma; alcohol/substance use disorders and CODs; and certain health conditions (e.g., chronic pain). Multiple meta-analyses (Magill & Ray, 2009) have demonstrated efficacy in the treatment of mental and substance use disorders. CBT originally was primarily based on the works of Marlatt and Gordon (1985) and Beck. From these foundational works have grown models for relapse prevention for SUDs and newer applications (e.g., mindfulness-based CBT, dialectical and behavioral therapy, acceptance, and commitment therapy) addressing a range of behavioral health conditions and substance use. These interventions target cognitive, behavioral, affective, and situational triggers for substance use, mood disorders, and anxiety and provide clearly defined skills trainings in support of abstinence and recovery. CBT manuals have been developed since 1985 and adapted for use in a variety of clinical settings, with CBT interventions tested to examine their cost-effectiveness and utility in real-world settings (Carroll, 1996; Marlatt & Gordon, 1985).

All people develop habits to address life's complexities more efficiently and effectively. CBT clinicians view some mental health coping strategies, in part, as negative and repeated habits (often unconscious) reinforced by the neuropsychological effects of the behaviors. The role of the clinician is to elevate the seemingly repeated, ineffective, and unhealthy coping strategies (e.g., behaviors such as self-harm, avoidance, negative looping thoughts, and/or substance-linked habits) into conscious awareness. Awareness is created through a functional analysis discussion that reviews the relationships between the negative coping reactions (e.g., substance use, avoidant, and mood-dependent behavior) and internal and external factors.

The clinician's integration and proficient use of MI skills to create a therapeutic alliance is a critical element in utilizing CBT, especially the Life Movie and functional analysis, to realize and change negative habitual patterns (e.g., substance misuse, avoidance, and mood-dependent behaviors). Providing the therapeutic environment for honest dialogue more readily brings the triggers, feelings, thoughts, and underlying belief systems that help drive repeated patterns into conscious awareness. The clinician must be adept at using MI to promote readiness and to evoke awareness and equally adept at teaching and coaching to help patients develop new skills.

Previous writings on CBT (Monti et al., 2002) have described the value of skills training in the treatment of substance use and mental disorders. Determining the targeted skills to be addressed requires some form of assessment (functional analysis is sometimes defined as situational and personal awareness, situational awareness, the ABCs of CBT, etc.). For each issue defined as a priority, the clinician works in partnership with the patient to assess readiness to address the issue, identify mastering the necessary skills as priorities, and develop reasonable expectations about intended outcomes.

Skills deficits are significant factors to be addressed, as these challenges often lead to or perpetuate the use of maladaptive coping strategies. To the extent the individual does not develop more healthy coping skills, the risk for recurrence remains high if the deficits are not addressed. Similarly, certain kinds of skills deficits are associated with anxiety and depression (addressed in ICBT sessions). Managing these affective states is important in recovery and to the overall patient well-being.

This treatment guide organizes sessions into three broad and interrelated categories: intrapersonal skills training, interpersonal skills training, and recovery support. These categories are based on the most common factors supporting recovery:

- Situational awareness
- Managing uncomfortable feeling states
- Stronger communication skills (e.g., assertiveness)
- Healthy committed relationships
- Healthy replacement activities
- Guilt-free intimacy
- Engagement with a spiritual community/connection to something greater than the self

Skills training also addresses causes of relapse (e.g., interpersonal and intrapersonal challenges that result in negative emotional states), leading to a recurrence of the problem behavior (substance misuse) and/or other associated problems (Marlatt, 1996).

Why Focus on Skills?

Motivation Leads to Skills Development

Once the individual commits to changing their behavior, treatment focuses on building and/or strengthening skills for recovery from negative mental health symptoms and/or becoming and remaining abstinent from substance use. The patient's motivation and commitment may vary, so the use of MI techniques and MET strategies remains integral to treatment. The clinician begins by reexploring the patient's commitment to change and by using motivational strategies (e.g., identifying discrepancies, increasing change talk, and exploring values) when the patient's motivation wavers. In these sessions, the clinician and patient work on developing specific skills (e.g., assertive communication and coping with cravings or distress). This approach is usually slower and somewhat less structured than typical CBT approaches, but many individuals find this emphasis on collaboration and internal motivation helpful.

What Is a Skills-building Approach?

The treatment skills-building approach is founded on the CBT social learning model, which focuses on learning interpersonal and self-management skills (Center for Substance Abuse Treatment [CSAT], 1999). The emphasis is on skill building rather than a deficit-oriented counseling approach. Negative coping behaviors or thought patterns (e.g., SUD or depression) is considered a learned behavior that developed in response to external (e.g., environmental and relational) and internal (e.g., beliefs, feelings, thoughts, and neurobiology) conditions. The skills-building treatment model suggests that habitual negative responses (e.g., addictive behavior) have become a favored strategy because of repeated associations with predictable outcomes. For example, someone cuts themselves; avoids others; or uses substances when feeling sad, angry, lonely, or upset. The person feels less bad when cutting, alone, or using and associates the coping strategy with feeling better (at least in the short term). Over time, they select these immediately relieving strategies more and more often as the quickest way to escape negative feelings or thoughts.

A skills-building approach also can help in coping with depression, anxiety, and trauma, as well as in improving other mental illness symptoms (co-occurring or not).

Skill-building approaches view addictive behaviors, negative moods, or self-limiting coping strategies as learned and not the result of character defects. Because these behaviors are seen as learned, the patient can learn new and healthier behaviors that replace self-limiting behaviors. Change occurs through learning and practicing new skills and enhancing the patient's capabilities and self-efficacy. They develop skills to identify and cope with high-risk internal states and external situations that increase the likelihood of a recurrence. The clinician assigns the patient in-home challenges to practice the new skills and elicits patient commitment to when, where, and how they will practice the skills in the upcoming week. The patient's participation and the clinician's positive feedback enhance patient confidence in managing situations and create long-lasting behavior change. This perspective of substance use or depression as learned is therapeutic because it:

- Reduces blame and criticism
- Fosters hope and optimism
- Identifies development and improvement processes

This treatment approach differs from less structured "talking" models of treatment because it:

- Addresses interpretations of events as important cues for compulsive behavior
- Provides structure (i.e., every week, the clinician devotes a specific amount of time at a specific time in the session to a particular activity)

- Incorporates experiential strategies
- Informs and teaches but is still collaborative

With the use of the MI and CBT approach, the clinician selects skills sessions from a menu of possible choices, based on information that emerged during the earlier motivation enhancement sessions and functional analysis. The sequence of the sessions corresponds to those in many researched, combined MET and CBT intervention manuals (Moyers & Huck, 2011). The purpose of the sequence of sessions is to immediately offer patients methods for increasing awareness and developing coping strategies.

For example, one patient may describe struggling with depression or other difficult emotions and might benefit from sessions that focus on thoughts and emotions. Another patient may present with a history of difficulty expressing thoughts and feelings constructively and might be helped by assertiveness skills. Mindfulness and meditation may be helpful for the large majority of patients who are referred for treatment, as these strategies have broad applications for treating difficulties with mood, substances, and anxiety.

Intrapersonal Skills Training

Intrapersonal skills training begins with building personal awareness (mindfulness), identifying and managing thoughts and urges to use substances, managing powerful emotions (e.g., fear or anger), and addressing negative and self-defeating thoughts (e.g., those associated with depression, low sense of self-efficacy, catastrophic expectations, and feelings of helplessness and hopelessness). On the positive and strengths-based side of treatment, skills training helps patients learn how to become or remain calmer, problem solve, internally assess thoughts and feelings, and successfully manage and navigate what can be powerful and uncomfortable emotional states. Skills that have proven effective include relaxation training, mindfulness, skills for the positive use of unstructured time, mastering healthy physical and mental activities, decision-making, and planning for the unexpected.

Interpersonal Skills Training

Interpersonal skills target the management of situations where other people are an important factor or are actually part of the problem. Developing assertiveness skills in social situations is important for patients experiencing substance misuse because most will be confronted with the opportunity to use substances and faced with a choice. For people experiencing anxiety and depression, learning how to assert oneself convincingly and in a manner that works for the patient in their world and context is an important skill to develop.

Developing appropriate boundary management and assertiveness skills is important in multiple domains of a person's life. Failing to develop these skills often leads a person to feel unsafe, imposed upon, and resentful and can serve as a trigger for trauma, anxiety, depression, and/or substance use. Addressing potentially contentious situations is important. It is challenging to be the recipient or the bearer of criticism; both can provoke feelings of frustration or anger.

Building and strengthening intimate relationships is essential for most people's happiness. Many patients have trouble expressing their feelings, communicating their thoughts, and being sensitive to the thoughts and feelings of others, especially when there has been considerable conflict or trauma in the past. Skills sessions can help patients learn how to self-disclose appropriately, share both positive and negative feelings in appropriate ways, and develop listening skills to become better partners in relationships.

Too often, intimate relationships become problem saturated and problem focused. Strengthening intimate relationships can include learning how to make the best use of positive and restorative time for a couple or within a family. In one effective model for couples therapy (O'Farrell & Fals-Stewart, 2006), an initial task is given to plan and have an enjoyable time with each other in the coming week.

Enhancing Social Support

Adequate social support is fundamental for most people. When individuals have struggled with depression, trauma, social anxiety, and/or substance use, they can perceive their social networks as threats to continued safety and sobriety. Nurturing a vibrant social support system helps manage stress and reduce isolation and loneliness.

Treating Co-occurring Disorders

Large-scale, population-based epidemiological surveys have shown that people with a mental illness are more likely to have an SUD and that the more incapacitating disorders have a higher incidence of substance use problems. Lifetime prevalence rates of 25–30% of patients with depression or anxiety have co-occurring SUDs (Miller & Carroll, 2006). People with primary SUDs have similarly high incidents of co-occurring mental disorders (37% of adults with an alcohol use disorder [AUD] and 53% with a drug use disorder) (Regier et al., 1990).

The incidence rates of post-traumatic stress disorder in the US health care systems have increased in part because of the number of veterans returning home after serving in recent wars. Prevalence varies by a population's traumatic exposure but is estimated to be 12–14% among troops returning from Afghanistan and Iraq and 7% of all patients in routine primary care.

All clinicians in behavioral health care need to maintain a high sensitivity for trauma, traumatic stress, symptoms of depression or anxiety, or other signs of psychological distress, alcohol or substance use, or excessive health care utilization (Lecrubier, 2004). The continuing COVID pandemic increased depression, anxiety, and traumatic stress. Alcohol misuse and suicidality have also increased significantly. Further, people who are impacted by disparities are affected profoundly. The Kaiser Family Foundation's analysis of the US Census Bureau's Household Pulse Survey (Kaiser Family Foundation [KFF], n.d.) documented 35% of adults experiencing anxiety symptoms, 28% depressive symptoms, and 11% suicidal ideation. As reported in the *Journal of the American Medical Association*, there has been a significant increase in alcohol use and a 54% increase in US alcohol sales during the pandemic.

This MI/MET and CBT model helps to reduce the gap in care by providing a flexible and structured treatment protocol that integrates two effective clinical interventions (MET and CBT) and medications when appropriate. The session activities are common to many evidence-based interventions for substance use, mental, and co-occurring disorders. MI/MET and CBT employ a model for care that is staged and recovery based and uses MI and skill building. Clinicians can address the disorders and their symptoms in stages, while delivering the chosen session activities. The session activities known to be effective across common mental health conditions (i.e., depression, anxiety, and traumatic stress) and SUDs are the following:

- Reflective assessment discussions
- Motivational enhancement strategies
- Self-awareness (situational and mood)
- Monitoring (functional analysis)
- Cognitive restructuring
- Relaxation training
- Problem solving
- Communication skills
- Social support skills
- Increasing pleasant/mastery activities
- Relapse prevention

We have laid out the sequence of the sessions in this guide based on the session activities listed above and on our own clinical experience. However, this sequence should be modified based on your patient's needs. For example, if your patient has a high level of anxiety or a significant trauma history, we suggest that you sequence the clinical process differently in the beginning. The next section of the manual describes this approach.

Table 1 illustrates the functionality of the model addressing mental, substance use, and/or co-occurring disorders.

Table 1 Clinical Interventions Addressing Substance Use and Mental Disorders

Treatment Sessions	Substance Use	Depression and Anxiety	Traumatic Stress
Session 1 Eliciting the Life Movie	P	P	P
Session 2 Enhancing Situational Awareness	P	P	P
Session 3 Learning Assertiveness	P	P	P
Session 4 Supporting Recovery Through Enhanced Social Supports	P	P	P
Session 5 Supporting Recovery Through Healthy Replacement Activities	P	P	P
Session 6 Problem Solving	P	P	P
Session 7 Handling Urges, Cravings, and Discomforts	P	P	P
Session 8 Working with Thoughts	P	P	P
Session 9 Working with Emotions	P	P	P
Session 10 Making Important Life Decisions	P	P	P
Session 11 Enhancing Self-awareness	P	P	P
Session 12 Using Mindfulness, Meditation, and Stepping Back	P	P	P
Session 13 Addressing Suicidality	P	P	P
Session 14 Using Medication in Support of Treatment and Recovery	P	P	P
Session 15 Engaging with Self-help	P	P	
Session 16 Using the MET/CBT Approach for Traumatic Stress and Substance Use	P	P	P

Recovery Supports

While many recognized recovery support services have emerged over the past 20 years—driven substantially by an appreciation of recovery-oriented systems of care principles—this guide addresses only two widely used recovery supports: the use of medications and self-help. The reason for this choice is that firm evidence supports the benefits of medications as a method of recovery support (Kelly & Yeterian, 2011), and not all recovery support services are available and accessible in all communities. However, nearly every community in the United States and elsewhere is home to 12-step, self-help meetings.

Session 14 addresses decision-making related to the use of medications in the treatment of substance use and other disorders. Session 15 includes information about Alcoholics Anonymous and Narcotics Anonymous. The placement of these sessions after the skills training sessions is not intended to reflect when and how a clinician would use this information; the handouts and discussion tips may be used to inform patients about these essential recovery tools during any phase of treatment. In fact, depending on patient needs, it could be beneficial to introduce both substance use disorder medications and self-help strategies early in ICBT treatment.

Patient Activation Within the Context of ICBT

This model offers clinicians a structured and systematic approach to support the transfer of learning and patient empowerment. This is done by enhancing the patient's motivation to engage in the therapy process and working to maintain a high level of engagement with in- and out-of-session therapeutic activities. The goal of patient activation in ICBT is to systematically support and guide the patient to increase purposeful action such that the patient experiences opportunities to manage and solve life problems with newly acquired skills and to increase self-efficacy in their ability to do so. While meaningful work can be done during the session, patients learn to become more effective in their lives by applying what is learned to real-life situations. Patient activation focuses on supporting the patient to plan and take action outside the clinical session to address problematic thoughts, feelings, and behaviors that inhibit purposeful action and self-efficacy, replacing them with healthy internal and external coping skills. Evidence shows that the more actively engaged the patient is in doing planned and purposeful actions outside the clinical encounter, the greater the likelihood of their long-term success in recovery.

On Spirituality

Spirituality is more commonly referenced today in clinical literature than in the past (Hayes et al., 2012; Miller, 2003). It is important to define the term and to place spirituality and its relationship to the treatment of behavioral health conditions within a theoretical change framework.

We conceptualize spirituality not as an attribute that human beings possess but rather as activities we do. Spirituality emerges from our actions, which are informed by self-knowledge and activated skills. From our perspective, spirituality is an action verb, not a noun or adjective. To quote Erich Fromm (2007), "We are what we do." We define spirituality as mindful awareness of, and participation in, the process of choosing based on our core values. Spirituality means taking actions (risks) based on our values, being fully present in this moment, relating intentionally to others, and recognizing we are all works in progress.

Unpacking These Interconnected Parts

Mindfulness refers to the practice of increasing one's capacity to remain in the present moment and accept experience without judgment. The practice recognizes our minds are busy; distracted; and reactive to events, situation, thoughts, and feelings. Building a capacity for mindfulness involves becoming increasingly aware of one's moment-to-moment experience and approaching the present moment with acceptance. The intended outcome is a move toward "present-centeredness," which creates greater clarity about the nature of one's struggles, builds capability for accepting situations and feelings as they are, and sheds light on new pathways for recovery and growth.

Cultivating mindful awareness can generate a sensation in which the boundaries between ourselves and others and even the world around us can become indistinguishable. This sense can be experienced as a connection greater than ourselves. Some people find this sense in religion and others by gazing at an infinite night sky, beholding vast and majestic mountains, feeling the rhythm of ocean waves, or becoming enchanted with art or music. These moments fill us with wonder and awe and can foster a sense of connection and belonging. Those moments affirm our connectedness to all things. This connectedness helps us understand our place, better equips us to embrace the uncertainty of life, and develops the resilience to lean in and learn from pain rather than allowing it to victimize us.

Being present in the moment means that you are aware and intentional of what is happening at this very moment. You are not distracted by inner chatter about the past or by worries about the future. In the present moment, you are not distracted by what has already happened or what is yet to come. Rather, you are aware of yourself—your physical body, your heartbeat, your breathing. You may be aware of your body temperature or whether you are hungry or thirsty. You notice the ways your body is communicating with you. You notice what you are thinking and feeling. You are more aware of your surroundings, including sights, sounds, and smells. Being in the present moment takes practice, just like any other skill we learn, but it is an important one to develop.

Taking actions based on our personal values means living and acting intentionally and making conscious choices guided by what we hold most important. **Values** are our True North, our guiding principles, that keep us headed in a direction that is who we are and seek to be. Values are distinct from goals. **Goals** are targets we want to achieve during a period of our life.

Some examples of values include being an active community member; being a loving and compassionate friend and partner; supporting others through good times and pain; or being a good parent by helping your children to become strong, kind, and confident. These are values in action, and they unfold over a lifetime.

Goals have distinct start and end points (e.g., saving money for a child's college tuition, becoming an electrician). These are life goals.

Relating intentionally to others is aligned with the MI spirit. Intentionality brings presence and power to each relationship important to us. Whether relationships with co-workers, intimate partners, or personal friends, what we value grows if we pay attention to it. Intentionality helps us understand the purpose and importance of every relationship we have.

We acknowledge that the concept of spirituality we have outlined here differs from some religious views of spirituality. Our perspective of spirituality is an active and interactive lifelong practice, central to overall health and wellness and to behavioral health treatment and recovery. From a clinical and recovery perspective, if spirituality is an active process (i.e., something that we do), then we can be supported and offer others support more fully as part of the intervention. In this context, it is helpful to think of our spirituality as actions made real by these four interconnected attributes of our humanity. When we embody this spirit, we understand that the energy of relating within the space between two individuals is far more affirming and potent than the end transaction of the relationship itself. This is the mindful experience of wonder and awe that fosters healing, wholeness, and connection.

Enhancing Cultural Relevance in Clinical Practice

> *Even more than other areas of health and medicine, the mental health field is plagued by disparities in the availability of and access to its services. These disparities are viewed readily through the lenses of racial and cultural diversity, age, and gender.*
> —U.S. Department of Health and Human Services (HHS) (1999, p. vi)

What Is Culture?

Culture is the product of group values, beliefs, norms, practices, expectations, and experiences (Alegria et al., 2010; Cooke & Szumal, 1993; López & Guarnaccia, 2005). Culture is social, complex, and continually evolving (Alegria et al., 2010). Culture—*our own and our clients'*—affects our health and work in substantive ways. It informs how we conceptualize our understanding of illness and wellness, problem severity, the treatment system, attitudes toward medication, and the decision to seek care. Its influence cannot be overstated.

Culture is frequently a synonym for diversity, referring to individual characteristics (e.g., race, ethnicity, gender identity, sexual orientation, religion, country of origin, and ability) that are essential to include in our conceptualization. Yet, our conceptualization of culture can be more expansive. Culture can also refer to other identities people hold, such as their profession or membership in a social group (e.g., military culture, police culture, in recovery, first-time parent, and caregiver). Hinting at the complexity of culture and how we interact with it, we must also understand culture through an intersectional lens. It is important to recognize that every individual carries within themselves multiple identities, like a Venn diagram with overlapping layers (Alegria et al., 2010), and that different layers are activated depending on the social context (e.g., at home or at work, with friends from country of origin or from school).

> **TASK** *Consider the experience of Jackie, a Black female police officer. Jackie is of Haitian descent. She has two children. Six months ago, her 16-year-old shared that they identify as queer. In the past, Jackie was very active in her church, but she recently stopped attending. Overcoming her concerns, she has come in to talk to you about feeling depressed.*
>
> - In what ways do you think culture plays a role in her life?

Importance of Culturally Relevant Practice

An essential component of culturally relevant practice is an awareness of how historical events shape the current cultural climate and embedded disparities. For example, the legacy of slavery, colonization, and White supremacist beliefs embedded within institutional policies and practices continue to impact the experiences of racial and ethnic minorities and of marginalized individuals living in the United States. An awareness of this history and an openness to understanding how it affects clients today is a cornerstone of culturally relevant clinical practice. Disparities in terms of access to quality behavioral health care treatment, lower service use rates, higher attrition rates, and poorer health outcomes—based on race, ethnicity, and other marginalized identities—are well documented (Alegria et al., 2008; Jimenez et al., 2013; Nakash & Saguy, 2015).

The social determinants of health (SDOH) framework is useful for identifying how this history affects your clients and their communities (Marmot & Wilkinson, 2005). Using a life-course approach, the SDOH framework recognizes the impact of where we are born, live, and age on our overall health and well-being. It considers the non-medical factors that influence our health, including economic stability, access to work, neighborhood safety and the built environment, social supports and community context, and access to education and health care services. These factors also influence culture and are worth exploring with your client when developing a culturally relevant treatment plan.

Betancourt (2003) defined cultural competency in health care as "the ability of systems to provide care to patients with diverse values, beliefs, and behaviors, including tailoring delivery of care to meet patients' social, cultural, and linguistic needs." Culturally competent practice has been shown to improve engagement and retention in treatment (Huey Jr. et al. 2014; Sue et al., 1992) and health outcomes and symptoms post-treatment (Gainsbury, 2017; Huey Jr. et al. 2014). The shifting demographics of the United States have played an important role in raising the importance of cultural competency and culturally relevant practice and will continue to do so. The US Census Bureau has predicted that Black, Indigenous, and other people of color will comprise half of the population by 2044 (Colby & Ortman, 2015, p. 1). As the nation becomes more and more diverse, it is vital for all practitioners to consider the role of culture and to develop culturally relevant treatment plans.

Strategies to Improve Cultural Relevance
Part of being a culturally responsive clinician is taking the time to do your homework. Find out what you can about your client's identity and culture, history, and any major milestones or events. Understanding these can be useful and inform your practice. However, clinicians should also be aware of what researchers refer to as *ecological inferences* and *ecological fallacies* (Freedman, 1999). An ecological inference is made when we infer information about an individual based on group- or population-level data (e.g., children like candy, so this child must like candy). An ecological fallacy happens when we believe that a relationship observed at the group level holds for individuals (e.g., we observe a relationship between smoking and heart disease and infer that because my client smokes, they must also suffer from heart disease) (Freedman, 1999). To be culturally responsive means doing general research about the population and possible relationships between things but being prepared to discover that none of that information applies to your client (i.e., seeing the tree, regardless of the surrounding forest).

A culturally responsive clinician takes the time to learn about the client or family member's culture, with the goal of developing a treatment plan that acts as both a mirror and a window. It should reflect the cultural nuances you have learned about the client. It should also be a window into greater understanding, allowing the client to give feedback on its cultural relevance to the clinician, encouraging a dynamic, interactive exchange between the clinician and client that deepens knowledge and enriches the experience for both.

Making the journey from the first session to a place where dynamic, interactive exchange can happen takes purposeful action and time. The following content will help you identify strategies to navigate how to (1) address culture and explore experiences of discrimination, (2) discuss differences in understanding of the problem, (3) explore cultural perceptions of cause, and (4) examine the role of cultural identity and coping with your client.

Importance of Initial Engagement

Addressing Culture and Exploring Experiences of Discrimination

Many clinicians worry about broaching the topic of culture with their clients, concerned that they will cause offense or say the wrong thing. The worst thing you can do is ignore this issue. When choosing to engage in that conversation, the two most important things to know are that (1) no one is expecting you to be an expert on all cultures or identities and (2) this work begins with you.

Clients are hoping for a clinician who wants to understand them and their experiences. They are not expecting perfection; they are coming to you for help. In these vulnerable moments, they are looking for respect and for someone who will see their humanity and individuality. They want and need a clinician who is interested in learning about their values, beliefs, views, and perspectives on the issue that brought them in to see you and is willing to invest the time in getting to know them. Your role is to practice thoughtful curiosity and demonstrate cultural humility by asking questions in a respectful and sincere way with intention and purpose. Use open-ended questions like: "Can you tell me what happened that made you decide to come in today?" "What do you think is causing the problem?" "Why do you think this is happening now?" "What would 'better' look like?" "Are there any cultural practices or beliefs about the problem that inform how you have chosen to navigate it so far?" "How can I be helpful?"

However, asking good questions is not enough. Prior to working with any client, it is essential to reflect on your own assumptions and biases and on how they may influence your level of engagement with your client and your treatment planning decisions. When working with your client, if appropriate, name the elephant in the room: "How are we different? How are we similar?" Even if you share a common thread, do not assume a shared understanding or experience. When there are differences that you feel are salient to your understanding, acknowledge them in a way that is thoughtful and clear, especially for ascribed identities, like gender or race. For example: "As a [CLINICIAN IDENTITY], I can appreciate that our experiences might be really different. I want to understand your experiences, and what's important to you. When I have misunderstood something, please correct me. In our work together, if I say something that feels off-key, I'm hoping that you will let me know, correcting my misunderstanding and giving me a chance to learn and improve. I hope that we can have that kind of relationship."

Always be prepared to challenge your assumptions about your client, their beliefs, what they will share, or how they will work with you. After the session, reflect on how well you did. How did bias or assumptions influence the direction of your conversation or of your treatment plan ideas? Discuss this with your supervisor and come up with a plan for addressing it in your next session.

As part of this inquiry process, it is also important to get a sense of the individual's previous experience(s) with the treatment system, either for themselves or a loved one. Was it a positive experience? If so, why? Was it challenging or upsetting? If so, why? While it may take time for them to share the details of a difficult experience in the moment, letting them know that you are aware that systems can sometimes feel (or be) unfair, unkind, overwhelming, or scary signals your interest in learning more and in being able to hear a critique of the system you are part of without getting defensive. In addition, it is vital that your treatment plan incorporate what you learned from your work together and that you revisit your treatment plan on an ongoing basis as trust is built.

In your first meeting, be sure to explain your role and confidentiality and to ensure that their expectations in terms of what you can and cannot do are clear. At all times, reflect on your language and vocabulary. Are you using jargon or unnecessarily complicated terms that would be difficult for anyone in distress to understand and remember? Check in with your client; make sure they understand your recommendations and treatment plan.

Finally, remember that you have skills! Your clients are looking to you for assistance in a difficult moment. They are counting on you to bring your knowledge, skills, and expertise to the table.

Differences in Understanding or Defining a Problem

It is important to recognize that we all make sense of our experiences and the world around us based on our values and beliefs. Individuals, families, communities, and cultures have different understandings of mental health, mental health treatment, what constitutes a problem, and when a problem rises to a level of concern. Even if there is consensus about the problem, different interpretations or understandings of the cause of and potential solutions to the problem will likely exist. Our beliefs may lead us to different conclusions, with implications for the next steps.

Patients share their understanding of the problem with us, providing us their interpretation. We apply our knowledge, training, experience, and cultural filter to their interpretation, generating our own interpretation. We then convert their interpretation into the language of our profession to develop a treatment plan and to funnel our interpretation through the treatment system, where others will add their own interpretation and understanding (Alegria et al., 2018).

Having an awareness of the inherent bias and flaws of the interpretation process is important. While this is changing, in our profession in the United States, care typically centers on the experience of White, cisgender, heterosexual, able-bodied, non-neurodiverse, adult men with stable housing and employment and through a Western medical model of care, making adjustments for everyone that falls outside those parameters as they interact with the treatment system. Recognizing how this starting point informs or skews our interpretations can help us course correct and provide the client with the necessary resources and options they will need to receive the quality care they require.

So far, we have focused on differences between the client and the clinician. However, it is also important to recognize within-group differences. For example, every member of a family may have a different interpretation of the problem, its causes, and ideas about the best response. Let us say your client is feeling intense anxiety. When they shared this with their family members, they got a range of responses based on each individual's beliefs and understanding about the cause of the problem and an appropriate response. This would likely be confusing for your client. This could be an important and rich topic for discussion when developing your treatment plan.

- Family Member 1: "Let's get a prescription and get this taken care of."
- Family Member 2: "I need time to pray on this; I am not sure what to do."
- Family Member 3: "Let's give therapy a try."
- Family Member 4: "I don't see anything wrong here; everyone is entitled to have a bad day"

Cultural Perceptions of Cause

Definitions, understandings, and theories about the cause of a problem will vary. As noted above, family members may disagree. Providers are also apt to develop different theories, based on their approach to clinical practice; relationship with the client; circumstances that brought the individual in for treatment; and, of crucial importance, the questions they ask. The Clinical Formulation Interview (CFI) embedded within the Diagnostic and Statistical Manual of Mental Disorders, 5th Edition (DSM-5), was designed to assist providers in any setting by offering possible questions to ask and tips when asking them (American Psychiatric Association, 2022). As Table 2 illustrates, the CFI addresses several areas and subareas.

Cultural Identity: Strength and Coping

Cultural identity often focuses on the aspects of interactions with the majority culture or systems of care that are challenging for the client to navigate. Valid worries and concerns about access to treatment and the quality of care for racial and ethnic minorities and for other marginalized identities exist. We do not need to look far to hear news about a racist incident or to feel the sting of

Table 2 Domains and Sample Questions from the Cultural Formulation Interview

CFI Content Areas	Subarea and Sample Question
Cultural Definition of the Problem	People often describe their problems in their own way, which may be similar to or different from how doctors describe the problem. How would you describe the problem?
Cultural Perceptions of Cause, Context, and Support	**Causes:** • Why do you think this is happening to you? What do you think are the causes of [PROBLEM]? **Stressors and Supports:** • Are there any kinds of support that make your [PROBLEM] better, such as support from family, friends, or others? • Are there any kinds of stressors that make your [PROBLEM] worse? **Role of Cultural Identity:** • For you, what are the most important aspects of your background or identity?
Cultural Factors Affecting Self-Coping and Past Help-Seeking	**Self-Coping:** • Sometimes, people have various ways of dealing with problems, like [PROBLEM]. What have you done on your own to cope with [PROBLEM]? **Past Help-Seeking:** • Often, people look for help from many different sources, including different kinds of doctors, helpers, or healers. In the past, what kinds of treatment, help, advice, or healing have you sought for your [PROBLEM]? **Barriers:** • Has anything prevented you from getting the help you need?
Cultural Factors Affecting Current Help-Seeking	**Preferences:** • What kinds of help do you think would be most useful to you at this time for your [PROBLEM]? **Client–Patient Relationship:** Sometimes doctors and patients misunderstand each other because they come from different backgrounds or have different expectations. • Have you been concerned about this, and is there anything that we can do to provide you with the care you need?

inequity or discrimination in our own lives. However, these situations do not define any group. It would be incredibly misleading and a disservice to discuss culture only through a negative lens. For those who identify as a member of a racial or ethnic minority or of a marginalized group, there is true beauty, strength, and pride in these identities, both at the individual and the community level. Great joy and a determination to thrive, despite the challenges, inhabit these spaces. Clinicians who take the time to ask about the strengths, benefits, and pride of a client's cultural identity and what it means to them are better able to access this precious resource when it is needed.

In conclusion, taking the time to explore and understand the ways that culture influences the client's experience in the world generally, and in the treatment system specifically, is of vital importance. Taking the time to acknowledge difference and to approach difference with thoughtful curiosity is essential to good practice. Reflecting on your own identity and on the biases and assumptions that you carry is a crucial first step. Be prepared to explore what some researchers have referred to as the cultural transference and countertransference that comes into play in your clinical work (Rosenfield, 2020).

It takes a great deal of courage to seek treatment. Clients who are from racial and ethnic minorities and/or hold a marginalized identity are looking for a clinician who has an awareness of how scary and intimidating it can be to engage with providers who are unknown to them and are part of systems that may be unfamiliar or where they have had negative experiences. In these moments, these clients want what all clients want. They want to know: (1) *Are you a person of goodwill?* Are you going to approach them from a place of thoughtful curiosity, without judgment? (2) *Are you skilled?* Are you prepared to apply your skills and knowledge to the problems with which they are struggling? They are counting on you to bring your expertise, seek support if you need help, and communicate clearly with them especially when there are moments of tension or confusion. (3) *Will you respect my values?* Are you open to learning about their values and beliefs? Will you respect their values in the treatment planning process? If you can commit to these three things, you will have gone incredibly far in building trust and in creating an environment that promotes culturally relevant practice.

Section 2

Clinician Guidance for 16 Sessions of Integrated Cognitive Behavioral Therapy

Introduction

As a framework for treatment, this section provides detailed guidance to clinicians for delivering any or all of the included sessions. Each session is organized according to the following headings:

- Introduction to the session
- The patient's experience: what the patient learns (intended outcome)
- Clinician preparation for the session
- Session outline, steps
- Protocol with scripts (and sidebar tips; some appear in the appendices)
- Handouts (appearing in corresponding sections at end of guide)

Sessions 1–7 are viewed as core skills and may be completed by all patients. Session 1 supports engagement and developing a richer understanding of your patient's life. This session can aid both clinician and patient to gain a richer contextual understanding. Session 2 initiates the process of functional analysis to help the patient build situational awareness of internal and interpersonal factors affecting mental and substance use disorders and is used to individualize treatment strategies. Sessions 3–7 are universally beneficial and necessary skill-training sessions for addressing SUD and behavioral health concerns. The clinician and patient may decide to target other sessions based on identified needs. While the model is flexible, the clinician should not assume that the patient has sole responsibility for deciding the number or sequence of sessions. Rather, the clinician should guide the course and plan for treatment with considerable input from the patient. The clinician must balance patient motivation and needs with clinical judgment when deciding on a reasonable duration of treatment for each patient.

> 💡 We recommend that Sessions 1 and 2 are completed first and in order. These two sessions provide you (and your patient) valuable insights for setting priorities and for individualizing care. However, beyond that, we encourage you to sequence sessions based upon your patient's need. For instance, early in treatment, some patients might benefit from mindfulness training and from working with self-limiting thoughts. Also, we know that trauma is common in many patients; if your client seems easily triggered for a trauma response (e.g., heightened anxiety/panic), before Session 2, consider completing Session 7, which targets basic mindfulness to better manage uncomfortable affect.

Clinicians using the MI/MET and CBT approach are encouraged to integrate the skills and techniques Section 1 describes in detail. You are encouraged to undertake the following activities and to practice the skills outlined:

- Review relevant sections of the manual before each session.
- Develop and practice a natural style of conveying the material; avoid reading text to the patient or appearing overly didactic, dogmatic, or as though presenting a lecture. Practice helps you develop a more natural style.
- Maintain a motivational style; use open-ended questions and reflections, and avoid a directive, resistance-building style.
- Always provide a rationale for what you are doing. In this context, a patient rationale is describing why this activity is important to the patient.
- Encourage involvement and participation by the patient.
- If working with a patient of a different culture, review Enhancing Cultural Relevance in Clinical Practice. With humility, reinforce that your patient is the expert in their life.
- Allow time for practice and feedback.
- Build self-efficacy; help the patient identify and acknowledge skills already in use.
- Avoid overwhelming the patient; present only one or two new skills per session.
- Remember to take a few minutes to review the between-session exercises at the start of each session.
- Attend to shifts in the patient's motivation and readiness for change.
- Explain practice exercises carefully; probe for the patient's understanding.

Law of Thirds

ICBT is a structured treatment grounded in the "law of thirds." Studies in psychotherapy have determined that most successful therapy sessions occur in three phases, known informally as the law of thirds (Carroll, 1996) or the 20/20/20 rule. The law of thirds describes the first third of the therapy session as engaging, building, or reestablishing rapport and reviewing progress since the last contact and between-session practice activities. The second third is the core of that session's activity and addresses a particular skill to be introduced and practiced during the session. The final third summarizes what took place during the session, and the clinician and patient identify a real-life practice opportunity and make a mutual commitment to practice the new skill in the coming week outside of the session (Figure 1).

First Third	Second Third	Third Third
▸ Establish and strengthen rapport ▸ Review progress ▸ Review between-session challenge	▸ Provide session rationale ▸ Teach session skill(s) ▸ Lead demonstration/role play ▸ Facilitate patient-led practice (assess skill transfer)	▸ Identify real-world application ▸ Negotiate and prepare between-session challenge ▸ Elicit commitment ▸ Summarize and conclude

Figure 1 Sample Therapy Sessions According to the Law of Thirds

First Third

The key goal of the First Third of the session is to **connect** and **engage**. Using the MI spirit is especially useful within this part of the session, which involves three key activities:

1) **Establish and Strengthen Rapport.** The clinician works to develop or strengthen rapport by using the MI spirit (compassion, acceptance, autonomy, evocation) and core MI skills (open-ended questions, affirmations, reflections, summaries) while engaging the patient in non-problem-focused rapport building (i.e., exploring areas of their life not directly related to treatment).

2) **Review Progress.** This is the clinician's opportunity to identify and explore any changes in the patient's substance use, mental health, and related experiences since the previous session. The clinician asks the patient about what has gone well, what has not gone so well, changes they have made since the last session, and any other element of the patient's experience that is related to their identified challenges and treatment goals.

   Using the MI core skills of open-ended questions, affirmations, reflections, and summaries allows the clinician to learn more about the patient's thoughts and feelings around what they think is going well or not so well and why. In addition, progress review serves as a feedback loop for the clinician to learn how the treatment to date is or is not working and the reasons for the treatment response (or lack thereof). Some clinicians may find it beneficial to structure their review of progress, using a tool that suggests key domains relevant to most patients, on an ongoing basis over the course of treatment. We provide an optional ***Review of Progress*** handout at the end of this chapter. The domains assessed include physical activity, sleep, diet, pleasurable activities, mastery activities, work/school, substance use, and mood states.

3) **Review Between-session Challenge.** In addition to reviewing progress over the course of treatment, it is critical in the ICBT framework to directly review the progress of between-session challenges. These give patients the opportunity to apply the awareness and skills they are learning in the sessions so they gain more confidence and practice applying the skills on their own in the real world. By reviewing the patient's application of newly learned skills, the clinician can reinforce the patient's efforts, explore how skill application worked or did not work, and support the patient in identifying how to best continue working toward that skill on an ongoing basis. Some patients will benefit from re-training of the skill to maximize its utility for them.

   - It is imperative for the clinician to ensure the patient knows the importance of the between-session challenges and is expected to report on the application of new skills in every session. When a between-session challenge has not been completed, the clinician explores with the patient the barriers that led to that outcome. Common barriers include lack of motivation or perceived relevance of the skill, uncertainty about how to apply a newly learned skill, and external challenges outside of the patient's control (e.g., sudden crisis situation that takes priority, medical illness). The clinician continues to use the core MI skills and other MI tools (e.g., decisional balance) to explore motivation around skills application. Revisiting the rationale for the skill and its relevance to the patient can increase the patient's willingness and perceived importance to complete the between-session challenge.
   - General troubleshooting can also be helpful to identify solutions to other barriers. By focusing attention on the review of between-session challenges, the clinician reinforces the expectation of patient skills practice outside of the session. Where appropriate, the clinician can use a portion of the session to support the patient applying any missed between-session challenges. For example, if a patient previously committed to making an assertive request to a colleague, the patient and clinician could role play a similar scenario to provide the patient an opportunity to practice and explore the outcome of their use of assertive communication.

Second Third

The key goal of the Second Third of the session is to **transfer a new skill** to the patient. It represents the core of a session's activity, when teaching and skill building occur. The Second Third involves four key activities:

1) **Provide Session Rationale.** ICBT sessions are designed to support the patient in learning and applying new coping skills. Just as patients may experience fluctuations in motivation for treatment, they may also feel ambivalent or have misconceptions about a particular skill or set of skills. Prior to delivering any intervention activity, the clinician should explain the rationale for using it to the patient. Delivering a **personalized session rationale** helps the patient understand the activity and its potential benefit, facilitating their increased engagement in sessions and a commitment to skill learning and application. The rationale is not just a review of the planned session activity, but an individualized discussion of how and why the session activity is important, relevant, and aligned with patient values and priorities for their own clinical progress and recovery. A sample rationale is presented within each of the ICBT session chapters in this guide.

2) **Teach Session Skill(s).** To effectively teach coping skills, the clinician shares relevant information to enhance the patient's understanding of the skill and engages in collaborative step-by-step application of the skill. The clinician does not simply talk "at" the patient but, rather, engages them in discussion along the way, eliciting their baseline knowledge, resolving misconceptions, and addressing questions or concerns.

3) **Lead Demonstration/role Play.** To reinforce the teaching of new skills, the clinician models skill application in sessions through demonstration. Clinician demonstration most commonly occurs with the clinician coaching the patient through skill application (i.e., walking the patient through the application of the skill using the patient's experiences as content while going through the step-by-step teaching the skill). The clinician may also role play a scenario in which the clinician acts out the skill.

4) **Facilitate Patient Led Practice/assess Skill Transfer.** Observing the patient deliver or apply a skill is essential to assessing whether skills transfer has occurred. Following clinician modeling of the skill, the patient practices skill implementation in session. Patient practice helps to build confidence in their use of the skill while allowing the clinician to reinforce skill application and provide feedback.

Third Third

The key goal of the Third Third of the session is to prepare the patient for transferring the skills they are learning in the ICBT sessions into their everyday life. The clinician uses core MI skills and strategies to help them make a connection between what they have learned in session and their daily life. The Third Third involves four key activities:

1) **Identify Real-world Application.** The clinician works with the patient to connect newly learned skills to meaningful opportunities in their life. Patients will be more likely to practice and ultimately adopt skills if they perceive them to be relevant. The clinician helps the patient identify real-life situations to which they can apply a coping skill.

2) **Negotiate and Prepare Between-session Challenge.** The clinician elicits from the patient how and where in their life they can apply awareness raising and other coping skills they are learning in session. The negotiation of a challenge is a patient-centered, collaborative process, not an assignment given by the clinician. The more active the patient is in identifying

real-world opportunities for skill application, the more relevant its implementation will be, thereby increasing buy-in and the likelihood of follow-through. Between-session challenges need to be specific (i.e., it should be clear to both patient and clinician what the patient will do, when they will do it, and how often it will be done). To prepare the patient for the between-session challenge, the clinician walks through the application of the newly learned skill and supports the patient for how they will think through, approach, and/or deliver the skill in the identified scenario. This mental rehearsal sets the patient up for greater success in completing the activity. Generally, it is recommended that patients complete at least two practice applications of newly learned skills to derive the intended benefit.

3) **Elicit Commitment.** After the patient has identified an area for real-world skill application, the clinician elicits their commitment for engaging in skills practice. As needed, commitment can be directly assessed using the MI ruler and other MI skills used to strengthen patient commitment. The clinician also supports the patient in establishing a plan for success by having them write down their plan and think through any strategies they will use to succeed and overcome possible obstacles.

4) **Summarize and Conclude.** The clinician summarizes what has been covered during the session and elicits the patient's feedback. While summaries are intended to be brief and follow the general timeline of the session, they help reinforce relevant themes, set the stage for what comes next, and allow the patient to provide targeted feedback. The clinician directly asks the patient about how the session went for them, what was particularly helpful or less helpful, and other areas in which the patient would like to provide feedback.

Delivering clinical sessions consistent with the law of thirds requires some accommodation in approach for many clinicians. However, with practice, this soon becomes second nature.

Review of Progress and Between-session Challenges

Directions: The table below supports weekly progress review in key domains relevant to the patient's substance use and overall well-being. This table can also be used to review the between-session challenges. The table can be truncated for specific targets when indicated.

Domain	Sun.	Mon.	Tues.	Wed	Thur.	Fri.	Sat.
Physical Activity							
Sleep							
Diet							
Pleasure/ Replacement Activities							
Mastery Activities							
Work/School							
Mood States							
Tobacco/Nicotine							
Alcohol							
Marijuana							
Other Drugs							
Between-Session Challenge							

CBT Process Skills

Within the law of thirds structure are process skills (sometimes referred to as microskills). These process skills are new for some clinicians and build on the customary skills of clinical training, as summarized below:

1) **Motivational Interviewing.** MI is the conversational platform for ICBT delivery.
2) **Providing a Rationale.** Providing a rationale **is not** a review of the session agenda. A rationale is a discussion with your patient describing why this session or activity is important for their recovery and aligned with their values.

> **Enhancing Social Supports Example**
>
> For any challenge in life, it is helpful to have support, whether you have chronic health problems or employment trouble or are going through a tough time. Figuring out whom you can trust and who can help you in different types of situations creates a sense of stability in life. That is what many people call their social connections, net, or network—it supports us through many life experiences.

3) **Use of Handouts/Worksheets.** Handouts and worksheets bring focus to a particular issue, support reflection and increased self-awareness, help to facilitate understanding, and provide tips for action or guides for planning. Completing handouts is not an end in and of itself. Rather, handouts are tools that support clinical objectives. *Remember: Do not confuse the menu for the meal.*
4) **Significant Practice Elements of CBT.** For the clinician, this can include teaching and demonstrating skills, conducting roleplays with patient teaching back, and coaching to support skills acquisition. To do these activities well, it is important to understand the skill and skill delivery from both a patient and clinician perspective.
5) **Negotiating Between-session Challenges.** Negotiating a between-session challenge helps the patient transfer what is learned in session to real-life practice. This core behavioral activation empowers the patient. Following through on negotiated plans of any sort are good indicators of positive outcomes. This activation is what makes CBT more potent. Remember, it is your patient's plan and not yours. Even if your patient commits to and does something in the coming week that is modest, that's great news!
6) **Having an Uncomfortable Conversation.** When your patient does not follow through with their commitment for the between-session challenge, it is necessary to discuss and explore what happened. If you do not, you are unintentionally sending a message that the activity is not that important. Here are the key principles for having these conversations:
    - Saying nothing does not serve your client.
    - It is important to communicate that these challenges are an essential step for someone to make changes.
    - Saying something lets your client know that you care and that the work is important. Explore what happened.
    - People who have a substance use history or are depressed or anxious may not have great memory. It is often useful to work on memory strategies.
    - If they agreed to the challenge with you to people-please or placate, address that directly.
    - If the challenge that was agreed to was overly optimistic and beyond capacity, next time, set more modest expectations.

Beyond Clinical Sessions 1 and 2

Just as we have recommended that all patients complete Sessions 1 and 2 in order, we suggest completing Sessions 3–7 in order. However, clinicians are encouraged use clinical judgment in sequencing further sessions. We also want to remind clinicians that some session strategies may need to be repeated multiple times.

Session 1. Eliciting The Life Movie

Introduction and Session Goals

This session focuses on building rapport, raising awareness, and building motivation for change through the Life Movie conversation. Eliciting the Life Movie is an important part of ICBT. It is a semi-structured discussion designed to explore the domains of the patient's life and of how these domains may be related to their primary reasons for seeking treatment. An opportunity to explore themes identified from the initial assessment in greater depth, the Life Movie can

> One of the greater challenges to building rapport and collaboration is when the patient experiences the clinician as not listening and not appreciating their struggles. A central clinician objective is to offer affirmation of their challenges so that the patient feels understood.

increase the clinician and patient's insight and contextual understanding, motivation, and readiness to enact changes. The graphic below helps illustrate contextual understanding.

Building A Contextual Understanding for Treatment

What behavioral science and experience tell us: When we change a behavior like depression or alcohol misuse, this involves one or more changes in context.

Prior to this first session, the clinician uses the patient's assessment and screening information to further understand their current substance use, depression, and other mental health issues and their connections to the domains of their life. In this way, the clinician begins to more fully understand the patient's concern, how it has affected their life, and potential areas to explore further to build motivation for change and to target areas for intervention. Then, the clinician and patient discuss the core areas of the Life Movie to begin the conversation about where the patient stands in relation to the presenting concern and what they would like to accomplish.

See Session 1 handouts at the end of the guide, which provide the necessary framework to facilitate and deliver competent Life Movie discussions. The handouts include a *Treatment Information Sheet*, as well as material to help guide the Life Movie discussion.

> The needs of your patient and your clinical judgement matters! Where there is benefit, any session can be delivered multiple times.

With the approach described here, the patient experiences a nonjudgmental conversation with a skilled health professional providing support, empathy, and a desire to collaborate on a journey toward wellness. The patient develops an awareness of related health risks, begins to question their readiness to address the risks now, and commits to following through on any number of "readiness" tasks prior to the next meeting.

This following conversation segment demonstrates clinician effort openness, humility, and recognition of our differences. Both the clinician and patient bring expertise supporting patient self-efficacy.

A First Encounter Illustration

This brief conversation might often precede the first clinical session, the Life Movie.

Clinician (C): Hello, thank you for coming in today. As we get started, I would like to spend a few minutes getting to know one another. My name is Jonathon M. Please feel free to call me John. What name do you want me to call you?

Patient (P): OK, John. You can call me Andrea.

C: Thank you, Andrea. I try to be open and upfront about what's going on, and I want to talk a minute about what how we can work together. While we may have a shared understanding of universal emotions, such as joy, sadness, anger, etc., our unique life experiences and circumstances will influence how we navigate these emotions, as well as the choices we make when seeking to make a change in our lives. As a middle-aged white man, my experiences may be different or similar to your own experiences in many ways. While I have skills and abilities that believe could be of value for you in our work together, you are the expert in your life.

P: Yep, you got that right!

C: As we are working together, I will put forth thoughts and ideas about what's going on for you. I know that I might not with you. How does that sound to you, that you would let me know?

P: Yes, I can do that.

C: Is there anything you would like to share now as we get started?

Note to clinician: Policies vary from state to state as to when a treatment plan must be completed. Some states require a treatment plan after completion of the intake assessment, others after the first, second, or fourth session. We assume each clinician will document in accordance with their respective policies. In ICBT, Sessions 1 and 2 provide a wealth of understanding of the person's internal and social world.

Clinician Preparation

Session 1. Eliciting the Life Movie	
Materials • *Treatment Information Sheet* • *Eliciting the Life Movie: MI Conversation* handout • *Change Plan* handout • Optional: *Learning New Coping Strategies* handout	**Session Length** 45–60 minutes **Delivery Method** MET-focused individual therapy

Strategies
- Follow OARS techniques (Open-Ended Questions, Affirmations, Reflections, Summary).
- Use EDARS (Express Empathy, Develop Discrepancy, Assist in Awareness of Ambivalence, Roll with Sustain Talk/Discord, Support Self-Efficacy).
- Identify stage of change.
- Engage in the four phases of MI: Engage, Focus, Evoke, and Plan.
- Discuss and offer feedback to help emphasize personal reasons for change.
- Use the MI readiness ruler and decisional balance.
- Develop a "real-life practice challenge" and generate commitment.

Goals for This Session
- Build the alliance between the patient and clinician.
- Orient the patient to what might be expected in treatment sessions, the demands on time to attend, and the time needed for practice between sessions.
- Build on the data gathered during the assessment session by engaging the patient in the Life Movie conversation.
- Explore the domains of the Life Movie, eliciting the patient's core values and enhancing the patient's motivation for change by:
  - Discussing the patient's behavioral health concern(s) and associations with other challenges in the Life Movie domains
  - Exploring the patient's attitudes about change, including ambivalent attitudes
  - Eliciting, acknowledging, and reinforcing the patient's expressions of motivation to change
  - Affirming any patient expressions of readiness to develop a "change plan" and to identify change strategies
- Develop a between-session challenge focused on having the patient complete the *Change Plan* handout.

Note to clinician: Today, multiple terms are used to describe the person seeking care: patient, client, participant, or consumer. Please use the term that best suits you and your institution.

Session 1 Outline and Overview

First Third

1) Establish rapport.
   - Welcome the patient.
   - Share the session agenda. Invite items for discussion or updates since the initial intake assessment.
   - Engage in non-problem-focused rapport building, exploring areas of the patient's life not directly related to treatment.
2) Review progress.
   - Ask the patient for their feelings and thoughts about the assessment session.
   - Engage the patient in a brief review of their progress related to their substance use or mental health issue and related experiences since the previous session.
     – How well were they able to manage their mental health or substance use since the last session?
       o Did they have any successes or setbacks managing their issue?
       o Did the patient make an effort to change their behaviors based on the conversation during the initial assessment?
       o Did the patient experience any high-risk or triggering situations?
   - Reinforce expressions of motivation.
3) Review between-session challenge.
   - Using the *Treatment Information Sheet*, discuss treatment expectations.

Second Third

4) Provide session rationale.
   - Explain the rationale for the Eliciting the Life Movie discussion.
   - Ask the patient if they understand why the activity will be helpful in their treatment.
5) Teach session skills.
   - Explore each domain of the Life Movie, conveying the MI spirit and using MI strategies.
   - Elicit and reflect any problems related to presenting concerns (e.g., substance misuse, depression) and any positive reasons for change, including living by core values.
   - Reinforce confidence in efforts to create positive change.
6) Summarize the Eliciting the Life Movie discussion, emphasizing ambivalence and readiness.
   - Elicit and reinforce the patient's readiness to change.

Third Third

7) Negotiate the between-session challenge.

   For the patient ready to make change:

   - Assist the patient in preparing for change.
   - Ask and elicit a commitment from the patient to complete the **Change Plan** handout before the next session.
   - If appropriate, discuss and help the patient develop a specific behavioral target, for example:
   - Selecting a "sampling sobriety period" or a stop date (if the patient has not already stopped using)
   - Monitoring their mood and the quality of their interactions with others
   - Review previous successful experiences of navigating challenges to identify useful strategies.

Specific to substance use: If time allows and if appropriate, discuss the following:

- What the patient will do with the current supply of alcohol or other substances and paraphernalia
- How the patient will disclose plans to family and friends
- How the patient will address problems in maintaining abstinence
- In the next session, communicate that you will explore what may be effective strategies, skills, and supports for the patient to reach their personal goals.

If the patient is not ready to make changes, ask to have an open discussion about use. The goal is to explore and build awareness regarding the patient's experiences and challenges. An effective and nonconfrontational approach is to ask the patient to discuss an episode or episodes in the recent past where they have used substances or their depression, anxiety, or other mental health condition negatively affected their relationships or choices. The clinician's role is to be open and reflective and to clarify the pros and cons of the patient's behavior. The discussion also starts to build situational awareness of factors associated with the problem behavior and the impact of making or not making a change.

For the patient not ready to change:

- Using the MI approach of looking forward, explore what might need to happen for them to help them think more critically about the impact of their choices and of their motivation to change.
- Explore what they might be willing to examine now and what might be some initial goals.
- Discuss the **Learning New Coping Strategies**.

8) Assign an appropriate between-session challenge. Often it can be something new from the **Learning New Coping Strategies** handout to try.
   - Discuss with the patient the rationale and need to adopt or continue doing substance-free pleasurable activities.
9) Summarize and conclude.

Session 1 Protocol with Scripts

Establish Rapport
The clinician welcomes the patient and provides an overview of the first session, in which the clinician further builds rapport and explores domains of the patient's life, with the goal of exploring the potential relationship between these domains, patient's personal goals, and their substance use. The clinician invites the patient to provide additional agenda items for the session.

As part of building rapport, the clinician should ask the patient about nonproblem areas of the patient's life. For example, the clinician may offer:

> **Clinician:** Thank you for coming in today. I realize that you are here to explore your goals. Before we get to that, though, I would love to learn a little more about you. What do you feel it might be important for me to know about you, for example, your interests or ways you spend your time?

Review Progress
Next, the clinician may ask the patient to express their thoughts regarding the assessment process and any major changes that have occurred since the assessment session. Possible responses from the patient might be:

- Changes in the pattern or frequency of problematic thoughts or behaviors
- Decision to seek additional treatment or attendance at a mutual-help program
- Conversations about their issue with others

The clinician responds empathically, uses opportunities to support the patient's self-efficacy for change, and reinforces expressions of motivation. See two examples below.

> **Example 1: Shirley (S)**
>
> *Clinician (C):* I know last time you were here, you completed our assessment. I'm wondering how things have been since then.
> *S:* After answering all those questions, I am more aware than ever of what's been going on these last months! Nothing has changed yet, but I'm thinking about it. My husband has been very supportive.
> *C:* And his support means a lot to you.
> *S:* You bet! He's someone I can count on.
> *C:* That's good to hear. Let us be sure to talk about specific requests you might make of him for support in the future.

> **Example 2: Doug (D)**
>
> *C:* You arrived a little late for your appointment. Is this a good time for you, or would a different time work better?
> *D:* No; this is fine. There was a lot of traffic.
> *C:* How are things?
> *D:* Worse. My wife and my son are on my back; they are treating me as if I'm a leper.

> **C:** That sounds like an uncomfortable situation for you.
> **D:** Yeah. I feel like everyone is against me.
> **C:** How has this affected you?
> **D:** At times, I find myself using just to prove that it's not a problem for me!
> **C:** It's more of a problem for them.
> **D:** That's right. I do not think either one really understands me.
> **C:** You'd like them to understand you; that might remove some reasons for getting high.
> **D:** Yeah. At least I would not be trying to get back at them.

Review Treatment Information Handout
The clinician gives the patient the *Treatment Information Handout.* They review the handout together, with the clinician inviting questions and/or input from the patient.

Introduce Eliciting the Life Movie and Provide Rationale
The clinician shares the rationale for Eliciting the Life Movie by expressing a desire to learn more about the patient, in addition to the assessment, with the goal of being able to collaborate better. The clinician also fosters patient collaboration by asking permission to engage in the activity.

> **Clinician (C):** I would really like to understand more about you, your everyday life, and important aspects of your background, such as family, other relationships, your work, and other passions. This better prepares us to work together. How does this sound to you?
> **Shirley (S):** Sure, but did not I just answer all those questions in the assessment?
> **C:** Yes, you did, and those were very helpful. However, those assessment questions tell me when the problem started, how it affected you, and how often it was taking place. That information is important as it helps me begin to get a picture of the problem and other areas of your life. The discussion I want us to have today builds on that by exploring areas of your life we may not yet have touched on, as well as by exploring connections between different areas of your life and your mood or your drinking/use. This conversation is different from the assessment because it helps me better understand how you think and feel about your life. It also helps you to see how different parts of your life may be related to why you are here.
> **S:** OK. That makes sense. I just did not want to feel like I was telling you everything all over again.
> **C:** I get that, and I do not want you to feel that way either. Can I ask you: If you do start to feel that way, can you please let me know? I do not think you will, but just in case, it is really important that you feel you can give me that feedback.

Engage in Eliciting the Life Movie Discussion
The clinician progresses through the *Eliciting the Life Movie* handout, covering all of the more relevant domains. The session activity should feel like a conversation that builds or seeks elaboration beyond the initial assessment results. The goals are to build rapport and collaboration, acknowledge and reflect patient core values, and develop discrepancies between the patient's goals and values and their current problematic behaviors in order to build motivation for change. The clinician should not feel they need to ask every question in the handout. Rather, the focus is on areas that seem more relevant to the patient's life and circumstances and that build on what is known already from the assessment.

Within the Life Movie, as different domains are discussed, it is important for the clinician to help explore connections between those domains and the patient's presenting concerns. Some clinicians will seek those connections with discussion of each domain. Other clinicians may do a collective summary at the end of the discussion. Summarizing following each domain can sometimes disrupt the conversational flow. The clinician listens reflectively to the patient's responses to questions in the Life Movie domains, inserting additional open-ended questions or reflections to help elucidate connections between the domain and the patient's substance use or other issue. The goal in making these connections is to acknowledge the importance of the perceived benefits and expressions of potential readiness for change. This is an opportunity to use MI techniques(e.g., expressing empathy, identifying discrepancy, eliciting self-motivational statements, rolling with sustain talk/discord, supporting self-efficacy).

The clinician may also affirm—with the patient's active and thoughtful engagement in this process (rolling with resistance)—their willingness to explore these domains and their potential relationship to substance use. In keeping with the MI/MET approach, the clinician uses open-ended rather than closed-ended questions. For example, "Did you say you used in unsafe situations?" is a closed-ended question that invites a mere yes or no answer and possible disagreement with the PRS item. Saying instead, "Tell me about using in unsafe situations" invites elaboration and discussion.

Below is an example of what an exchange might look like within the family domain.

> **Clinician (C):** I know you shared that you currently live with your husband and two daughters. I'd like to ask you a bit about your family growing up. What were things in your family like for you growing up?
>
> **Shirley (S):** They were OK, I guess. My mom was a single parent. She worked pretty hard between her job and raising my brother and me. We saw my dad occasionally. I think we had a pretty good childhood.
>
> **C:** So, your mom was there to provide for you and your brother and make sure you were cared for.
>
> **S:** She was. She really was. I do not think it was always easy, but she clearly put us first. I just think it was hard because she worked full time, and then, when she got home, she had us to take care of. Plus, as a mom, I realized how much she may have felt she missed out on because she was working so much.
>
> **C:** Being a mom yourself has helped you gain perspective of what it was like for your mom raising you. How do you feel all of this has shaped your own views or beliefs about being a parent?
>
> **S:** I want to be the best parent I can be for my kids. I want to be able to have the energy to be there for them. I do not want to miss anything.
>
> **C:** Being there for your kids—really there, present for each day—is a core value for you. You really want to be fully engaged with them.
>
> **S:** Yes, I do, and that is part of why I want to stop being so anxious. It makes me so tired at the end of the night. I just need a better way to handle stress and worry.

At the end of the Life Movie, the clinician should summarize the key themes voiced by the patient. The summary focus on themes that reinforce and help build motivation and a commitment toward change. Ideally, within the summary, the clinician will be able to include the following:

- Problems caused by the presenting issue (e.g., substance use, depression, anxiety)
- Reasons for change
- Risk factors for recurrence (i.e., the clinician points out possible risky situations the patient identified as risk factors for recurrence.)

- Connections and strengths within the patient's world
- Reinforcement of the patient's values and priorities and how change may help the person to live a life worth living

After summarizing the Life Movie discussion for the patient, the clinician asks the patient for reactions and responds to them with empathy.

Summarize the Eliciting the Life Movie Discussion
The clinician summarizes the highlights from the Life Movie:

> **Clinician (C):** Let us review and summarize what we have talked about so far. How does that sound to you?
> **Shirley (S):** I'm ready!
> **C:** You stated your evening smoking and drinking are the only way you have found to really relax and reduce stress. But you also acknowledged that your [drinking or anxiety] your anxiety has caused several problems, including missing work, difficulty sleeping, and feeling bad about yourself. Is there anything else you want to add?
> **S:** No; those are the main problems.
> **C:** You mentioned one of the main reasons for making a change is because one of the things you value most is your relationship with your kids. You want to be a mom who is really present and engaged with her kids.
> **S:** Being the best parent I can be is really important.
> **C:** Being a good parent is important to you, and your using gets in the way. You get tired and feel like you just do not have the energy to be fully with them at night.
> **S:** It's my biggest reason for wanting to stop.
> **C:** When you talk about being a parent and your kids, you get enthusiastic, and you light up, but when you talk about your using, you get discouraged and seem a bit down.
> **S:** I never noticed that before, but you are right.
> **C:** You also stated that high-risk situations for you would include being with others who smoke and seeing them enjoy it. Anything else?
> **S:** Not really, but that is a major concern for me as I try to [quit/change]. So many people in my life use alcohol or other substances.
> **C:** You've already identified how difficult it may be, but you have also identified some very strong reasons for change.
> **S:** I know it'll be difficult, but I think it's worth it.
> **C:** Despite the obstacles, you are ready to take on this challenge.
> **S:** I really am.

Elicit and Reinforce the Patient's Readiness to Change
When the patient expresses motivation to change, the clinician acknowledges these expressions, seeks elaboration, and offers reinforcement:

> **Clinician (C):** You said your drinking has caused problems, including feeling that you have lower energy. Could you tell me about that?
> **Shirley (S):** I mean to do things, but they never get done. It seems that I'm so tired and down all the time. I cannot help thinking it's related to my drinking, but alcohol also makes me relaxed and feel better.

> **C:** Hmm. So, there are times drinking makes you feel better, and you think your drinking makes you tired, and you do not get your responsibilities done?
> **S:** I did not feel this way when I was young. But now, well, I just do not know what to do.
> **C:** So, you worry about your drinking; you feel down. You are feeling stuck and do not know what to do.
> **S:** And, like we talked about, I am so tired at home that I do not feel I'm there for my kids in the way I want to be. And I feel terrible about that.
> **C:** So, you think that if you quit drinking, you will increase your energy at nigh, when you are with your family.
> **S:** Yeah. I hope so.
> **C:** You'd like to regain your energy and have a better time with your children and do better at work.
> **S:** I really would like that.
> **C:** Shirley, it seems like we have two areas to work on, and they likely are connected. First is your drinking, and second is how you have been feeling. Let us start first with your drinking, and let us see how that influences how you are feeling.

Negotiate Between-session Challenge
Assist the patient in preparing for change

The clinician assists the patient in preparing to reduce and, if ready, stop using alcohol by discussing several key issues. At the same time, the clinician needs to be prepared to promote contemplating change regardless of the patient's current stage of change. The goal is to support the patient to identify healthy change and to begin to move toward what that would be like for them. The clinician provides the rationale for goal setting by explaining that most successful change processes, including this treatment, begin with a roadmap of where the "driver" (the patient) wants to go and what they would like to accomplish in a specific time period. This helps the patient choose options for achieving the goals. Writing down goals for change also helps measure progress once started. The idea is to plan a journey with the best potential for success within a specific period of time. The journey may change as the process unfolds, but it is critical to identify the goal, reasons for wanting to achieve it, and specific directions for success—called the "action steps."

Elicit from the patient a commitment to complete the ***Change Plan*** on their own as the between-session challenge, which will be discussed at the beginning of the next session.

> **Clinician:** The Life Movie conversation is designed to help you think about what changes in your life you might be willing to make to achieve your goals and have a healthier life overall. The Change Plan can apply to identifying any kind of change you want to make in your emotional and physical health. I would like to give you a Change Plan as your between-session challenge. It can be helpful for you to take time to think about these different aspects of making these changes: your specific goals, why they are important, and specific steps you want to take to achieve them.
>
> If you are focusing on substance use, it can be helpful to think about times when you have not used in the past or when you have cut down or quit. In general, it can also be helpful to think about when you have made changes and what helped you to make those changes. If you get stuck, do not worry. Just do the best that you can. If you feel comfortable, you could talk to a support person about any part of the Change Plan. The goal would be for you to think through each of the questions or prompts and write out your responses. I would ask you to bring the Change Plan to our next session. We will start our next session by checking in on what you came up with. How does that sound to you?

If the patient is seeking assistance regarding substance use, the clinician might ask if the patient is willing to select a day to begin the process by reducing use by a specific amount, thus "sampling sobriety" or quitting. The clinician helps the patient consider several alternative stop dates. Topics to contemplate include:

- What the patient will do with their substance supply and paraphernalia
- How the patient will disclose the plan to family and friends (both supporters and those who might sabotage the patient's efforts)
- How the patient will address challenges to maintaining abstinence (e.g., sleep difficulties, boredom, anxiety, restlessness) in the first week

In addition to the **Change Plan**, another between-session challenge involves engaging in healthy coping strategies. The clinician summarizes the patient's readiness by briefly reviewing the main reasons for and against changing use. Then, regardless of the patient's stage of change, the clinician provides the rationale for adopting or continuing substance-free pleasurable activities and completing the challenge to use at least one of the coping strategies from the **Learning New Coping Strategies** handout.

> **Clinician (C):** *Regardless of how ready you are to change your use, it is important to remain healthy and happy. One of the most proven approaches to feeling good is doing pleasurable activities. These pleasurable activities increase chemicals in the body that make us all feel good and can also help us remain calm through daily stressors, like a decision to cut back or not use substances. We have a worksheet I can give you that defines the types of activities that can be beneficial. Before I do that, though, what activities can you think of that you would enjoy doing and would help release stress?*
> **Shirley (S):** *I used to go for walks with my children and with a group of my girlfriends. I have not gone in a long time. I really liked it when I did that each week.*
> **C:** *I get that. When you continue to try rewarding or pleasurable activities, they also become easier like a good habit. So, if it's OK with you, I'm going to ask you to commit to doing one or two pleasurable activities in the next week. If you want to try something new, you could pick from this worksheet (**Learning New Coping Strategies** handout) and commit to doing them. And, of course, remember that when walking with children or friends or something new, you will not use any alcohol.*
> **S:** *OK*

The clinician elicits a commitment from the patient that identifies specific activities and when the patient is going to do them, including the day of the week and possibly the time of day. The more specific, the better.

Summarize and Conclude
The clinician reviews the session, asks the patient for feedback, responds empathically to their comments, troubleshoots any difficulties, and reminds them to review the handouts over the next week.

Note to clinician: There is much material to successfully address in this session. If, in your judgment, the patient is still processing this information and appears undecided or ambivalent, continue the discussion in a second or even third session to address the motivational concerns. To move forward before your patient is ready invites greater resistance to change and a higher likelihood of prematurely leaving services. See the sample language provided below for addressing several high-risk situations that confront people who use and suggestions for coping without using.

Specific Suggestions for Addressing Common High-risk Situations
Tension Relief and Negative Emotions (e.g., depression, anxiety, nervousness, irritability). Develop relaxation techniques and exercises. Write down your feelings, or talk to a friend or clinician. Do something enjoyable that requires little effort. Figure out what you are feeling and whether you can do anything about it. Sessions specific to depression and anxiety are included in Sessions 8 and 9. **Anger, Frustration, and Interpersonal Conflict.** Try to handle the situation directly rather than hiding your feelings. If appropriate, be assertive. Get some release by squeezing a rubber ball, pounding a pillow, or doing some physical activity. Write down your feelings, or tell them to someone. Take deep breaths. **Fatigue and Low Energy.** Do muscle relaxations. Take a brisk walk. Do something enjoyable. Eat properly, and get enough sleep. **Insomnia.** Do not fight being unable to sleep. Get up and do something constructive or relaxing. Read a book, watch television, or do muscle relaxations until you feel sleepy. Remember that no one dies from losing a night's sleep. **Timeout.** Read. Do a crossword puzzle. Prepare a healthy snack. Take up a hobby. Knit or do other needlework (things you can carry with you for easy access). **Self-Image.** Try a new image: get a new haircut, or buy new clothes. **Social Pressure.** Be aware when others are using. Remember your commitment not to use. Be assertive, and request that people not offer you alcohol or substances. If appropriate, ask that they not use around you for a while. If necessary, be prepared to leave the situation, especially when you have recently quit. **Cravings and Urges.** The only way to interrupt cravings is to break the chain of responding to them, that is, do not give in. Eventually they will decrease. Do something to distract yourself. Use the techniques suggested. Breathe deeply. Call a friend. Go for a walk. Move around. Time the urge; you'll find that it will disappear like a wave breaking.

The ***Change Plan*** handout is optional and offered to patients ready to think about immediate ways of changing. This will be reviewed with the patient during Session 2.

Session 1 Handouts: The Life Movie and Change Plan

Treatment Information Sheet

I want to take a few minutes to discuss what you can expect from us and what we expect from you. Over the coming weeks, we will be meeting (individually or as part of a group) and developing goals that are important to you and that seem reasonable for you to achieve in this amount of time. You can set the pace of our work together and let me know if, at any point, I am moving too quickly or too slowly. I have some ideas for how we can work together on the goals that you have identified already. I hope to share these ideas and help you develop effective skills or build on abilities you already have but may not recognize or be using to your best advantage. Following are some general guidelines:

- **Regular Meetings.** It is most helpful if we can meet on a regular basis, such as weekly. If you need to cancel or are running late, I would appreciate your letting me know with as much advance notice as possible.
- **Commitment to Treatment.** Change is difficult for everyone. I ask that you make every effort to participate fully in the treatment by coming to sessions; sharing your thoughts, feelings, and frustrations; and staying the course, even if you feel at times that our work is not helping as quickly as you would like.
- **Therapy Process.** I will do my best to help you feel comfortable, and my hope is that we can work as a collaborative team. Therapy can be uncomfortable at times because different thoughts and feelings may come up. This does not mean that treatment is not working. However, if at any point you find yourself upset with something that has happened, or something I have said or done, I encourage you to bring this up and let me know so that we can continue with a positive connection.
- **Substance Use.** I ask that you refrain from using alcohol or substances on days or at times when we will be meeting together. I think our discussions together can be most productive and helpful to you if you are not under the influence of any substances.
- **Structure of Meetings and Practice Exercises.** We will meet together for about an hour each time. I will usually want to hear about how things have been going the previous week and anything you want to share about events in your life. Then we will spend some time on a particular topic area or skill that will be helpful to you in accomplishing your goals. I may ask you to do some writing or thinking about what we have discussed between sessions. It is up to you whether you do this, and the goal is not to make you feel pressured or burdened. You will never be graded or judged on what you write. The purpose is to keep the material alive between the times we meet and to encourage you to practice or apply some of the new ideas and skills in your real life, as opposed to merely discussing them. If I ask you to write or practice something that you are not comfortable with, please let me know so we can come up with an exercise that is more suitable.
- **Questions.** You may have regarding treatment, what is involved, or my background and role.
- **I look forward to working together with you.**

Eliciting the Life Movie: MI Conversation

Goal
Using MI interviewing strategies focusing primarily on open-ended questions and reflections, the goal of this conversation is to get a deeper understanding of the person's life. Use open-ended questions and complex and compassionate reflections to promote an initial sense of the person's values, beliefs, and priorities.

Provide rationale for the life movie

> I would really like to understand more about you, your everyday life, and important aspects of your background, including family, other relationships, your work, and other passions. This better prepares us to collaborate in ways that make sense for you.

Ask permission

How does this sound to you as a place for us to start our work together, so you feel I understand you better and that we are on the same page?

General questions to start off with:
What was your last week like?
What do you feel has gone well for you recently?
What has been troubling for you?
Has there been anything you'd like to change?

Explore areas of the life movie
Any single question can open significant dialogue.

- Family of origin
    Tell me about what it was like for you growing up in your family.
    What are the ways in which your family has influenced you? What are the ways you feel your early experiences with your family affect you now?
    What are some values you developed growing up that are important to you now?
- Today's significant others
    Tell me about the people in your life that you are closest to.
    What is your relationship with your spouse/partner/significant other like?
    How does your significant other feel about your alcohol and/or drug use (if any)?
- Work (or school)
    What is work/school like for you?
    What are the ways work/school cause stress or challenges for you?
    Ideally, what would you like to be doing for your work?
    How has alcohol and/or drug use affected your work/school?
- Health (physical and mental)
    How do you feel physically? Emotionally?
    What are the ways you try to take care of yourself?
    What challenges are you experiencing in your health?

- Life activities that bring personal satisfaction
    What do you enjoy doing? What brings you happiness or joy?
    What is it like for you when you can do these activities more often?
    What gets in the way of being able to pursue these activities regularly?
- Spirituality
    How would you describe your spirituality? By spirituality, we do not necessarily mean a religion but, rather, what helps ground you, what feeds your spirit and your soul. It could be what grounds you and helps give you a sense of purpose and direction in life.
    What are the ways in which spirituality has been helpful to you in your life?

The conversation does not need to be complicated. Be present and curious. We have offered some possible questions within each domain that can serve as a starting point. However, do not feel you have to ask these questions if there are others that feel more natural and relevant to your conversation. Use your MI skills to explore deeper into feelings, values, and beliefs.

Note to clinician: Some of our patients have had very difficult histories, and in these early sessions, your patient may be willing to go only so far in these disclosures. That is understood and normal. You can respectfully "flag" content for future explorations.

> *From what you are saying, it sounds like there is a lot going on there. Perhaps at a future time we can revisit that.*

Note to clinician: Remember, use deeper/compassionate reflections, affirmations, and summaries to better understand patient values, beliefs, areas of internal conflict, drivers of use behavior, etc.

In your final summary, link the key themes, especially values, you hear from your patient to help develop discrepancy and to build motivation for change. Through the Life Movie discussion, both the patient and you gain a richer understanding of the person's life, some of the drivers for suffering and its impact, substance use, and the impact that has had. The Life Movie conversation can add depth and context to these areas that may not have been explored during the clinical intake.

Change Plan

It is important to think about the changes you would like to make in your life now. The Change Plan should be expressed orally at a minimum but can also be in writing. Ideally, making changes and sticking to commitments works best when you actually write out your goals. Responses to the following questions will create a simple-but-powerful plan for change.

Name _____

1) The changes I want to make are: (specifics)

_____

_____

_____

2) The most important reasons I want to make these changes are:

   a) _____

   b) _____

   c) _____

3) The steps I plan to make in changing are:

   a) _____

   b) _____

   c) _____

Learning New Coping Strategies (Optional)

Developing alternatives
Substance use reduction

You can do many things to change your behavior. Some may work better than others. Some help you resist the urge to use substances, avoid tempting situations, or satisfy your needs in more constructive ways than using. Expect to try several new strategies and add any that may be helpful for you. Think about what worked when you gave up (e.g., drinking, smoking, using substances) before or when you made other changes in your life. Be kind to yourself as you begin this change process—you are doing something to take care of yourself, and you deserve all the comfort and self-acceptance you can get! Remind yourself that learning and changing inevitably mean giving up old ways and that, in time, you will feel more comfortable. Remember the changes your body and mind went through when you learned to drive, got to know a new person, started a new job, or learned a new skill. Chances are you felt awkward, uncomfortable, silly, dumb, nervous, frustrated, impatient, or anxious, in addition to hopeful, excited, and challenged. What helped you then? How long did it take you to feel relaxed? Did you learn all at once, or were improvement and progress gradual?

Managing mood and anxiety

Most of the following actions work well for both managing substance use urges and mood and anxiety problems.

First Actions

- **Avoid situations** that make you want to use or that feel emotionally overwhelming; sometimes this is the easiest and most effective way, especially at the beginning.
- **Get enough sleep.** For lots of people, disturbed sleep can be both a trigger and a symptom of episodes.
- **Think about what you eat and drink.** Eating a balanced and nutritious diet can help you feel well, think clearly, and calm your mood.
- **Exercise regularly.**
- **Change your physical position.** Stand up and stretch, walk around the room, or step outside.
- **Carry things to put in your mouth** (e.g., toothpicks, gum, mints, plastic straws, low-calorie snacks).
- **Carry objects to fiddle with** (e.g., rubber ball to squeeze, small puzzle, pebble, worry beads).
- **Have a distracting activity available** (e.g., phone call, crossword puzzle, magazine or book, postcard to write).

New Activities

- **Exercise or take a brisk daily walk.** Get your body used to moving (e.g., use stairs instead of elevators, park farther away from your destination, walk instead of drive).
- **Practice relaxation or meditation techniques regularly** (we will have an opportunity to learn and practice these techniques later in our work together).
- **Take up a hobby,** or pick up an old hobby you used to enjoy.
- **Drink less coffee.** Switch to decaf or drink herbal teas.
- **Engage in an enjoyable activity** several times a week that is not related to work.

New Thoughts

- **Self-talk.** Give yourself a pep talk. Remind yourself of your reasons for making changes and of the consequences of staying the same. Challenge any wavering in your commitment.
- **Thought-stopping.** Tell yourself loudly to STOP. Get up and do something else when you are feeling consumed by negative thoughts or beliefs. Remind yourself that a thought is a thought, and it's not necessarily real.
- **Distraction.** Focus on something different (e.g., the task at hand, a daydream or fantasy, counting).

Social Interactions and Environment

- **Go to places where it feels safe and comfortable** (e.g., a library, theater, swimming pool, sauna, steam bath, restaurant, public gatherings [not loud rock concerts]).
- **Spend time with friends.** Enlist support from family and friends. Announce that you have begun to make some changes; ask people not to offer you alcohol or other substances, to provide emotional support, and not to use drugs around you.
- **Learn to be appropriately assertive** and to handle frustration or anger directly.

Specific Suggestions for Some Common, High-risk Situations

Below are several high-risk situations that people who use confront, along with suggestions for coping without using.

- **Tension Relief and Negative Emotions** (e.g., depression, anxiety, nervousness, irritability). Develop relaxation techniques. Exercise. Write down your feelings. Talk to a friend or counselor. Do something enjoyable that requires little effort. Figure out what you are feeling and whether you can do anything about it.
- **Anger, Frustration, and Interpersonal Conflict.** Try to handle the situation directly rather than hiding your feelings. If appropriate, be assertive. Get some release by squeezing a rubber ball, pounding a pillow, or doing some physical activity. Write down your feelings or tell them to someone. Take deep breaths.
- **Fatigue and Low Energy.** Do muscle relaxations. Take a brisk walk. Do something enjoyable. Eat properly. Get enough sleep.
- **Insomnia.** Do not fight being unable to sleep. Get up and do something constructive or relaxing. Read a book, watch TV, or do muscle relaxations until you feel sleepy. Remember that no one dies from losing a night's sleep.
- **Time-out:** Read. Do a crossword puzzle. Prepare a healthy snack. Take up a hobby. Knit or do other needlework (things you can carry with you for easy access).
- **Self-image.** Get a new haircut or buy new clothes.
- **Social Pressure.** Be aware when others are using substances. Remember your commitment not to use. Be assertive and request that people not offer you alcohol or substances. If appropriate, ask that they not use around you for a while. If necessary, be prepared to leave the situation, especially when you have recently quit.
- **Cravings and Urges.** The only way to interrupt cravings is to break the chain of responding to them; that is, do not give in. Eventually they will decrease. Do something to distract yourself. Use the techniques listed under **New Thoughts**. Breathe deeply. Call a friend. Go for a walk. Move around. Time the urge, and you'll find that it will disappear like a wave breaking.

This handout is optional and offered to patients ready to think about immediate ways of changing. This will be reviewed with patients during the next session.

Session 2. Enhancing Situational Awareness

Introduction and Session Goals

This session focuses on building rapport further, developing situational awareness, setting priorities based on what is important to the patient, and defining the goals and activities of the upcoming therapeutic journey. The clinician continues to use motivational strategies to increase change talk and reduce sustain talk. They also introduce the process of functional analysis to help the patient build situational awareness of internal and interpersonal factors affecting substance use or trauma symptoms and/or of depression and anxiety. Situational awareness, also referred to as functional analysis, is the backbone of CBT. Through enhanced awareness, we create psychological space to make decisions and change. Clinicians may refer to the eliciting change talk strategies presented in Section 1 and reinforce any successful efforts at initiating change.

As the clinician expresses genuine interest in the patient's well-being since the last meeting, the patient experiences how a therapeutic relationship can provide the necessary support and guidance to push past obstacles and begin to change. Use and continued practice of the *Awareness Record* is a potent strategy and set of patient skills for bringing unconscious thoughts, feelings, and beliefs into conscious awareness and enabling the patient to make conscious decisions about behavior change. Awareness raising is empowering. This awareness-raising process better enables both patient and clinician to prioritize and individualize treatment sessions. As a result of this exploration, the patient can gain a deeper understanding of their target issues (e.g., substance use or anxiety, including internal and situational factors). The patient can receive support, guidance, and assistance in creating a personalized plan for change.

> The first goal of Session 2 is for your patient to build skills in self-awareness, specific to the targeted area of concern (e.g., depression, anxiety, substance use). This increased awareness of these often-unconscious processes opens psychological space between a triggering stimulus and a habitual response. This creates opportunity for change.

This experience can result in a rich conversation that may span more than one session. Patients often experience strong affect as they explore. Frequently, the clinician instructs the patient to continue completing the *Awareness Record* handout as a between-session challenge over several weeks and possibly months.

Note to clinician: The *Awareness Record* is a universal strategy throughout all CBT. It can as easily apply to anxiety, depression, or anger management.

Important note to clinician: Trauma experiences exists within portions of the populations we serve. When this is true for your patient, we advise that, in advance of the awareness-raising session, certain mindfulness practices are learned, so that if the patient is activated, they can ground and decompress. See Sessions 7 and 12.

Clinician Preparation

Session 2. Enhancing Situation Awareness	
Materials • *Review of Progress* • *Learning New Coping Strategies* and *Change Plan* (see Session 1 handouts) • Blank Copy of the *Awareness Record* handout • *Awareness Record* example • Optional: *Planning to Feel Good* handout	**Total Time** One hour **Delivery Method** MET-focused individual therapy with case planning elements
Strategies • Follow OARS techniques. • Use EDARS. • Identify stage of change. • Discuss and offer feedback to help emphasize personal reasons for change. • Develop "real-life practice challenge," and generate commitment.	
Goals for This Session • If not completed in a previous session, review the patient's initial Change Plan. • Support the patient to enhance awareness around the internal and situational factors associated with their use, mood, and other behaviors.	

Session 2 Outline and Overview

First Third

1) Strengthen rapport.
   - Welcome the patient and, if present, the support person.
   - Share the session agenda; invite items from the patient.
   - Engage in non-problem-focused rapport building, exploring areas of the patient's life not directly related to treatment.
2) Review progress.
   - Engage the patient in a brief review of their progress related to their substance use, mental health, and related experiences since the previous session. Use the ***Review of Progress*** handout as a guide.
     - Did the patient make an effort to change?
     - Did the patient experience any high-risk situations?
     - If the patient engaged in substance use, explore their use event(s), using the ***Awareness Record*** to assess internal and external triggers, cravings, and consequences.
3) Review between-session challenge.
   - Review any between-session challenges from the previous session.
     - Did the patient complete the ***Change Plan***? If so, review it as a personalized reflective discussion.
     - Did the patient use any strategies from the ***Learning New Coping Strategies*** handout? Were the strategies successful?

Second Third

4) Provide session rationale.
   - Provide a personalized rationale for the session activity.
   - Ask the patient if they understand the reasons why the activity or skill will help build recovery strength.
   - Teach session skill. Share relevant information to help the patient understand the skill and to provide the step-by-step approach of how to implement it.
   - Describe the components of the ***Awareness Record*** to the patient.
5) Lead a demonstration/role play.
   - Demonstrate the skill by leading the patient in its practice to model the way it is done.
     - Be clear and make sure the patient understands the lesson.
     - Have the patient identify two incidents of concern in recent history.
   - Walk the patient step by step through the ***Awareness Record*** using the identified event.
     - Use open-ended questions, reflections, and summaries to gain a deeper understanding of the patient's experiences within each of the components on the ***Awareness Record***.
     - Respond to any questions the patient has regarding skill application.
6) Facilitate patient-led practice/assess skills transfer).
   - Have the patient lead a practice of the skill.
     - In practice, encourage the patient to use real-life examples.
     - Have the patient walk through each component of the **Awareness Record,** step by step and aloud, for two recent incidents of use or craving to use substances or for episodes of depression, anger, or anxiety. Ideally, these incidents will reflect a situation in which the patient was triggered but did not use.
     - Use open-ended questions, reflections, and summaries as the patient completes the activity to elicit a deeper understanding of their experiences.

Third Third

7) Identify real-world application.
   - Help the patient identify real-life situations in which they can apply the skill.
8) Negotiate and prepare between-session challenge.
   - Elicit from the patient how and where in their life they can apply awareness raising and other coping skills they learned in session in their daily life.
     - The patient is encouraged to continue practicing awareness raising by completing the **Awareness Record**.
   - Make sure the challenge is specific and support the patient by rehearsing their application of the new skill.
     - What will they do?
     - When will they do it?
     - How often will it be done (e.g., at least two times)?
9) Elicit commitment.
   - Elicit commitment for completion of the between-session practice at least two times before the next session.
   - Use MI strategies, as needed, to strengthen commitment.
10) Summarize and conclude.
    - Present a session summary of what has been covered during the session, and elicit the patient's feedback.
      - What did the patient learn through the awareness-raising activity?
      - Use the information generated in completing the Awareness Record to discuss relevant skills and associated treatment sessions.
      - Explore supporter involvement.
    - Conclude the session.

Session 2 Protocol with Scripts

Strengthen Rapport

The clinician welcomes the patient and provides an overview of the second session, in which the clinician further develops and reinforces the patient's change process and helps them increase their awareness around substance use or other issues of concern.

Review Progress: Examining the Patient's Recent Experiences

The clinician uses the ***Review of Progress*** handout to briefly review of the patient's progress in key domains since the last session, including substance use, mental health symptoms, and related wellness areas.

The clinician asks the patient to describe their recent experiences with alcohol or other substances:

- Did the patient stop or attempt to discontinue use since the previous session?
- Was the patient confronted with any high-risk or triggering situations?
- Has the patient experienced high anxiety or depressive episodes?
- What strategies did the patient use? Did the patient try any of the strategies in ***Learning New Coping Strategies***? Were they successful?
- Were there any instances when the patient effectively handled a "hot" situation?

As the patient talks, the clinician's objective is to elicit information and to use that information to provide reflections, express empathy, identify discrepancies, elicit self-motivational statements, and roll with sustain talk/discord. See the sample language provided.

> ***Shirley (S):*** *Well, I've almost completely stopped smoking weed since our last session.*
> ***Clinician (C):*** *You seem very pleased with yourself! How did you do that?*
> ***S:*** *Right after the last session, I kept thinking about how weed has kept me from doing the things I want to do. I really want to be a teacher, and I realized that as long as I kept smoking, I would always feel bad. So, I went home and smoked one last time, then got rid of the remainder of my stash into the sink! During the last week I've wanted to use several times, but I did not.*
> ***C:*** *What did you do when you felt like smoking?*
> ***S:*** *Well, I talked to my husband. I read about that in the handout you gave me last week.*

Review Between-session Challenge: Assessing the Patient's Progress and Readiness to Proceed

The clinician asks the patient how they feel about the previous session and responds to any concerns, addressing any comments or questions about the ***Change Plan*** or ***Learning New Coping Strategies*** activities. If the patient has completed the ***Change Plan***, they are asked to read it and discuss the choices. The clinician reviews the ***Change Plan*** as a personalized reflective discussion. Specifically, the clinician:

- Reaffirms the patient's written statements
- Provides feedback
- Discusses adjustments (e.g., is the patient setting unrealistically high standards that may set them up for failure? has the patient identified salient reasons for wanting to make changes?)
- Evokes the personal meaning of the Change Plan elements to the patient

- Enhances motivation and resolves ambivalence about change
- Reinforces the patient's commitment to their goals

The clinician then photocopies the change plan as a record of the patient's goals.

The clinician must be vigilant about maintaining the patient's level of motivation for change and engagement in treatment. If the **Change Plan** was **not** completed, the clinician elicits the patient's reasons for not engaging in the change process at home to assess, for example, ambivalence, other obstacles, or both. Strong ambivalence may manifest in nonverbal behavior (e.g., level of comfort, reluctance to establish treatment goals). If the reason appears to be ambivalence, the clinician uses MI strategies described in Section 1, asking open-ended questions, reflecting, etc. Specific MI strategies depend on the nature of the sustain talk and of the assessed stage of change (i.e., precontemplation or contemplation). If the patient still is uncertain or unaware of any need to change, the clinician can focus the discussion on reflections, normalizing uncertainty, reviewing health risks again, asking future-oriented questions, or imagining extreme questions (e.g., "What would it take or what would have to happen for you to want to make a change?").

> Sessions 1 and 2 are always done first and in order. Priorities for intervention emerge during these sessions, and subsequent sessions should be individualized.

If there is awareness of a need to change, the clinician can use the **Decisional Balance** form (Session 8 handout) and reemphasize the benefits and risks. This technique can help the patient develop further discrepancy and swing the balance toward change. If the lack of follow-through was the result of more simple obstacles (e.g. being too busy, forgetting), the clinician can brainstorm solutions and have the patient choose and commit to the choice. (Session 6 presents one method for problem solving, I-SOLVE.) Forgetfulness is a common challenge for persons in treatment. A strategy that can help a patient remember the between-session practice is to encourage use of a smartphone calendar, typing in the assigned challenge using the alarm function. Regardless of why the assigned challenge was not completed, the clinician should reinforce the need to complete the practice work to achieve goals.

Provide Session Rationale

The clinician shares the rationale for the awareness-raising activity by describing how and why building personal awareness is essential in the change process. They also personalize the rationale by sharing how personal awareness skills will support the patient's own recovery process.

Substance use example

> **Clinician (C):** I want to explain how we think about substance use. When someone has used alcohol or other drugs over time, we think of it as a negative habit, similar to other habits, like biting your nails or eating junk food. We try to help the person figure out what has been keeping the habit going. This way, if someone wants to stop the habit and knows what is keeping it going, they can use this information to help stop it. Does thinking of it as a habit make sense to you?
>
> **Shirley (S):** Completely! It's like to just start pouring my first drink without even thinking about it the second I walk into the door after work.
>
> **C:** Yes, and after a while of drinking in similar situations, just being in those situations can make that person feel like drinking. We call that a trigger. It could be anything about the situation, like the time of day, whom you are with, or even something like a type of music. You have mentioned some things that sound like triggers for you. What do you think some of your triggers are?

> **S:** Well, definitely the time of day. In fact, I even start thinking about drinking as I'm pulling out of the school parking lot and heading home from the day. On the weekends, I drink a lot with my close group of friends. So just getting together in the evening to hang out is a pretty strong trigger for me.
>
> **C:** For you, some of the external aspects of a situation are strong triggers. Another type of trigger can be how someone is feeling. Some people say that they feel more like using alcohol or other drugs when they are feeling bad, like feeling bored, nervous, or angry. They say that using is a way of trying to cope with the bad feelings. Some people especially feel like using alcohol or other drugs when they are happy or excited. Does this part of it—someone using to affect how they feel—make sense to you?
>
> **S:** You know, I think that my desire to drink after work is probably in large part due to having such stressful work days. There is very little downtime in my job.
>
> **C:** Stress is a very common trigger. I wonder whether you sometimes find yourself having certain thoughts or ideas about your use as these can also lead to urges to use. These might be thoughts like, "My friends will think I'm boring if I do not drink," or "I deserve this after the day I've had."
>
> **S:** I often feel like my thoughts are my own worst enemy, and I really do believe that I deserve some type of reward for all the hard work of the day."
>
> **C:** Based on all the triggers you just identified; this shows how substance use does not just suddenly happen. Usually there are things going on around a person or in the way someone is thinking or feeling that affect whether or not they make a choice to use. Knowing what affects your own use gives you more power to decide whether or not to use. And looking at both the pros and cons of what happens after you use also helps you understand why you use and helps you make decisions about what you want to do in the future.
>
> Figuring out the factors that lead to your own alcohol use, like the time of day, being around friends, work stress, and your town thoughts, gives you more power to decide what to do next and to break the habit, if you want to. That's the main thing that we are trying to do in this treatment—to give you a lot of different ways to take back control instead of being under the control of the habit.

Depression example

> **Clinician:** I want to first explain how we think about depression. What we do and what we think profoundly influences what we feel. We know that some people may be more sensitive than others to feelings. And we know that by learning how our behaviors and/or thoughts influence how we feel, we can change how we feel by changing our behaviors and/or our thoughts. In this awareness-raising session, we will explore your triad of thoughts, behaviors, and feelings and how they work together to keep you feeling the way you feel. We know that these thoughts, feelings, and behaviors can become fused and seem automatic. We also know that by raising your awareness of this triad, you then have the psychological space to make small changes that can make a big difference.

Teach Session Skill

Introduce the patient to the ***Awareness Record***. Provide them with a blank copy, and retain one for yourself. Describe the ***Awareness Record*** by walking the patient through each column and by explaining each component in depth, checking in to assess the patient's understanding along the way.

The components of the *Awareness Record* include:

- **Trigger.** Triggers refer to internal, external, and situational factors that invite depressive feelings, negative and self-limiting thoughts and beliefs, and avoidant behaviors. Triggers also invite urges to use substances. Identifying triggers involves pinpointing the stimuli that may be present in a given situation.
- **Thoughts, Feelings, and Beliefs.** These internal experiences serve as triggers for depressed feelings. The way people respond is largely shaped by the thoughts people have about those events, feelings that are generated, and belief systems that are activated.
- **Behavior.** Behavior refers to the action(s) taken in response to thoughts and feelings, which are triggered by external events and by internal thoughts, feelings, and beliefs. Behavioral responses often serve to decrease or lessen the intensity of the feelings and can range from healthy and helpful behaviors to unhealthy and less helpful behaviors.
- **Positive Results.** The person's behavior has potentially both positive and negative outcomes. We will explore the good things that came out of the behavioral choice. In addition to positive outcomes, we explore the not-as-good things that resulted from the behavior response.

Lead Demonstration/Role Play

The clinician demonstrates the awareness-raising activity by walking the patient through a detailed exploration of one incident of substance use or of heightened depression in recent history. The patient identifies the situation, and the clinician uses core MI skills (i.e., open-ended questions, reflection, summaries) to gain a deeper understanding of the patient's experiences. It is important to probe enough within each component of the *Awareness Record* to gain a comprehensive, thorough understanding of the incident. The clinician will most often need to ask multiple follow-up questions within each element to dive deeper into the details of the patient's experience. They check in with the patient as to their experience in completing the awareness-raising activity and address any questions regarding how to complete it.

Note to clinicians: It is important to remember that completing a handout like the *Awareness Record* **is a means to an end** for your patient and you to gain a deeper awareness of the target behavior and of the thoughts, feelings, beliefs, and actions that invite it.

Facilitate Patient-led Practice/Assess Skills Transfer

The patient then takes the lead at walking the clinician through each component of the awareness record for up to two recent incidents in which the patient did use or and was triggered but did not use, as well as thoughts and behaviors they listed in the depressive feelings. The purpose for focusing on an event in which the patient did or did not do is to bring understanding to the factors that led to the choice in a given situation. During the patient's application of the awareness-raising activity, the clinician affirms the patient's skill application and offers follow-up questions to encourage the patient to explore the incident more thoroughly.

Identify Real-world Application

The clinician helps the patient to think through opportunities for how they might continue strengthening their awareness through additional awareness-raising practice throughout the week. These might be situations in which the patient can benefit from "slowing down" their automatic behavioral response to use when having cravings. Relatedly, the patient may consider using the awareness-raising activity before a potentially triggering event to prepare for how they may experience the trigger and to plan for health choices. The patient may also consider reflecting on incidents in which they did use to bring clarity to the multiple factors that led to their behavioral response and to the outcomes of that response. For a patient with mood or anxiety issues, you can invite them to scale the emotional severity on a scale of 1–10 (low to high).

Negotiate and Prepare Between-session Challenge

The exploration of real-world skill application is a natural transition into negotiation of a between-session practice. The clinician encourages the patient to continue reviewing the materials handed out at this and last week's sessions. They ask the patient where, when, and how they can apply awareness raising in their daily life, working to generate a specific plan for continued practice of the *Awareness Record* and completing one of the newly developed specific steps in the *Change Plan*. If the patient is uncertain which one to choose, discuss options, and indicate that one good initial choice would be the step the patient is most ready to complete. For any identified between-session challenges, the clinician works with the patient to ensure that they know what they will do, when they will do it, and how often it will be done, mentally rehearsing its application in their daily life. Most patients benefit from writing down this plan somewhere accessible to also serve as an ongoing reminder.

Elicit Commitment

The clinician explores the patient's commitment for completing the between-session practice and uses MI strategies, as needed, to assess and strengthen commitment. They also ask the patient to think through any potential obstacles to their skills practice, working with them to identify solutions and to activate resources as needed to support their skill application.

Summarize and Conclude

The clinician reviews the session, asks the patient for feedback, responds empathically to their comments, and troubleshoots any difficulties. Specifically, they will want to explore the patient's response and perceived utility of learning the awareness-raising activity. Through completing the *Awareness Record* with several different incidents, the clinician begins to identify patterns and common challenges the patient experiences. The clinician engages the patient in their identification of patterns and associated areas of difficulty (e.g., boredom, not asserting oneself, lack of coping skills to manage strong emotions).

With this information, the clinician and patient should also discuss the likely scenarios for future treatment sessions. At this point, the clinician reminds the patient they will be meeting for 4–15 more sessions (in most cases) and that they have some flexibility as to what they can do for those meetings. The clinician should suggest the kinds of skill topics they might cover, based on what they have learned about the patient's use experiences thus far, and seek input from them about how to spend the remaining sessions. Explain that the sessions focused on skills are meant to give the patient new tools to make the important changes they have begun. See the sample language.

> **Clinician:** I appreciate being able to get to know you over these few weeks and admire your courage in undertaking the important goals you have started to work on regarding your use of cocaine. What I'd like to do is help you learn some new skills that are meant to support you with keeping your resolve. One of these sessions focuses on learning a skill called mindful awareness, which can be very helpful for people trying to make a change the same way you are. I also want to help you with the problem you described where you said it's sometimes difficult to communicate with friends and families. There are other tools I want to share with you that I think will be useful. How do these ideas sound to you? Any questions so far?

Session 2 Handouts: Enhancing Situational Awareness

Review of Progress and Between-session Challenges

Directions: Use the table below to support weekly progress review in key domains relevant to the patient's substance use and overall well-being. This table can also be used to review the between-session challenges. This table can be tailored to address target areas of concern.

Domain	Sun.	Mon.	Tues.	Wed	Thur.	Fri.	Sat.
Physical Activity							
Sleep							
Diet							
Pleasure/Replacement Activities							
Mastery Activities							
Work/School							
Mood States							
Tobacco/Nicotine							
Alcohol							
Marijuana							
Other Drugs							
Between-Session Challenge							

Awareness Record

To increase awareness, use this form to identify situations, thoughts, feelings, and consequences that are associated with your alcohol/substance use or other behaviors of concern.

Note to clinician: The **Awareness Record** can be applied to all manner of concerns (e.g., mood, anxiety, anger).

Describe incident:

Trigger	Thoughts, Feelings, and Beliefs	Intensity of Feeling	Behavior	Positive Results	Negative Results
(What set me up to be more likely to use alcohol or drugs?) or (to feel heightened depression or anxiety?)	(What was I thinking? What was I feeling? What did I tell myself?)	Low–high, 1–10	(What did I do then?)	(What good things happened?)	(What bad things happened?)

Date and Time: _____

Awareness Record—Substance Use and Mood Examples

To increase awareness about your patterns of use, use this form to identify the kinds of situations, thoughts, feelings, and consequences that are associated with your alcohol/substance use or depressive mood. Below is an example of how the form might be used.

Describe incident: Spent evening with my friend smoking weed and drinking beer.

Trigger	Thoughts, Feelings, and Beliefs	Intensity of Feeling	Behavior	Positive Results	Negative Results
(What sets me up to be more likely to use alcohol or drugs?)	(What was I thinking? What was I feeling? What did I tell myself?)	Low–high, 1–10	(What did I do then?)	(What good things happened?)	(What bad things happened?)
Friend called and invited me to get high with him. Nothing else to do.	"I want to reward myself." "I'm bored." "Felt good about going 15 days without using so felt OK about getting high today."	It was like a 7 or an 8. I really wanted to get high.	Went out with friend and used	Had fun. Felt good to get high, having gone 15 days without	Broke the 15-day abstinence (although wasn't too worried about this). Didn't get as much done. Didn't feel as healthy.
What triggered me to feel really depressed.	(What was I thinking? What was I feeling? What did I tell myself?)	Intensity of Feeling	Behavior	Positive Results	Negative Results
My ex-wife called me, yelling at me for being late with my child support. She called me a failure as a father.	I felt terrible, like I just wanted to hide. I thought to myself, she's right. I am a loser and a terrible father.	It was like an 8 or 9	I did not do anything. I sat on the couch and felt like crap.	I guess there was positive because I did not call her up and start yelling at her.	I did not make anything worse by getting into an argument with her.

Planning to Feel Good (Optional)

I am doing this right now.	I used to do this, and I want to try again.	I have never done this, and I want to try.

Session 3. Learning Assertiveness

Introduction and Session Goals

Communication skills are perhaps our most important coping skills. During Session 3, the clinician first provides a rationale explaining the critical need for effective communication to get needs met and, more specifically, when trying to change behaviors. The clinician then discusses the different communication styles illustrating effective and less effective communication. Through a series of engaging interactive discussions and practice, the clinician helps the patient identify their own style of communication and the communication style of family and friends. They then assist the patient with practicing ways to be assertive in a variety of everyday situations and in challenging situations they are facing, while moving toward change. The clinician helps the client realize the difference between their expression of a definite, more assertive "no" and one where the client feels less definite and uncertain. The patient learns about effective and ineffective communication and develops increased awareness of their own communication and of those of their social network. Patients become familiar with expressing their needs assertively in a variety of real-life situations and practices in and out of sessions. They commit to practicing assertiveness and assertive limit setting in the upcoming weeks.

A main goal of all ICBT skill sessions is activating the patient in and out of treatment. Sessions are not just discussions, but a chance to introduce and practice skills, where the patient takes the lead and transfers these skills into real-life practice.

Clinician Preparation

Session 3. Learning Assertiveness	
Materials • *Review of Progress and Between-Session Challenges* • *Awareness Record* (see Session 2 handouts) • *Learning New Coping Strategies* (see Session 1 handout) • *Communication Styles* handout • *Between-Session Challenge: Assertiveness* handout	**Total Time** One hour **Delivery Method** CBT-focused individual or group therapy

Strategies
- Follow OARS techniques.
- Use EDARS.
- Identify stage of change.
- Demonstrate skill, role play, and give feedback.
- Review handouts to help transfer knowledge and skills.
- Develop "real-life practice challenge," and generate commitment.

Goals for This Session
- Enhance the patient's understanding of different styles of communication.
- Explain the four different communication styles:
    1. Passive
    2. Passive-Aggressive
    3. Aggressive
    4. Assertive
- Practice relevant scenarios and different communication styles.

Session 3 Outline and Overview

First Third

1) Strengthen rapport.
   - Welcome the patient and, if present, the support person.
   - Share the session agenda; invite items from the patient.
   - Engage in non-problem-focused rapport building, exploring areas of the patient's life not directly related to treatment.
2) Review progress.
   - Engage the patient in a brief review of their progress related to their substance use, mental health, and related experiences since the previous session. Use the **Review of Progress** handout as a guide.
     - Did the patient try to change behavior?
     - Did the patient experience any high-risk or triggering situations?
     - If the patient engaged in substance use or a significant affective event, explore their use event(s), using the **Awareness Record** handout from Session 2 to assess internal and external triggers, cravings, and consequences.
3) Review between-session challenge.
   - Review any between-session challenges from the previous session.
     - Did the patient complete the **Awareness Record**? If so, review their triggers, beliefs, urges, behavior, pros, and cons.
     - Discuss the different situations recorded and see if patterns emerge to the reactions. Note any signs of internal or external triggers that can be addressed through better communication to self or others.
     - Did the patient use any strategies from the Session one **Learning New Coping Strategies** handout? Were the strategies successful?

Second Third

4) Provide session rationale.
   - Provide a rationale for assertive communication in general, as well as specific assertive skills, including refusal/limit setting and help seeking.
   - Explore with the patient if they understand why the activity or skill will help build recovery strength.
5) Teach session skill.
   - Share relevant information to help the patient understand the skill and provide them the step-by-step approach of how to implement it.
   - Engage and elicit patient communication styles:
     - Offer to reveal the patient's communication style. For example, offer the patient a food you know they dislike or even despise or ask them to lend you $20. The objective is to make a request that you know the patient can refuse or say "no" to without internal conflict or guilt.
     - Discuss how the patient expressed their refusal.
   - Define aggressive, passive, passive-aggressive, and assertive communication.
   - Discuss benefits of assertiveness:
     - Increases likelihood person will achieve goal or objective
     - Increases chance the person will feel more satisfied with a situation

6) Lead demonstration/role-play.
   - Model different styles of communication.
   - Identify scenarios exemplifying these styles.
   - Develop role-play exercise of relevance for patient.
   - Practice assertiveness in the context of role-play. Identify obstacles and barriers.
7) Facilitate patient-led practice/assess skills transfer.

Third Third

1) Identify real-world application.
   - Help the patient identify real-life situations in which they can apply the skill.
2) Negotiate and prepare between-session challenge.
   - Review the patient's communication style and the skill of assertiveness.
     - Hand out **Between-Session Challenge: Assertiveness**.
   - Ask the patient to commit to a weekly between-session real challenge using assertive communication in several upcoming situations.
   - Discuss the real-life "assertive" situation details: when, with whom, and where.
   - If time allows, practice the between-session challenge to help the patient prepare.
3) Elicit commitment.
4) Summarize and conclude.

Session 3 Protocol with Scripts

Strengthen Rapport
The clinician welcomes the patient and provides an overview of the third session, where the clinician further strengthens recovery skills through understanding and learning the most effective types of communication. They invite the patient to provide additional agenda items for the session.

Review Progress: Examining the Patient's Recent Experiences
The clinician uses the **Review of Progress** handout to briefly review of the patient's progress in key domains since the last session, including substance use, mental health symptoms, and related wellness areas.

The clinician asks the patient to describe their recent experiences with alcohol or other substances:

- Did the patient make any behavior changes since the previous session?
- If relevant, did the patient make an effort to stop? If so, what was the result?
- Was the patient exposed to any high-risk situations? If so, how were they handled?
- What strategies did the patient use? Did the patient try any to see what triggers were most inviting to use, and, if so, did they try any of the strategies in the handout on **Learning New Coping Strategies**? Were they successful?
- Were there any instances when the patient effectively handled a "hot" situation (i.e., very high risk)? How were they handled?

Again, and throughout the model when the patient talks, the clinician's objective is to elicit information and to use that information to provide reflections, express empathy, identify discrepancies, elicit self-motivational statements, and roll with sustain talk/discord.

Review Between-session Challenge: Assessing the Patient's Progress and Readiness to Proceed
Inquire about any between-session practice. Did the patient find recording situations in the **Awareness Record** helpful? If appropriate, praise the patient's efforts in accomplishing the between-session challenge and maintaining changes, if any. If the patient did not complete the **Awareness Record**, ask them what happened and why they did not complete the challenge. If they state they did not understand the challenge, it is fine to go ahead and complete the challenge with them, but emphasize their taking the lead in the activity. Holding patients accountable in a clear manner but one that is not off putting is essential to potent CBT. Thus, the clinician again reaffirms that between-session challenges are an expectation of work in treatment and explains the reason for the between-session challenge again. Elicit a confirmation of patient's understanding. Then have the patient do the challenge with you now to demonstrate its importance.

Provide Session Rationale
Introduce the current topic involving styles of communication.

> *Clinician:* Have you ever been in a situation where you wanted to tell someone how you felt but could not for some reason? Can you explain to me what made it difficult? Did not saying anything to help or hurt the situation or your feelings in general?
>
> What about a time when you felt really upset or angry but waited to tell the person so that when you finally spoke up, you ended up saying a lot of negative things that you later regretted? Many of us can identify with these kinds of situations.

Provide the rationale for the benefit to use assertive communication to get needs met and the need for assertive refusal skills to strengthen the path toward recovery. Sample language follows.

> **Clinician:** Communication is much more complex than it seems, so we all struggle with miscommunication. Any conversation includes a speaker and a listener. Both verbal and nonverbal expressions are used to determine the meaning during the conversation. The listener has a filter already in place to influence and interpret what is seen and heard. Therefore, to be clear and have our needs met, we all must rely on practiced and effective communication strategies.

There is an extra burden to use effective communication when trying to change any behavior, especially substance use behaviors. The repetitive nature of negative habits increases the likelihood there will be an increase in situations to use, along with associated thoughts and feelings. Sample language follows.

> **Clinician:** When we are really stressed, there's a funneling effect or narrowing of your own thoughts and coping strategies. Your coping outlets, like your circle of supportive friends, gets smaller, while your circle of using friends gets bigger. This increases relapse risk.
> When was the last time you celebrated without using? When was the last time you handled a negative situation, feeling, or thought?

Teach Session Skill
Begin the in-session practice of assertive communication with real situations to evoke natural skill level for being direct with refusal.

> **Clinician:** Tell me a food you dislike and would not eat.

Pressure the patient to eat the disliked food, and see how they respond. Use any strategy necessary to try to get the patient to accept it, such as saying, "I made it just for you," or "I made it a way that it tastes like candy." Discuss the patient's response and how clear they were about refusing the food.

Incorporate the patient's communication style from the discussion above. Ask about the patient's understanding of the terms assertiveness or assertive communication. Discuss whether and when the patient has been successfully assertive.

Teach Communication Styles
Different Styles of Communication. The clinician identifies types of communication and asks the patient to define their understanding of them. Next, they provide definitions of each style and compare them to the patient's definitions—not to evaluate but to ensure accurate understanding. The clinician clarifies any areas of misconception according to the definitions below.

Passive Communication. With this style, a person is often unable to or fearful of expressing themself directly. They tend to acquiesce or go along with what another person wants. The person may not feel entitled to their opinions or believes the other person will not listen or care. For example, someone is asked to attend an event for work that is inconvenient, and, rather than asking to be excused or to reschedule, the person agrees immediately. With this form of communication, the individual does not express their needs and wants in a clear way.

Passive-aggressive Communication. With passive-aggressive communication or behavior, someone may appear to agree or go along with a plan of action but engages in other behavior that conveys true feelings. For example, a woman asks her husband to attend a family gathering. He is not enthusiastic about family events and has somewhat difficult relationships with some of his wife's family members. He would much prefer to stay home and watch a tennis match on television. Instead of telling his wife his feelings, he agrees to go to the family party and arranges to meet her there after he completes some errands. He ends up being "held up" with some of his chores and arrives at the party two hours late. This would be considered passive-aggressive because on the surface he seemed willing to go along with his wife's wishes, but, by arriving late, he conveyed his real preference indirectly. Passive-aggressive communication can be difficult to identify because often people are not aware of their behaviors. See the example provided.

> *Yes, that sounds just great. I want to go to the party, but I really have a few things I must do beforehand, so why do not I meet you there? It starts at 3:00, right? Oh, 2:00. OK, see you then.*

Aggressive Communication. When someone behaves or communicates in an aggressive manner, the person tends to ignore the rights or feelings of others. That person prioritizes their own experiences and needs above others'. The person may communicate through loud tones, yelling, threats, and intimidation. They may be insensitive to how a message is conveyed to others. This individual may not be willing to hear how someone else feels or wants in a particular situation. A fairly benign example: A group of friends goes out to dinner and begins talking about their children. One member of the group proceeds to comment and give unsolicited advice to each of the parents about all the mistakes they are making and how they are damaging their children through their behavior. See another example below.

> *I hope you understand that you are working for me. I am in charge. You'd better be willing to stay late or come in early if I tell you to, and I do not want to see any mistakes, or you will not be seeing a paycheck too much longer. Is that clear enough?*

Assertive Communication. With assertive communication, a person expresses thoughts, feelings, or needs directly and clearly and is respectful and sensitive to the rights and feelings of others. This person does not yell or intimidate, but they also do not sugarcoat a message to the point of meaninglessness. An example appears below.

> *When you tell me I'm stupid or will never accomplish anything important, I feel hurt. In the future, I ask that you communicate in a more constructive and respectful way, or I'll have to consider how to continue in this relationship.*

Assertive people decide what they want, plan a constructive way to involve others, and then act on the plan. It can be very effective to state one's feelings or opinions and to request the changes one would like from others, without being threatening, demanding, or negative. In sum, assertiveness means recognizing one's right to decide what to do in a given situation rather than giving in to others. Assertiveness recognizes the following rights to:

- Inform others of your opinion
- Inform others of your feelings in a way that is not hurtful
- Ask others to change their behavior that affects you
- Accept or reject what others say to you or request from you

Next, the clinician discusses the patient's understanding of the terms discussed and asks for examples they could share of each style. The examples could be situations the patient has experienced, heard about, or imagined. The clinician also asks the patient to identify how they speak to themself (self-talk). For example, "Given that most of us are critical when we make mistakes, it is also important to realize the style of communication we use for self-talk and how practicing assertiveness with ourselves will likely lead to a better feeling inside and perhaps an increased desire to change."

Explain the benefits of assertiveness. The clinician explains the benefits of assertiveness below.

> Assertiveness is the most effective way to let others know what's going on or what effect their behavior has. By expressing themselves, assertive people resolve uncomfortable feelings that otherwise build up. Because being assertive often results in correcting a source of stress and tension, it can lead to feeling more in control of life. Assertive people do not feel like victims of circumstances. However, their goals cannot be met in all situations; it is not possible to control how another person will respond. Nevertheless, behaving assertively has two benefits: It increases the chances goals will be met, and it makes people feel better about their role in the situation.

Introduce Skill Guidelines

The clinician explains that the guidelines in the *Between-Session Challenge: Assertiveness* handout can help the patient become assertive.

> *Take a moment to think before you speak. What did the other person do or say? Try not to assume the other person's intentions. Do not assume that they know your mind. Plan the most effective way to make statements. Be specific and direct. Address the problem without bringing in other issues. Be positive. Do not put others down; blaming others makes them defensive and less likely to hear your message.*
>
> *Pay attention to your body language: eye contact, posture, gestures, facial expression, and tone of voice. Make sure your words and expression communicate the same message. To get your point across, speak firmly, and be aware of how you appear.*
>
> *Be willing to compromise. Let others know you are willing to work things out. No one has to leave the situation feeling as if they have lost everything. Try to find a way for everyone to win. Give others your full attention when they reply, try to understand their views, and seek clarification.*
>
> *If you disagree, have a discussion. Do not dominate or submit to others. Strive for equality in the relationship. If you feel you are not being heard, restate your assertion. Persistence and consistency are necessary parts of assertiveness. Changing how you respond requires effort. The first step is to become aware of habitual responses and to try to change.*

The most difficult situations to respond assertively are those that may end with negative consequences. The clinician asks the patient to examine the thoughts that prevent them from acting assertively with others and themselves (e.g., "My boss will fire me if I cannot work overtime because I have my counseling session"). This examination uses many skills discussed in other sessions.

- **Determine the thought or fear.** What am I afraid will happen? What's the worst that could happen?
- **Assess the probabilities.** How likely is the negative consequence?
- **Evaluate the catastrophe.** What would happen if the worst occurred? Would it really be so terrible?
- **Identify the rules.** What assumptions and beliefs govern feelings?

Lead Demonstration/Role Play
The clinician and patient role play a situation in which the clinician plays a person refusing the offer of substances from a friend; the patient plays the person offering the substance. The clinician models passive, aggressive, passive-aggressive, and assertive responses. After each response, the clinician asks the patient to identify the behavior and to determine the success of that approach.

Facilitate Patient-led Practice/Assess Skills Transfer
After discussing and reviewing the different styles of communication, the clinician asks the patient to identify a current problem or situation where they have difficulty communicating needs in an effective manner. The situation might be one involving alcohol or substance use (e.g., being able to resist or refuse offers to use at a party or from a long-time drinking buddy). It could also involve the patient expressing feelings in an important relationship. If they have difficulty generating a role-play scenario, the clinician can suggest some general topics or relationships or a specific idea based on knowledge about the patient where assertive communication could be of benefit. The clinician gives the patient the ***Assertiveness*** between-session challenge handout and asks the patient to try at home.

Identify Real-world Application
After summarizing the assertive communication session, get a specific commitment for the patient's completion of the between-session work and prepare for the next session. The summary is an opportunity to reinforce the patient's personal awareness and assertiveness refusal skill learning to increase a sense of self-efficacy. The preparation statement could sound like the following.

> *Today we covered a lot of information about your use, what sets you up to use, and communication skills that are helpful in working toward your recovery goals. You most frequently reported your triggers are likely to be [___] and that knowing these triggers ahead of time and avoiding certain places and people has helped increase successful experiences without use." (Summarize the types of triggers: the time of day, situation, or feelings and thoughts—positive and/or negative). But, as you have stated, you cannot avoid all people, places, or situations all the time, and trying to do is also stressful. As today's lesson has demonstrated, it's possible to practice assertive refusal skills that allow you to be clear on how to get your needs met and to refuse in ways others will understand.*
>
> *For example: Today you practiced refusal skills in several situations with others and in self-talk to help you gain confidence in saying no and to not feel guilty or confused during risky times or events in the upcoming weeks.*
>
> *I wonder if you can tell me how you would use the assertive refusal skills in the next weeks to help you meet your goals?*

Negotiate and Prepare Between-session Practice
Hand out the **Between-Session Challenge: Assertiveness** worksheet. Ask the patient to use assertive communication for self-talk and with others when confronted by a trigger to use (e.g., negative thought, feeling, celebration, social pressure situation).

> *During the next week, I would like you to practice using the **Awareness Record** worksheet and your assertive refusal skills, like how we did today. How does that sound to you?*

If the patient says it will be hard, try to help remove any obstacles.

Elicit Commitment
If the patient agrees, say:

> *I am asking you to commit to filling out the sheet and using your refusal skills in two situations between sessions.*
>
> *Please identify a specific day, time, and place when you will complete the worksheet. Is there anything I can do to help you complete the real-life practice at the times you committed to?*

Provide a brief summary of the next session topic and how the lessons will help the patient strengthen recovery. The clinician might say:

> *In our next session together, we will focus on [___], working with your thoughts and learning a method to change them to enhance how you feel and what you do.*

Summarize and Conclude
Review and summarize session activities and key points. Prepare the patient for the next session by introducing the topic and by explaining how it will be helpful on the path toward wellness.

Session 3 Handouts: Learning Assertiveness

Review of Progress and Between-session Challenges

Directions: Use the table below to support weekly progress review in key domains relevant to the patient's substance use and overall well-being. This table can also be used to review the between-session challenges.

Domain	Sun.	Mon.	Tues.	Wed	Thur.	Fri.	Sat.
Physical Activity							
Sleep							
Diet							
Pleasure/Replacement Activities							
Mastery Activities							
Work/School							
Mood States							
Tobacco/Nicotine							
Alcohol							
Marijuana							
Other Drugs							
Between-Session Challenge							

Communication Styles

Passive-Aggressive	Aggressive
With passive-aggressive communication or behavior, someone may appear to agree or go along with a plan of action but engage in other behavior that conveys their true feelings. Passive-aggressive communication can be difficult to identify because often people are not aware they are doing it. **Example:** A woman asks her husband to attend a family gathering. He is not enthusiastic about family events and has somewhat conflicted relationships with some of his wife's family members. He would prefer to stay home and watch a tennis match on television. Instead of telling his wife his feelings, he agrees to go to the family party and arranges to meet her there after he completes some errands. He ends up being "held up" with some of his chores and arrives at the party two hours late. This would be considered "passive-aggressive" because, on the surface, he seemed willing to go along with his wife's wishes, but, by arriving late, he conveyed indirectly his preference to be elsewhere.	When someone behaves or communicates in an aggressive manner, they tend to ignore the rights or feelings of another person. They prioritize their own experience and needs over and above others involved. They may communicate through loud tones, yelling, threatening, and/or intimidating. They may be insensitive to how their message is coming across to others. They also may not be willing to hear how someone else feels or what they want in a particular situation. **Example:** A group of friends goes out to dinner and begins talking about their children. One member of the group comments and gives unsolicited advice to the parents about all the mistakes they are making and how their behavior is damaging their children.

Passive	Assertive Communication
This style occurs when someone feels unable to or fearful of expressing themselves or their feelings directly. They tend to acquiesce or go along with what the other person wants. They may not feel entitled to their opinions or believe the other person will not listen or care. **Example:** Someone is asked to attend an event for work that is inconvenient, but rather than asking to be excused or reschedule, the person agrees immediately. With this form of communication, an individual does not express their needs and wants in a clear way.	With assertive communication, a person expresses their thoughts, feelings, or needs directly and clearly and is respectful and sensitive to the rights and feelings of others. They do not yell or intimidate, but they also do not sugarcoat their message to the point of meaninglessness. *Benefits of being assertive:* • Is the most effective way to let others know what is going on or what effect their behavior has • Resolves uncomfortable feelings that otherwise build up • Can lead to feeling more in control of life • Increases the chances that goals will be met • Makes people feel better about their role in the situation

Between-session Challenge: Assertiveness

Remember the following points in practicing assertiveness:

- Take a moment to think before you speak.
- Be specific and direct in what you say.
- Pay attention to your body language (i.e., use direct eye contact; face the person you are addressing).
- Be willing to compromise.
- Restate your assertion if you feel that you are not being heard.

Practice exercise

The following exercises will help you become aware of your style of handling various social situations. The four common response styles are **passive, aggressive, passive-aggressive,** and **assertive**.

Pick **two** different social situations. Write brief descriptions of them and of your responses to them. Then decide which of the four common response styles best describes each response.

Situation 1

Describe:

_____

_____

_____

Your Response:

_____

_____

_____

Circle response style: *passive*   *aggressive*   *passive–aggressive*   *assertive*

If your response was not assertive, think of an assertive response and write it down here:

_____

_____

_____

Situation 2

Describe:

_____

_____

_____

Your Response:

_____

_____

_____

Circle response style: ***passive***   ***aggressive***   ***passive–aggressive***   ***assertive***

If your response was not assertive, think of an assertive response and write it down here:

_____

_____

Source: Monti et al. (1989).

Session 4. Supporting Recovery Through Enhanced Social Supports

Introduction and Session Goals

Effective therapy starts with building rapport and trust and enhancing the therapeutic alliance developed in earlier sessions. The therapeutic alliance is essential to honest appraisal and recall of situations, triggers, and consequences of behaviors. A main goal of all ICBT skill sessions is activating the patient in and out of treatment. Sessions are not just discussions, but a chance to introduce and practice skills where the client takes the lead.

In Sessions 4 and 5, the clinician and patient address two essential areas of recovery: (1) social support and (2) healthy replacement activities. Both aspects of the patient's life are a necessity to finding a life worth living without using substances. The clinician facilitates a discussion with the patient about the quality and scope of their social network (using the ***My Social Atom Diagram***). Session 4 includes skills introduced in Session 3. The clinician discusses and asks the patient how they might use their assertive communication skills from the previous session to engage social support in a clear fashion that helps to build connections. The patient will have an opportunity to better understand and resolve reluctance in reaching out for support. They will identify potential allies and develop and activate a plan for building a more vibrant network of support.

A main goal for this first part of the session is not only discussing social supports, but practicing the social interaction and eliciting a commitment to asking for support from an identified person.

Note to clinician: Yes, some individuals recover from a use disorder without social support. However, research demonstrates that social support is strongly associated with recovery from anxiety, depression, and substance use (Atkins Jr. and Hawdon, 2007). In fact, social support is understood as so crucial that most evidence-based treatment maintains a significant focus on social support (Miller et al., 2011).

In Session 5, Supporting Recovery Through Healthy Replacement Activities, the clinician offers insights into the rationales that underlie most substance use/drinking habits, which are often maintained because they increase feelings of pleasure and/or take away pain. Such experiences result from chemical changes in the brain after drinking or using drugs. One of the primary neurochemicals involved is dopamine. Dopamine and other reward sensation chemicals (e.g., serotonin) can also be produced by healthy and pleasurable activities; these are called replacement activities.

Consider asking, "What are the aspects of a relationship that brings you peace? What about connection, kindness, loyalty, compassion, and empathy?"

One of the best ways to increase dopamine is through physically new and challenging activities that require making effort and practicing skills. In Session 5, the patient brainstorms both activities that give immediate pleasure (effortless) and those that require mastery (effortful) and commits to engaging in both types in the next weeks.

Clinician Preparation

Session 4. Supporting Recovery Through Enhanced Social Supports	
Materials • *Review of Progress* • *My Social Atom Diagram* handout • *Social Support* handout	**Total Time** One hour **Delivery Method** CBT-focused individual or group therapy

Strategies
- Follow OARS techniques
- Use EDARS and identify stage of change.
- Demonstrate skill, practice, and give feedback.
- Use handouts to focus the session, helping to transfer knowledge and skill.
- Develop "real-life practice challenge," and generate commitment.

Goals for This Session
- Enhance the patient's understanding of their social network as it pertains to connections that strengthen recovery.
- Discuss, elicit, and discuss how a helpful, supportive relationship in the patient's life can become aware of their role as a recovery support.
- Identify internal barriers that may limit your patient's willingness to seek out new social supports.
- Enlist other clinical sessions (e.g., Sessions 8 and 9, Working with Thoughts and Emotions) to address internal barriers.
- Identify a current situation or relationship that could benefit from the patient communicating in a more assertive way about needing help and offering help.

Session 4 Outline and Overview for Enhancing Social Support

First Third

1) Strengthen rapport.
   - Welcome the patient and build rapport.
   - Share the session agenda, and invite items from the patient.
   - Engage in non-problem-focused rapport building, exploring areas of the patient's life not directly related to treatment.
   - Use this as an opportunity to
     - Explore patient's social connections and strengths
     - Continue to explore patient's passions, interests, and strengths
2) Review progress.
   - Engage the patient in a brief review of their progress related to their substance use, mental health, and related experiences since the previous session. Use the *Review of Progress* handout as a guide.
     - Where is the patient in their readiness to change?
     - If applicable, did the patient make an effort to stop? Cut down?
     - Did the patient experience any high-risk or challenging situations?
     - If the patient engaged in substance use, explore their use event(s), using the *Awareness Record* to assess internal and external triggers, cravings, and consequences.
3) Review between-session challenge.
   - Did the patient experience any high-risk or tempting situations?
   - Did the patient use the communication assertiveness strategies from the previous sessions?
   - Were the strategies successful?
   - Did the patient complete the between-session practice? How did it go?
   - If the patient did not complete the between-session challenge, explore what got in the way, practice it if time allows, and potentially problem solve in anticipation of this week's challenge.

Second Third

4) Provide session rationale.
   - Explain the rationale for building the patient's social support networks (*Social Support* and *My Social Atom Diagram* handouts).
   - Use the *My Social Atom Diagram* to get a snapshot of the people in your patient's life today.
   - Ask the patient about the qualities of people that the patient has and would like to have in their social network.
     - Elicit types of support the patient is currently receiving or has received in the past. Who provided it? What did it look like? In what ways was it helpful? Unhelpful?
     - What type of support does the patient feel is needed most? Why?
5) Discuss the different types of social support.
   - Continue reviewing the different types of support from the *Social Support* handout.
   - Elicit examples from the patient for each type.
   - Ask the patient to consider supports not used in the past but which they might be willing to consider. Reference the *My Social Atom Diagram* handout.
6) Develop a plan for enhancing social support.
   - Continue reviewing the different types of support from the *Social Support* handout.
   - Elicit examples from the patient for each type.

- Ask the patient to consider support they have not used in the past but might be willing to consider.
- Identify barriers to seeking social support and address those barriers.
- Have the patient activate seeking support in session, if possible (e.g., sending a text message, email, or making a phone call or text while in session).

Third Third

7) Identify real-world application.
   - Have the patient complete the ***Plan for Seeking Support*** handout.
8) Review tips on how to ask for support and address potential obstacles.
   - Continue reviewing the tips on how to ask for support from the ***Social Support*** handout (hint: Draw from the assertiveness guidelines from previous session).
   - Discuss any potential barriers to getting the support identified in the patient's plans and engage the patient in group problem solving.
9) Negotiate between-session challenge and elicit commitment.
   - Elicit commitment from the patient to seek out one support identified in the plan during the next week.
   - Have the patient define specifically how and when they will seek out the support.
10) Summarize and conclude.

Session 4 Protocol with Scripts

Strengthen rapport
The clinician welcomes the patient and provides an overview of the fourth session, where the clinician further strengthens recovery capital through understanding and learning about the patient's relationships, including their quality, depth, and type. The clinician and patient also explore the patient's healthy-action-based coping strategies. Both mastery and immediate pleasure replacement activities are discussed and activated. The clinician invites the patient to provide additional agenda items for the session.

Review Progress: Examining the Patient's Recent Experiences
The clinician uses the ***Review of Progress*** handout to briefly review the patient's progress in key domains since the last session, including substance use, mental health symptoms, and related wellness areas.

The clinician asks the patient to describe their recent experiences with alcohol or other substances:

- Did the patient stop use or reduce since the previous session?
- Did the patient experience any mental health symptoms since the previous session?
- Was the patient confronted with any high-risk or tempting situations?
- What strategies did the patient use? Did the patient try any to see what triggers were most inviting to use; if so, did they try any of the communication strategies from the last session or any other coping strategies? Were they successful?
- Were there any instances when the patient effectively handled a "hot" situation (i.e., very high risk, very high stress)?

Again, and throughout the model when the patient talks, the clinician's objective is to elicit information and to use that information to provide reflections, express empathy, identify discrepancies, elicit self-motivational statements, and roll with sustain talk/discord.

Review Between-session Challenge: Assessing the Patient's Progress and Readiness to Proceed
Ask about any between-session practice challenge. Did the patient find being assertive with themself or others helpful? If appropriate, praise the patient's efforts accomplishing the between-session challenge and maintaining changes or abstinence. If the patient did not complete the challenge, ask them what happened and why they did not. Holding patients accountable in a clear manner, but one that is not off putting, is essential to potent CBT. Remind the patient that the between-session challenges are an expectation of work in treatment, explain the reason for the between-session challenge again, and then have the patient do the challenge with you now to demonstrate the importance.

Provide Session Rationale
Introduce the concept of enhanced social support and of how vital that is to creating a stimulating and fulfilling lifestyle. Share with the patient that often when reducing substance use, there is a sense of absence or loss as old habits, people, and places may create risks for continued use. Or, when addressing mental health concerns (e.g., depression), patients have withdrawn from social connections and been more driven by avoidant, mood-dependent behavior. Social support is a very

powerful and beneficial force in the recovery process and in living well. The benefits of social support are many:

- Sense of belongingness and inclusion
- Sense of safety and security
- Reduced stress and decreased isolation and loneliness
- Enhanced sense of meaning and purpose
- Hope and optimism about the future
- Opportunity to escape the narrow world of substance use
- Counteracting of shame, isolation, and secrecy

> **Clinician (C):** Most of our patients talk about the importance of examining and rebuilding social supports. Let us face it: We are social creatures and social connection is part of our well-being.
> **Patient:** That's true, but a lot of my friends and family drink or do drugs. So, what do I do? Alternatively, I just feel so down, and it feels so hard to reach out. It's just easier to stay home.
> **C:** So, let us start with getting a better picture of who actually is in your world and can they be an ally for your making changes. Let us first use the **My Social Atom Diagram** to understand who all is in in your world today.

The clinician and patient complete the **My Social Atom Diagram** together.

> **Clinician (C):** So, when you think about social support that would work for you, what do you want in that relationship?
> **Patient:** I want someone who will respect my privacy, someone who I can hang out with, someone who does not judge me, and someone does not give me grief.
> **C:** This is good. You are clear about what's important for you in a person who could be a support. Let us take a look again at the **My Social Atom Diagram** and see who might have those characteristics you value.

Clinician and patient review it together and identify one or more persons who could be social supports.

> Can you imagine for a minute that I am this person. How would you reach out to that person and what would you say?

Clinician and patient role play the conversation. The clinician may first model the behavior, and, next, the patient demonstrates the behavior. The clinician may need to use MI skills to process uncomfortable feelings of the patient connected to help seeking.

> Is there something you might do right now in session that gets this started?

Facilitate Patient-led Practice/Assess Skills Transfer

> **Patient:** I'd feel too weird calling in the middle of the day, but I could send a text message about catching up tonight or over the weekend. And then when we talk, I can say what's going on and ask.

Clinician has patient send text message (i.e., activation in session).

The Clinician and patient complete the ***Plan for Seeking Social Support*** and discuss any potential internal or external barriers to the plan.

Identify Real-world Application and Negotiate and Prepare Between-session Challenge

The clinician and patient negotiate between-session practice.

Elicit Commitment

The clinician elicits the patient's commitment to seek out one support identified in the plan during the next week. Have patient define specifically when and with whom they will seek out the support and how.

Summarize and Conclude

Note to clinician: Mastery and immediate pleasure activities can be the focus of the seeking support from relationships in the social network. Again, since a main goal of the social support session is to activate supportive relationships, this can be accomplished by directly seeking support to do a mastery activity together—and then the patient's challenge commitment integrates parts of this and the next the session.

Internal thoughts and emotions can be significant barriers to seeking supportive relationships. Working with these thoughts and feelings may need to occur concurrent to this skills session.

Session 4 Handouts: Supporting Recovery Through Enhanced Social Supports

Review of Progress and Between-session Challenges

Directions: Use the table below to support weekly progress review in key domains relevant to the patient's substance use and overall well-being. This table can also be used to review the between-session challenges.

Domain	Sun.	Mon.	Tues.	Wed	Thur.	Fri.	Sat.
Physical Activity							
Sleep							
Diet							
Pleasure/Replacement Activities							
Mastery Activities							
Work/School							
Mood States							
Tobacco/Nicotine							
Alcohol							
Marijuana							
Other Drugs							
Between-Session Challenge							

Social Support

Why is social support important?
We all need support at different times in our lives. Having people in our lives to support us can help us reach our goals and deal successfully with any challenges that come our way. When trying to make changes, you may experience the following:

- Continuing to interact with family and friends that use alcohol or drugs
- Continuing to interact with family and acquaintances when significant discord exists
- Missing out on social interactions
- Feeling anxious about socializing
- Facing a diminished social network of people
- Having a network of people who understand and support your efforts to change can be extremely helpful.

What types of support are out there?
- Self-help groups
- Professional help
- Spiritual or religious affiliations
- Personal relationships
- Coworkers
- Community service agencies

How can you ask for support?
- Be specific about what type of support you need.
- Show appreciation for the person's support if it was helpful.
- Give feedback to the person if they are giving support that was not helpful.
- Find a way to support the other person.

My Social Atom Diagram

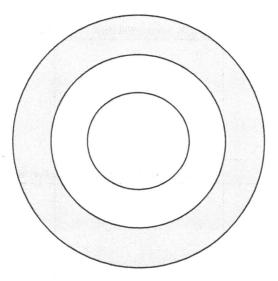

Instructions: The social atom is a direct way to better understand your social world. In the center, include yourself and those closest to you. In the next ring, include associates and others with whom you have somewhat-regular contact. In the third ring, include those with whom you have occasional contact. Outside the circles, put those with whom you have lost contact.

Plan for Seeking Support

Support	How This Support Will Help	Plan for Getting This Support
Support	How This Support Will Help	Plan for Getting This Support
Support	How This Support Will Help	Plan for Getting This Support

Session 5. Supporting Recovery Through Healthy Replacement Activities

Introduction and Session Goals

The goal of the healthy replacement activities is to help activate the patient's experiences through a focused conversation on how they obtain feelings of accomplishment, joy, and pleasure in life. The patient talks about past and present ways of feeling good and what it would take for them to reengage old activities or to consider trying new ones. They also experience having a supportive coach help them exchange their daily routines for ones that can become new, perhaps healthier, habits. The patient expresses optimism and commitment for trying to replace use by engaging in immediately pleasurable activities and longer term, skills-based activities.

Healthy Replacement Activities Rationale

Participating in healthy replacement activities is vital to creating an enjoyable and fulfilling lifestyle. Often when reducing substance use, patients feel a sense of absence, boredom, or loss owing to the physiological and psychological effects of no longer using or of using less. In a similar vein, people experiencing depression or high anxiety have retreated from activities and relationships through avoidance and mood-dependent behavior. Reengaging in healthy replacement activities helps to boost mood and confidence. Some of the best ways to increase feeling good is through physically new and challenging activities that require making an effort and practicing skills. In this session, the clinician and patient will brainstorm activities that give immediate pleasure and those that require mastery. Collaboratively, they will negotiate a commitment to engaging in both types in the coming weeks.

Note to clinician: For many patients, getting started is the hardest part. Scale the activity to a starting point that your patient will do and build incrementally.

Clinician Preparation

Session 5. Supporting Recovery Through Healthy Replacement Activities	
Materials • *Engaging in Replacement Activities* handout • *Increasing Pleasant Activities* handout	**Total Time** 45–60 minutes **Delivery Method** Skill-focused individual or group therapy

Strategies
- Follow OARS techniques.
- Use MI Eliciting Change Talk (Looking Back, Looking Forward, Pros and Cons, Decisional Balance Use).
- Brainstorm.
- Develop "real-life practice challenge" (e.g., prescription for fun).
- Follow CBT skills session reminders.

Goals for This Session
- Enhance the patient's understanding of their social network as it pertains to connections that strengthen recovery.
- Discuss, elicit, and discuss how a helpful, supportive relationship in the patient's life can become aware of their role as a recovery support.
- Identify internal barriers that may limit your patient's willingness to seek out new social supports.
- Enlist other clinical sessions (e.g., Sessions 8 and 9, Working with Thoughts and Emotions) to address internal barriers.
- Identify a current situation or relationship that could benefit from the patient communicating in a more assertive way about needing help and offering help.

Session 5 Outline and Overview for Healthy Replacement Activities

Note: If the session on replacement activities is done on its own and not coupled with the social supports, deliver all elements in a CBT session, including the first third of the session: Engage and Build Rapport, Review Progress, and Review Between-Session Challenge. Below, we assume the social support and replacement activities are being delivered in one session; therefore, some of the full CBT elements are truncated, but the goal of patient activation for the skills involved is met.

Second Third

1) Provide session rationale: Introduce increasing pleasant activities.
   - Explain the rationale that people often use *alcohol and/or other drugs* because of the pleasure they get from the experience or because they alleviate boredom and other uncomfortable emotions.
   - Explain the rationale that people experiencing anxiety and depression often retreat from pleasurable and socially connected activities because of the mood-dependent behavior of social anxiety.
   - Over time, it can be hard to have fun or enjoy oneself without using.
   - Related to this is the idea that drugs operate on specific reward centers in the brain.
   - Over time, as we retreat from or allow our moods to dictate our actions, our day-to-day lives become less enjoyable.
   - Our reward centers are also affected by other, exciting, nonsubstance-related activities (e.g., walking, running, playing basketball) and a wide range of other activities.
   - The clinician discusses the two different types of activities, including the differences between mastery and immediate pleasure and why having mastery activities is important (i.e., feeling better both immediately and longer term through accomplishment).
   - Finding activities that are rewarding, challenging, and stimulating can help increase long-term recovery.
2) Explore the patient's interests and passions.
   - Have the patient complete the top part of the **Increasing Pleasant Activities** handout by placing a "P" next to activities they select that are pleasurable and an "M" next to activities they select that incorporate a sense of mastery.
   - Brainstorm additional activities, if needed.

Third Third

3) Identify real-world application.
4) Elicit commitment from the patient to engage in one activity two times between sessions.
   - The patient completes the bottom portion of the **Increasing Pleasant Activities** handout.
   - Explore with the patient what could get in the way or pose a barrier to engaging in the chosen activities.
   - Problem solve to resolve any challenges to completing the task.
5) Summarize and conclude.

Session 5 Protocol with Scripts

Provide Session Rationale
Introduce the concept of participating in healthy replacement activities and how vital that is to create a stimulating and fulfilling lifestyle. Share with the patient that often when reducing substance use, there is a tremendous sense of absence or loss owing to the physiological and psychological effects of no longer using or using less.

Addressing SUD

> **Clinician (C):** Most of our patients tell us loud and clear that their substance use produced a sense of immediate pleasure and/or reward, both biologically and psychologically—feelings that they depend on to get through the daily boredom or stress of life.
> **Patient (P):** That's right! Using helps me spice up life when I need to, and, at other times, it chills me out so I do not feel so anxious and depressed.
> **C:** So, it does different things for you. Either way, it is mind altering, and you have come to rely on that experience. To replace the sense of loss as you reduce your use, most people find they need activities that include two important aspects of their life: pleasure and mastery. Pleasure activities bring us the immediate rewards that we all need to feel good, for example, watching a movie, reading a book, listening to music, and eating a nice meal. Mastery activities, because of the challenge they present, remain novel over time, lead to a long-term sense of accomplishment, and ultimately can produce feelings of passion for life (similar to passions for substance use). Mastery activities are challenging and demand creativity and effort in either or both the use of physical and mental skill.
> **P:** That makes sense because we'd even get bored of using the same thing in the same amount every day. Besides, I always switch it up and smoke weed sometimes and drink booze on other days or do both. It helps to give me different kinds of experiences.

Addressing mood

> **Clinician (C):** Most of our patients that avoid taking action do so even when we know it's good, because, in the moment, it reduces stress and anxiety.
> **Patient (P):** That's right! In the moment, I feel less stress because I do not have to get up, go out, and do something. I can just sit on the couch and watch something online. But, later that day, I have accomplished nothing and feel like a loser.
> **C:** So, when you do something, even something small like going for a walk, how do you feel?
> **P:** Better, I suppose. Like I actually did something. Of course, I will as often give myself grief thinking I should have done more.

Lead Brainstorm to Identify Real-world Application

> **Clinician (C):** Given the need for both pleasure and mastery activities, what can you do every day or week to engage in one type or the other so you feel better in your life? Let us take a minute to think about some possibilities, check off some listed ones, and discuss the choices in this handout on replacement activities.
> Offer the patient the **Increasing Pleasant Activities** handout.

> **C:** The handout lists a combination of Mastery activities (Ms) and Immediate Pleasures (IPs); you'll notice some could both be dependent on how you commit to doing them.
> **Patient (P):** How many of each should I choose?
> **C:** It is best to try to choose 3–5 of the different activity types. That way, you will have options should one or a few not work out.
> **P:** OK, I'll do the immediate ones, and some are not listed. Drinking tea, listening to music, calling a friend, and taking a brief walk outside all let me calm down and feel OK.
> **C:** Awesome list of pleasurable activities. What about the Mastery (Ms) effort activities that you find rewarding, enjoyable, and stimulating?
> If needed, prompt the patient with examples: playing a musical instrument, writing, singing, and playing a sport (e.g., golf, walking, distance running, skiing)
> **P:** There are many I used do a lot: dance, cook, and play the guitar. Dancing seems the most fun for next week as it lifts my mood, and I do not need to do it alone all the time.

Negotiate and Prepare Between-session Commitment

Once the patient has listed three or more choices for each type of activity on the sheet, the clinician elicits a commitment for the upcoming week.

> **Clinician (C):** Now, on the Engaging Replacement Activities handout, please write the choice in the appropriate space provided. Remember, all lifelong and stimulating habits take time to generate feelings of comfort. Even activities we think will be simple or enjoyable at first can become tedious or off-putting because of the effort needed to begin and learn the basic skills (i.e., "the devil is in the details"). Mastery activities can take more initial effort to pursue, but once you acquire some success, the activities can become habit and enjoyable.
> **Patient (P):** That makes sense, and I remember when I first started dancing, it was actually embarrassing, and I never thought I would get good at it. But I realized I could do it over time, and it got more fun as I could make the dance go with the music better and be in sync with my partner.
> **C:** Do you think your partner would like to go dancing with you, even though it's been a while?
> **P:** Oh, yeah. I think she would like that.

Cultivating the quality of persistence can be important in developing new skills and activities, solving a problem, or meeting a challenge. The ability to sustain effort in the face of difficulty or adversity is an important, lifelong skill worth pursuing. Delay of gratification is important to being able to put off immediate rewards or benefits for the purpose of having something more valuable and lasting over the long term (e.g., sacrificing the immediate pleasure of an ice cream sundae in favor of the larger goals of health and weight management).

Elicit Commitment

> **Clinician:** The handout titled **Engaging in Replacement Activities** is what you'll use to now write down your identified Ms and IPs and commit to one for next week.
> Take a couple of minutes to write down your ideas, and then we can go over it together and determine when, where, and with whom you will do your Mastery. It is harder to predict when you will do your immediate pleasure because you may have a stressful moment at any time during the week, but still it is good for you to commit to using the IPs when you are triggered.
> **Patient:** That's good! I now have a few ways to deal with triggers and cravings. And I think since I committed to dance, I will ask Maria to join me in dancing.

Summarize and Conclude Session

The clinician makes sure that the challenges are clear for both parts of the session (if it is done combined), and the client has specified how they will use the skill, where, when, and with whom.

If the session skills on social supports and replacement activities are done in two sessions, the sessions end with the challenge for the recovery skill discussed.

Session 5 Handouts: Supporting Recovery Through Healthy Replacement Activities

Review of Progress and Between-session Challenges

Directions: Use the table below to support weekly progress review in key domains relevant to the patient's substance use and overall well-being. This table can also be used to review the between-session challenges.

Domain	Sun.	Mon.	Tues.	Wed	Thur.	Fri.	Sat.
Physical Activity							
Sleep							
Diet							
Pleasure/Replacement Activities							
Mastery Activities							
Work/School							
Mood States							
Tobacco/Nicotine							
Alcohol							
Marijuana							
Other Drugs							
Between-Session Challenge							

Increasing Pleasant Activities

Below is a list of both effortful Mastery and effortless Immediate Pleasure activities that people find pleasurable. Please check those that seem appealing to you, either because you know you like them, or you imagine you would like them if you tried. *Please put an M = Mastery or a P = Immediate Pleasure on any item checked.* Also check any items that you are not sure about but might be willing to consider if you had some support or encouragement to try it out. There are no grades on this exercise. Check as many as you wish. If there are things not listed that you want to include, please add them.

❏ Reading a book	❏ Going to the movies	❏ Going out to a meal
❏ Exercising	❏ Listening to music	❏ Writing or journaling
❏ Dancing	❏ Singing	❏ Computer/Internet
❏ Photography	❏ Drawing	❏ Writing/calling a friend
❏ Yoga	❏ Baking/cooking	❏ Shopping
❏ Painting	❏ Swimming	❏ Boating
❏ Ice skating	❏ Knitting/crocheting	❏ Taking a bath
❏ Gardening/lawn	❏ Fixing things	❏ Refinishing furniture
❏ Going to live theater	❏ Library	❏ Visiting a park or garden
❏ Skateboarding	❏ Running	❏ Organizing
❏ Party/social event	❏ Hiking	❏ Fishing
❏ Skiing	❏ Playing competitive sports	❏ Yard sales
❏ Spending time with friends/family		

Other activities:

_____

_____

Commitment:
I will do the following activity, _____
number of times in the next week. I will do the activity on _____ (list specific dates) at _____ (list specific times).

Engaging in Replacement Activities

Why?
- When we reduce immediate pleasure/reward, it is important to replace it.
- Both Immediate PLEASURE type activities and more skill-based MASTERY activities are needed.
- They produce the same brain chemicals.
- They tap into life passions and keep us feeling better.

What types of immediate pleasure activities do you like to do?
_____
_____
_____

Which are you willing to commit to doing this week?
_____

What types of skill-based MASTERY activities would you like to do?
_____
_____
_____

Which are you willing to commit to doing this week?
_____
_____
_____

Session 6. Problem Solving

Introduction and Session Goals

Session 6 reviews the types of experiences and problems that cause stress for the patient and offers an easy-to-remember and effective method for how to choose the best possible solutions to most types of problems. The clinician explains that most recurrence may be attributed to either interpersonal (the self in relation to others) or intrapersonal (within the self) stress, which often leads to unpleasant feelings such as anger, fear, shame, sadness, or guilt. They explain that people successful at handling problems realize they cannot avoid all problems, but they can learn strategies to overcome them. The patient can develop ways of coping more skillfully and efficiently with predictable stresses that arise in daily life and the larger, more life-altering and disruptive types of stressful events.

As the clinician introduces and progresses through the session, the patient hears that they are not alone with troubles but shares them in common with most others as part of life's struggle. They also hear that the problems do not lie within oneself as flaws or deficits, but, rather, they reflect universal experiences that can be addressed practically and successfully in the context of supportive relationships (e.g., counseling). The patient also learns to approach problems or challenges in creative ways, recognizing multiple paths can lead to health and healing. Using the I-SOLVE acronym helps clinicians transfer a six-step model to patients. Providing formal training in solving problems may accelerate the development of higher-order coping strategies that go beyond situation-specific skills. This training helps the patient act as their own clinician when no longer engaged in a formal treatment situation. This guide uses a problem-solving approach adapted from D'Zurilla and Goldfried (1971) and Center for Substance Abuse Treatment (1999).

Clinician Preparation

Session 6. Problem Solving	
Materials • *Review of Progress* • *Problem-solving (I-SOLVE)* handout • Large paper, poster board, or dry-erase board to diagram problem-solving steps	**Total Time** One hour **Delivery Method** Skill-focused individual or group therapy
Strategies • Follow OARS techniques. • Support self-efficacy. • Demonstrate skill and practice, including transfer of skill, by having the patient go through an example on their own with you present. • Follow CBT skills sessions.	

Goals for This Session
• Introduce a strategy for solving problems.
   – Apply the problem-solving approach to alcohol or other substance use and other problems.
   – Apply the problem-solving approach to mood dependent behavior.
• Prepare for termination of treatment, if applicable.	

Session 6 Outline and Overview

First Third

1) Strengthen rapport.
   - Welcome the patient and, if present, the support person.
   - Share the session agenda; invite items from the patient.
   - Engage in non-problem focused rapport building, exploring areas of the patient's life not directly related to treatment.
2) Review progress.
   - Engage the patient in a brief review of their progress related to their substance use, mental health, and related experiences since the previous session. Use the **Review of Progress** handout as a guide.
     - How is the patient doing with changing their substance use? What is going well? What are they struggling with?
     - If the patient engaged in substance misuse, explore their use event(s), using the **Awareness Record** to assess internal and external triggers, cravings, and consequences.
3) Review between-session challenge.
   - Review any between-session challenges from the previous session.
     - Did the patient engage in pleasant activities? How did it go? If not, what got in the way?
     - Did the patient seek support? Explore their experience of doing so.

Second Third

4) Provide session rationale.
   - Discuss the importance of recognizing problems as opportunities to learn.
   - Explain the rationale that everyone has problems (e.g., the rich, famous, not-so-famous), and provide relevant examples.
   - Provide the rationale that we often cannot control much of what happens in life, so we say problems are not the problem; rather, how we react to problems is important. We can see problems as opportunities rather than roadblocks.
   - For patients, problem situations result and persist when people feel they have no effective coping responses to handle them or their range of abilities is narrow or constricted. However, these same situations can be managed by practicing effective problem-solving skills, so the choices diminish the negative consequences of the situations and even sometimes create opportunities.
5) Teach session skill.
   - Provide examples of problem-solving practice and how it is effective:
     - Explain how firefighters practice setting fires to be prepared for the real fire, similar to other emergency workers who develop response routines, so the incidents do not become overwhelming when they occur.
     - This problem-solving practice is like learning to do CPR or the Heimlich maneuver by gaining needed skills to respond to problem situations.
6) Brainstorm problems and describe problem-solving skills.
   - Recognize the problem.
   - Identify or elaborate on the problem.
   - Consider various approaches.
   - Select the most promising approach.
   - Evaluate effectiveness.

7) Lead demonstration/role play.
   - Practice problem-solving skills by identifying a problem and applying the problem-solving steps (*I-SOLVE* handout) to solving the identified problem.
   - Once it is clear the patient understands the problem-solving process, collaborate with them to identify another problem they can try to solve. When the problem is identified, ask them to go through the problem-solving steps, out loud, so that they demonstrate to you, the clinician, that they can use these steps on their own.
   - Role play solutions to one of the problems and evaluate effectiveness.
8) Facilitate patient-led practice/assess Skills Transfer.
   - Have the patient engage in a practice of the skill.
   - Have the patient identify another problem and engage in the problem-solving steps, the I-SOLVE model, on their own.
   - Be there for questions or if the patient feels stuck. Ideally, the patient can move through the steps to identify solutions to the problem on their own, and you are there to play a more supportive, affirming role.

Third Third

9) Identify real-world application.
   - Help the patient to identify a real-life problem in which they can apply the skill.
10) Negotiate and prepare between-session challenge.
    - Elicit from the patient when and where in their life they can use the problem-solving steps to address the identified problem.
    - Ensure that the challenge is specific, and support the patient by rehearsing their application of the new skill: What will they do? When will they do it?
    - Encourage the patient to continue (1) using the **Awareness Record** when they are triggered to use, (2) engaging in pleasant activities, and (3) build support.
11) Elicit commitment.
    - Elicit commitment for completion of the *I-SOLVE* between-session challenge for the identified problem before the next session.
    - Use MI strategies, as needed, to strengthen commitment.
12) Summarize and conclude.
    - Present a session summary of what has been covered during the session, and elicit the patient's feedback.
      - What did the patient learn through the problem-solving activity?
    - Conclude the session.

Session 6 Protocol with Scripts

Strengthen Rapport

The clinician welcomes the patient and provides an overview of the sixth session, in which they further support the patient to build coping skills by normalizing the experience of facing problems and by enhancing their ability to resolve problems independently using a step-by-step system that has been shown to be helpful to others. The clinician invites the patient to provide additional agenda items for the session.

Review Progress: Examining the Patient's Recent Experiences

The clinician uses the **Review of Progress** handout to support a brief review of the patient's progress in key domains since the last session, including substance use, mental health symptoms, and related wellness areas.

The clinician asks the patient to describe their recent experiences with alcohol or other substances:

- Was the patient confronted with any high-risk or challenging situations?
- What strategies did the patient use? Did the patient try any of the strategies in **Learning New Coping Strategies**? Were they successful?
- Were there any instances when the patient effectively handled a "hot" situation (i.e., very high risk)?

As the patient talks, the clinician's objective is to elicit information and to use that information to provide reflections, express empathy, identify discrepancies, elicit self-motivational statements, and roll with sustain talk/discord.

Review Between-session Challenge: Assessing the Patient's Progress and Readiness to Proceed

The clinician asks the patient how they feel about the previous session and responds to concerns, addressing any comments or questions about the patient's experience of seeking support and of engaging in pleasant, healthy activities.

> *What type of support did they seek and from whom? How did it go when they asked? Were they able to get the support they needed? What was it like for them to ask and then to receive support?*

Note to clinician: If the patient expresses discomfort or even shame at asking for support, it is important for the clinician to explore with them their experience of providing support to others in the past. How did they feel when they were asked to offer their help? Often, the patients will indicate that they had a positive experience in being able to support someone else. The clinician reflects this back to the patient and asks if the people from whom they ask for support might feel the same way. If the patient's thoughts and feelings appear to be part of deeper self-limiting beliefs, you may want to consider using Sessions 8 and 9 now.

Provide Session Rationale

The clinician explains the rationale for learning an approach to solving difficult problems by using examples from real life and how they affect every type of person, including the rich, famous, poor, and brilliant. The clinician might use examples of people in the media, in the community, on news programs, etc. The clinician also explains that all people have problems, and the problems come in all forms (e.g., emergencies, illness, loss of employment). However, even a seemingly positive event (e.g., a party) can be a problem for someone trying to avoid using.

> **Clinician (C):** As you know, life throws all of us problems; they are part of the fabric of life for everyone. We like to say problems are not the problem; it is what you do with them that matters. Every person, no matter how rich, poor, brilliant, or famous, can have problems, and the problems can come in as many forms as the types of people. Some problems are emergencies caused by health issues, the stress of job demands, and money issues. Even a party can be a problem for someone trying not to use.
> **Patient:** So, you mean that what I experience is not unusual, but it seems to bother me more than people who experience the same types of things. How does knowing that help me not to feel bad?
> **C:** Situations become problems when people think they have no effective coping responses to handle them. Individuals can be flooded by emotions when faced with a problem and may be unable to manage the problem constructively.

Give examples of firefighters and emergency responders who learn to overcome adversities more easily by practicing possible responses. The clinician will use this session to help the patient practice a problem-solving model to deal with situations that normally would trigger them.

The clinician describes steps to solve problems and situations where the approach is helpful. See the sample language provided.

> Effective problem solving requires recognizing when you are confronted with a problem and resisting the temptation to respond impulsively or to do nothing (i.e., fight, flight, freeze). Coming up with an effective solution requires that you manage your affect and assess the situation to decide the best course of action. Sometimes the problem involves a conflict with someone or wanting to use alcohol or substances, such as at a party. At other times, the problem may be the urge to find a quick and easy solution. Effective problem-solving strategies must be part of your recovery program because the occurrence of problems can set the stage for a slip or longer periods of recurrence.

Teach Session Skill

Elicit information from the patient, and review some of the problems mentioned in past sessions. Then describe the effective problem-solving approach called I-SOLVE.

I-SOLVE
- Identify the problem.
- State the problem.
- Consider options.
- Look at the consequences of the choices.
- Vote on the most promising approach.
- Evaluate effectiveness.

The clinician describes the steps in I-SOLVE, provides examples, and encourages questions and feedback from the patient as to how this fits with their situation.

OK, so we are going to go through the steps of problem solving using a tool called I-SOLVE. I will describe each and give an example. Please ask questions or make any comments as we go along, okay?

The first step is to **identify** the problem. What clues indicate there may be a problem? You may get clues from your body (e.g., indigestion, craving), your thoughts and feelings (e.g., feelings of anxiety, depression, loneliness, or fear), your behavior (e.g., have you been able to keep up with plans and commitments you make to others or yourself?), the way you respond to others (e.g., feeling irritable, impatient, having less interest in things, feeling withdrawn from people who might be supportive of you), and the way others respond to you (e.g., they appear to avoid you or seem frustrated or critical of you).

The second step is to **state** or elaborate on the problem. What is the problem? Having recognized that something is wrong, you identify the problem by gathering as much information as you can. Break the problem down into smaller parts; you may find it easier to manage several parts than to confront the entire problem all at once. State the problem beginning with an "I" statement. For example, if you must complete a large project at work, it can be helpful to break it up into smaller, more manageable parts and perhaps consult with colleagues on aspects that are particularly challenging for you. "I have a project due at work and will need someone with advanced computer skills to help me finish it on time."

The third step is to consider **options** in addressing the problem. Develop several solutions; the first one that comes to mind may not be the best. Use the following methods to find a good solution:

Brainstorm and generate ideas without judging or stopping to evaluate how good or bad they are. Write down all the ideas that come to mind, even ones that seem unrealistic. Later you will review and make decisions about which you will try actually try out. More is better. Do not evaluate these ideas at this stage.

Consider strategies that require action or behavior change on your part (e.g., changing your routines related to social activity) and also that involve your changing how you think about a situation. For example, when the problem involves negative emotional reactions to uncontrollable events, change how you view this situation and your role in it (cognitive coping). Some problems require both behavioral and cognitive coping.

Once you have generated a list of ideas for coping with the problem, the fourth step is to **look** at the long and short term, including positive and negative consequences of choosing those options. Consider the resources you'll need for each solution. Here it is helpful to list the options and then to write either +, –, or 0 (= neutral) next to each choice, depending on your thoughts about the outcome.

The fifth step is to **vote** for the most promising approach. Rank the possibilities by their consequences and desirability. The solution with the most positive and fewest negative consequences is the one to try first.

Finally, the sixth step is to **evaluate** effectiveness. How did it work out? Evaluate the strengths and weaknesses of your plan. What difficulties did you encounter? Are you obtaining the expected results? Can you do something to make the approach more effective? Use the same clues as before (e.g., from your body, thoughts, feelings, and other people) to decide whether your solution is effective. If you give the plan a fair chance, and it does not solve the problem, move to your second choice and follow the same procedure.

In this session, the clinician should try to address only a problem with a solution that is within the control of the patient. The model will not work if the answer to the problem relies on someone else's control. The following is an example of someone else's problems: *I need to make it so my family stops complaining. I need them to learn to speak in a different tone...*versus: *I need to figure out a way of expressing myself so my family quits complaining about my tone of voice.*

Note to clinician: In a situation that is truly outside your patient's control, the "solution" rests in how the patient comes to think and feel about the situation. This is sometimes referred to as "radical acceptance."

If the patient chooses a problem where the solution is not in their control, the clinician collaborates with the patient to clarify the difference between the self's and another's ability to influence change (use examples). Then, together, the patient and clinician reselect or redefine the problem to one where there is primary influence over the outcome, thus emphasizing self-efficacy.

The clinician wants to ensure the brainstorming of options feels fun, and the spirit is creative. At this point in the *I-SOLVE* discussion, it does not matter if the solutions are realistic, as long as the patient understands the problems can be better solved when the solutions are in their control. The clinician can gently guide the patient toward a realistic solution they have the skills and will to carry out successfully (e.g., planning to create an enormous quilt when one has never picked up a needle and thread may be a setup for failure).

When leading a patient in brainstorming, it is usually best to elicit at least five solutions to assess which option might be best. This facilitates a choice should the option chosen and evaluated turns out not to be helpful and highlights problem solving as a learning opportunity rather than a stagnant process. Problem solving can be revised to adapt to evolving awareness in a manner similar to the recovery process, which is characterized by a variety of external and internal triggers. Each situation affords another chance to problem solve and test which option leads to the healthiest outcomes.

Lead Demonstration/Role Play

The clinician encourages the patient to work through the problem-recognition stage: identifying problems, describing them, and writing solutions on paper. They ask the patient to weigh alternatives, select the most promising one, and describe both advantages and disadvantages for every alternative. Finally, the patient prioritizes the alternatives. The clinician and patient role play and evaluate the effectiveness of the most promising solutions. See the sample language provided.

Clinician (C): Your upcoming 4th of July picnic will put you in a difficult situation because you'll be around old friends and family members with whom you used to drink heavily. What is the problem as you see it?

Steve (S): Well, I have really enjoyed these parties in the past, even though they tend to be a blur because I've been so drunk. It will be difficult to be there and not drink with people. They will be offering me stuff for hours, and I'm worried I'll just get worn down. Then I'll be mad at myself for not sticking to my guns.

C: You anticipate it being difficult to stick to your plans when you are around people you have drunk with in the past.

S: Yeah, I also do not want to let them down. I know that sounds kind of weird.

> **C:** It does not sound weird at all. It also sounds like there's a tension between staying focused on your goals and plans and worrying about disappointing people you care about by not being "part of" things as usual.
> **S:** Yes, I guess that's just how I feel.
> **C:** Have you thought about any ideas for how you might deal with this situation? Maybe we could come up with some possibilities and then see which ones might work better than others.
> **S:** Okay.
> **C:** Great.

The patient now uses the I-SOLVE model in the session to state the problem in a brief "I" statement, generate options, examine long-term and short-term consequences, vote, and then commit to trying the option chosen and evaluating the results of that choice.

Facilitate Patient-led Practice/Assess Skills Transfer

The patient then takes the lead at walking the clinician through each component of the *I-SOLVE* model for a second problem the patient identifies. The purpose for focusing on a second problem in which the patient uses the *I-SOLVE* model is to allow them to demonstrate their ability using the model more autonomously unless they specifically ask for help. During the patient's application of the *I-SOLVE* model, the clinician affirms the patient's skill application and offers follow-up questions to encourage them to explore the incident more thoroughly.

Identify Real-world Application

The clinician asks the patient to commit to applying the *I-SOLVE* model to another problem before the next session. They commit to check in the next session on the outcome of the solutions identified and applied.

Negotiate and Prepare Between-session Challenge

The exploration of real-world skill application is a natural transition into negotiation of a between-session challenge. The clinician encourages the patient to continue reviewing the materials handed out at this session and previous sessions, including the ***Awareness Record, Assertiveness, Increasing Pleasant Activities,*** and ***Social Support*** handouts. The clinician asks the patient where and when the patient can commit to working through the *I-SOLVE* model for a problem in their life. For any identified between-session challenges, the clinician works with the patient to make sure that they know what they will do, when they will do it, and how often it will be done, mentally rehearsing its application in their daily life. Most patients benefit from writing down this plan somewhere accessible to also serve as an ongoing reminder.

Elicit Commitment

The clinician explores the patient's commitment for completing the between-session challenge and uses MI strategies, as needed, to assess and strengthen commitment. They also ask the patient to think through any potential obstacles to their skills practice and work with them to identify solutions and to activate resources, as needed, to support their skill application.

Summarize and Conclude

The clinician reviews the content of the session, solicits feedback from the patient, responds empathically to their comments, and troubleshoots any difficulties. They ask that the patient report back on their efforts to complete the between-session exercise at the next session. If the patient seems disinclined to complete the exercise in writing, ask them to think about a problem, go through the steps mentally, and report back during the next session. The clinician might remind the patient that treatment will be ending soon and solicit the patient's feelings about ending treatment and the best way to spend the remaining sessions.

Session 6 Handouts: Problem Solving

Review of Progress and Between-session Challenges

Directions: Use the table below to support weekly progress review in key domains relevant to the patient's substance use and overall well-being. This table can also be used to review the between-session challenges.

Domain	Sun.	Mon.	Tues.	Wed	Thur.	Fri.	Sat.
Physical Activity							
Sleep							
Diet							
Pleasure/Replacement Activities							
Mastery Activities							
Work/School							
Mood States							
Tobacco/Nicotine							
Alcohol							
Marijuana							
Other Drugs							
Between-Session Challenge							

Problem Solving (I-SOLVE)

Here is a brief list of the steps in the problem-solving process:

I = Identify. Is there a problem? Recognize that a problem exists. We get clues from our bodies, thoughts and feelings, behaviors, responses to other people, and the ways that other people respond to us.

S = State. What is the problem? Identify the problem. Describe the problem as accurately as you can using an "I" statement where the outcome is in your control. Break it into manageable parts.

O = Options. What can I do? Consider various approaches to solving the problem. Brainstorm to think of as many solutions as you can. Consider acting to change the situation; consider changing the way you think about the situation.

L = Look. What will happen if ...? Select the most promising approach. Consider all the positive and negative aspects of each approach.

V = Vote. Select the one most likely to solve the problem.

E = Evaluate. How did it work? Assess the effectiveness of the selected approach. After you have given the approach a fair trial, determine whether it worked. If it did not, consider what you can do to improve the plan, or give it up and try one of the other approaches.

Practice exercise

Select a problem that does not have an obvious solution. Describe it accurately. Brainstorm a list of possible solutions. Evaluate the possibilities, and number them in order of your preference.

Identify the problem:

_____

_____

_____

List brainstorming solutions:

_____

_____

_____

- Examine the (+, −, 0 [= neutral]) long- and short-term results.
- Select the achievable option that has the most benefits.
- Commit to using.
- Evaluate outcome.

Source: Kadden et al. (1994).

Session 7. Handling Urges, Cravings, and Discomfort

Introduction and Session Goals

Session 7 focuses on helping the patient gain an overall understanding of urges, cravings, and significant discomfort and to learn two basic mindfulness skills effective in managing (1) urges to use a substance (urge surfing) and (2) high levels of distress. (dropping anchor). Discomfort is commonly anxiety that can be moderate or severe. After normalizing the occurrence of automatic thoughts, associated feelings, or urges, the clinician helps the patient identify how and when they experience urges or automatic thoughts. They collaborate on developing a menu of coping or response strategies that are relevant to the patient's experiences and environment. The session concludes with the clinician encouraging the patient to track their urges and response strategies during the week and suggests reviewing them with the patient at the next session.

What are Automatic Thoughts?

Thoughts influence much of our experience of the world, including our emotional experience. In this guide, we refer to a specific kind of thoughts as "automatic thoughts." Automatic thoughts are the thoughts that automatically arise in our minds often associated with certain feelings or behavior. Often, we are completely unaware we are even having thoughts, and the patient can learn to easily identify them and, as a result, get a better handle on their mood and behavior connected with these thoughts

What is Urge Surfing?

Urge surfing is a technique that can be used to avoid acting on any behavior that the patient wants to reduce or stop (e.g., smoking, overeating, substance use). The mindfulness understanding of urges is that you cannot get rid of them, but you can practice ways to accept them and ride them out without giving in to them. An ocean wave is a metaphor for an urge that comes on, rises, peaks, and subsides. Urge surfing involves relaxation and deep diaphragmatic breathing when the urge is present. The patient focuses on where they feel the tension in their body, and, if they can, placing their hand on the tension. They breathe in for five seconds, hold for five seconds, and slowly exhale for seven seconds. This breathing pattern is repeated at least five times. We breath. Into and ride the wave. Most urges last 20 minutes or less.

What is Dropping Anchor?

Dropping anchor is a useful skill somewhat akin to urge surfing. It is often used as a first step in work with people experiencing flashbacks, panic attacks, chronic pain, and other issues. The patient uses it for staying present with difficult thoughts, feelings, emotions, and memories more effectively. The skill helps them to (Harris, 2021):

- Switch their brain's automatic response (i.e., fight, flight, freeze)
- Engage in the present moment
- Stay steady in difficult situations
- Disrupt automatic thoughts, obsessing, and worrying
- Focus attention on the activity in the moment
- Develop more self-control
- Take action on impulsive, compulsive, addictive, or other problematic behaviors

Practice differences exist between urge surfing and dropping anchor. The metaphor of dropping anchor is that you may be in rough waters, and you can drop anchor so that you are in a safe place to ride them out. In preparation for the practice, the clinician orients the patient to the three domains of the practice or ACE:

- **A**cknowledge your thoughts and feelings.
- **C**ome back or stay grounded in your body (e.g., breath, touch, other sensory experience).
- **E**ngage in what you are doing.

In this practice, different from other practices, the clinician suggests that the patient keeps their eyes open and to signal verbally or with hand gestures if the experience becomes too uncomfortable. The practice is not linear and does have an exposure aspect. Starting from a place of relaxation, the clinician invites the patient to explore thoughts and feelings in the moment. If or when feelings move from acceptable levels of discomfort to pain, the clinician guides the patient away from thoughts and feelings (for the moment) toward staying in the present moment. Slow, diaphragmatic breathing helps, as is a simple strategy of having your patient look around the room, identify objects, and say the names out loud (e.g., I see a bookcase. I see a table lamp.). When comfort is restored, the patient's thoughts and feelings may be revisited. This pivoting between thoughts and feelings and coming back to the present increases both distress tolerance and awareness. In concluding the session, the clinician reinforces practicing the skills at home. This conversation should intentionally be more present and forward thinking.

The patient will leave the session with:

- A general understanding of the nature of cravings and, urges.
- An increased understanding of their discomfort and automatic thoughts.
- The ability to identify specific triggers or cues and to increase awareness and distress tolerance.
- Practice of one or related skills to manage discomfort and cravings.

Clinician Preparation

Session 7. Handling Urges, Cravings, and Discomfort (Urge Surfing and Dropping Anchor)	
Materials • *Review of Progress* • *Coping With Cravings and Discomfort* handout • *Daily Record of Urges to Use* handout • *Urge Surfing* handout	**Total Time** One hour **Delivery Method** CBT-focused individual therapy
Strategies • Follow OARS. • Support self-efficacy. • Demonstrate skill and practice, including transfer of skill (e.g., have the patient go through an example on their own with the clinician present). • Discuss the value of journaling/logging the patient's urges or discomfort. • Follow CBT skills sessions	
Goals for This Session • Enhance the patient's understanding about cravings and urges. • Identify specific triggers or cues for cravings (see Carroll, 1998). • Review and practice specific skills for addressing higher levels of discomfort. • Examine the patient's high-risk situations, triggers, and coping strategies.	

Session 7 Outline and Overview

First Third

1) Strengthen rapport.
   - Welcome the patient.
   - Share the session agenda and invite items from the patient.
   - Engage in non-problem-focused rapport building, exploring areas of the patient's life not directly related to treatment.
2) Review progress.
   - Engage the patient in a brief review of their progress related to their substance use, mental health, and related experiences since the previous session. Use the **Review of Progress** handout as a guide.
     - How is the patient doing? What is going well? What are they struggling with?
     - If the patient engaged in substance use, explore their use event(s), using the **Awareness Record** to assess internal and external triggers, cravings, and consequences.
     - How is your patient managing high levels of distress.
3) Review between-session challenge.
   - Review any between-session challenges from the previous session.
     - Did the patient use the **I-SOLVE** problem-solving approach? How did it go? If not, what got in the way?

Second Third

4) Provide session rationale.
   - Elicit from the patient their experiences with cravings or discomfort and current coping methods.
   - Provide reasons for urge surfing, focusing on cravings, including basic information about the nature of cravings:
     - Cravings and urges are a part of the repeated use of any substance. Understanding urges and developing skills to address them is essential to recovery.
     - Cravings may feel very uncomfortable, but they are a common experience.
     - Dropping anchor is a practice for handling difficult thoughts, feelings, emotions, or memories more effectively.
     - It is important to recognize and develop realistic strategies to manage these difficult moments, which can be practiced almost anywhere and anytime.
5) Teach session skill.
   - Provide a framework for understanding urges or cravings. Give the patient the **Coping with Cravings and Discomfort** handout. Explain:
     - Urges/cravings as a subset of the universal experience of longing or desire
     - Role of urges or cravings in substance use
   - Discuss the patient's experience with and recognition of an urge.
   - Identify the patient's cues or triggers for cravings. Give the patient examples of common cues:
     - Exposure to alcohol, substances, or paraphernalia
     - Seeing other people using substances
     - Contact with people, places, times of day, or situations associated with using
     - Particular emotions and physical feelings
   - Distinguish external or environmental triggers from internal states.

6) Lead demonstration/role play.
   - Practice one of the strategies for coping with triggers by walking the patient through a brief demonstration of how to implement the urge surfing strategy. Focus on:
     - *How* the strategy is implemented (i.e., the steps involved)
     - The *experience* of the activity by walking through each step, while sharing out loud your experiences, as if you were engaging in the strategy in that moment.
   - Once it is clear the patient understands the urge surfing technique, have them demonstrate the skill.
7) Facilitate patient-led practice/assess skills transfer.
   - Have the patient identify a recent urge or craving.
     - With that experience in mind, the patient is encouraged to practice urge surfing using a similar talk aloud method.
     - The clinician may need to support the patient by reading the instructions and prompts to them.

Third Third

8) Identify real-world application.
   - Help the patient to identify real-life situations in which they can apply the skill.
   - Work with the patient to make a list of cravings triggers and a plan for responding to those triggers.
9) Negotiate and prepare between-session challenge.
   - Elicit from the patient how and where in their life they can apply urge surfing and other strategies they learned for coping with cravings.
     - Introduce and encourage the patient to use the **Daily Record of Urges to Use** handout to track their urge experiences throughout the week.
   - Ensure that the challenge is specific and support the patient by rehearsing their application of the new skill. What will they do? When will they do it? How often will it be done (i.e., at least two times)?
10) Elicit commitment.
    - Elicit commitment for completion of the between-session challenge at least two times before the next session. Use MI strategies, as needed, to strengthen commitment.
11) Summarize and conclude.
    - Present a session summary of what has been covered during the session, and elicit the patient's feedback.
      - What did the patient learn through the urge surfing and/or dropping anchor activity? Include a broader discussion of strategies for coping.
    - Conclude the session.

Session 7 Protocol with Scripts

Strengthen Rapport
The clinician welcomes the patient and provides an overview of the seventh session, in which they support the patient in developing awareness around their experiences with urges and cravings and learning strategies for coping with these experiences. The clinician invites the patient to provide additional agenda items for the session.

Review Progress: Examining the Patient's Recent Experiences
The clinician uses the ***Review of Progress*** handout to support a brief review of the patient's progress in key domains since the last session, including substance use, mental health symptoms, and related wellness areas.

The clinician asks the patient to describe their recent experiences with alcohol or other substances:

- How are their efforts to quit or cut down going?
- Was the patient confronted with any high-risk or tempting situations?
- What strategies did the patient use? Were they successful?
- Were there any instances when the patient effectively handled a "hot" situation (i.e., very high risk)?

As the patient talks, the clinician's objective is to elicit information and to use that information to provide reflections, express empathy, identify discrepancies, elicit self-motivational statements, and roll with sustain talk/discord.

- If the patient engaged in substance use, explore their use event(s), using the ***Awareness Record*** to assess internal and external triggers, cravings, and consequences.
- Similarly, ask patient to describe a recent event of high anxiety or depressed mood.
  - How were their efforts to manage their affect?
  - What was the situation that triggered this response?
- What strategies did the patient use? Were they successful?
- Were there any instances when the patient effectively handled a "hot" situation (i.e., very high risk)?

Explore these episodes and consider using the ***Awareness Record*** to help the patient better understand their internal and external triggers and consequences.

Review Between-session Challenge
The clinician asks the patient how they feel about the previous session and responds to concerns, addressing any comments or questions about the patient's experience with implementing the ***I-SOLVE*** problem-solving model. The clinician elicits how the patient's implementation of the ***I-SOLVE*** technique went, exploring what went well and what went less well. If the patient did not complete the activity, the clinician engages the patient in a discussion about the barriers that got in the way and how they might respond to similar barriers in the future.

Provide Session Rationale
The clinician asks about the patient's experiences with cravings and current coping methods. See the sample discussion provided.

> Many people report they have strong urges to drink or get high when they first stop using. In the beginning, the urges can feel overwhelming and hard to manage.
> Is this something you have experienced when you have tried to stop using?

Or

> Many people report experiencing powerful thoughts and feelings that are hard to manage.
> Is this something you have experienced?.

Some important messages the clinician conveys during this discussion include:

- Urges are common during recovery.
- Automatic thoughts and feelings, and even panic, are common for many who have experienced painful past experiences. These thoughts and feelings interfere with your living your best.
- Learning to identify urges (or automatic thoughts) is important for gaining control over them.
- These experiences are predictable and have understandable triggers.
- Identifying triggers can help in the selection of effective coping strategies.
- Everyone can learn to manage their distress.
- Urges or automatic thoughts are like stray cats: If you do not feed them, they go somewhere else.

Eliciting the patient's view first is the most desirable approach. However, if the patient is not able to provide this information, the clinician should be more direct in approaching the discussion to cover the points listed above. It is important to try to understand the patient's experience with urges in the past, including their overall perception of the predictability of urges and confidence in managing them. Once the clinician has reviewed the points, it is helpful to summarize what has been learned about the patient's perception of urges. See the sample discussion provided.

> Before we move on, let me see if I've heard you correctly so far. It sounds like you have experienced quite a few urges in the past when you have tried to stop using. There have been times when you were able to deal with them, but there have also been other times when you have given into them. Your urges are generally more frequent and intense in the first few months after you stop using. But when you have been able to hang in there, you have noticed you have urges even sometimes when you are really committed to not using. You tend to feel discouraged and disappointed in yourself for having these urges. When this happens, you also feel less confident about your ability to stay sober.
> Although part of you realizes that having urges is normal and to be expected, you worry about your ability to manage them some of the time and would like some help with that.
> So, it may be helpful to talk more about how you experience urges to get a better handle on them. What are your thoughts?

Rationale for substance use recovery

> Cravings and/or urges are a part of the repeated use of any substance. Understanding your urges and developing skills to address them is essential to recovery. One thing we know about cravings is that everyone experiences them differently, and, in the recovery process, how one person experiences them will change over time.

> *The good news is that urges are like stray cats: If you do not feed them, they eventually go somewhere else. There are a number of strategies that can be used to manage urges. These fall into a few categories: escape, distraction, avoidance, and embracing. Learning to use one or all of these strategies will help you to diminish the craving/urge.*
>
> *What I'd like us to focus on today is how we can work together to support you in recognizing urges and in developing realistic strategies to recognize your triggers, reduce your exposure to them, and cope with urges.*

Rationale for addressing self-limiting emotions
Heightened anxiety and depressed mood are often activated by experiences and our thoughts. Increasing our awareness of these thoughts and our interpretation of events (embracing) reduces their power and influence over our behavior. Through adopting this practice, you can reduce the influence these feelings have over your behavior.

Teach Session Skill
Provide a framework for understanding urges or cravings and their role in substance use
The clinician gives the patient the **Coping With Cravings and Discomfort Urges** or **Urge Surfing** handout and explains the importance of recognizing cravings and/or distressing thoughts and feelings. Provide your patient with a framework for understanding the role of cravings. Explain that when someone tries to quit using alcohol or another substance, they often have cravings or strong urges to use that could be triggers for relapse. Normalize the experience of cravings and distress, not just in the area of substance use. Cravings and discomfort are universal human experiences and can cause suffering.

Throughout life, people struggle with wanting things or the belief they would feel better and be happier if only they had [____] (e.g., a new house, better job, more satisfying relationship). The craving or urge for alcohol or substances is no different from this basic human experience. When one can recognize that craving, and the discomfort that comes from this unfulfilled experience, is universal, the craving may become more manageable. It is also important to understand that giving in to the craving or urge does not usually solve the underlying problem of discontent and can even reinforce it. The saying, "The only thing worse than not getting what you want is getting it" has relevance here. The clinician can help the patient to see craving as just another psychological state—like sadness, joy, or fear—that need not take on special importance.

Discuss the patient's experience with and recognition of an urge
The clinician shares a general overview of how cravings or urges are often experienced, then elicits from the patient their unique experiences.

Recognition of Cravings

Cravings often are experienced when a person first tries to quit, but they may occur weeks, months, or even years later. Cravings may feel uncomfortable, but they are common experiences. An urge to smoke does not mean something's wrong. Many people learn to expect cravings on occasion and how to cope with them.

Things that remind you of using alcohol or other substances can trigger urges or cravings. Physical symptoms include tightness in the stomach or feeling nervous throughout the body.

> *Psychological symptoms include thoughts about how using alcohol or other substances feels, recollections of using, developing plans to get alcohol or other substances, or feeling that you need alcohol or other substances.*
>
> *Cravings and urges usually last only a few minutes or, at most, a few hours. Rather than increase until they become unbearable, they usually peak after a few minutes and then die down, like a wave. Urges become less frequent and less intense as you learn more methods for coping with them.*

Discussing what the patient experiences when they have an urge may help them identify an urge early and respond before it becomes overwhelming. Many different ways of experiencing an urge, only some of which are recognized by most patients (e.g., physical sensations). Recognizing all aspects of the experience of an urge will help the patient label the experience and prevent automatic responses (i.e., returning to alcohol or drug use). This should enhance the patient's ability to manage urges. The clinician may explore with the patient the various ways an urge may be experienced. This is important before moving on to coping strategies to ensure the patient can recognize it.

Some examples appear below:

- Physical sensations (e.g., sweating, heart racing, queasy stomach)
- Thoughts (e.g., "Wouldn't it be nice to have a drink?" "I'd rather be with my friends getting high tonight.")
- Positive expectancies (e.g., "I'd feel better if I did some cocaine.")
- Emotions (e.g., anxiety, depression, irritability)
- Behaviors (e.g., pausing while passing the beer display in a store, going by an old neighborhood where the drug dealer hangs out)
- Experiencing hunger

The clinician can use open-ended questions about the patient's experiences with urges and discomfort to explore their awareness of the symptoms.

> *We've spent some time talking about your general experiences with urges. Before we move on to talking about coping with urges, I'd like to get a better sense of how you know when you are having an urge. Some urges may be very easy to recognize, but others are less obvious. I'm wondering how you know when you are having an urge.*
>
> *What is the first thing you notice when you are having an urge? How do you know that an urge is coming on?*
>
> *What is the most obvious sign that you are craving alcohol?*
>
> *If somebody were with you when you were experiencing an urge, would they notice anything?.*

As the discussion progresses, the clinician may want to ask more directed questions for the areas the patient has not already identified.

Physical Sensations

> *I'm wondering if you can tell me a bit about the physical sensations you experience when you have an urge to drink or use drugs.*

> **Thoughts**
>
> *What about your thoughts? What kinds of thoughts do you recall having when you wanted to use alcohol or drugs?*
>
> **Positive Expectancies**
>
> *People say they imagine something positive will happen if they drink or use drugs. For instance, they think it will help them unwind after a tough day, or they will have a better time with other people or simply feel better. What types of positive expectations have you had when you had an urge to use?*
>
> **Emotions**
>
> *Many people find their mood changes just before they use. They feel anxious or depressed, and other people report feeling excited. I'm wondering what types of mood changes you have noticed.*
>
> **Behaviors**
>
> *Do you find yourself becoming less tolerant or more irritable? Do you find yourself getting into more arguments or fights with people? Do you find yourself hanging around more in some of the old places or with people that you used to drink or get high with? Have you impulsively decided to leave treatment?*

Identify cues or triggers

At this point in the session, it might be helpful for the clinician to summarize what they have learned about the patient's experience of urges and transition to identifying triggers for having urges.

> *It sounds like you have a good sense of how you experience an urge, particularly when it comes to the physical sensations. You've noticed your heart starts racing, and you feel a knot in your stomach.*

The goal of the next discussion is to establish a link between triggers and urges or discomfort. Triggers are generally situations associated with a patient's use of alcohol or drugs in the past. With this repeated association, the patient tends to have urges in these situations when stopping or making attempts to cut down. If they understand this connection, it may make the urges more predictable. If the patient feels urges are somewhat predictable, this should help them feel more in control and also make it easier to identify specific coping strategies that may address urges in response to specific triggers.

The clinician should follow this brief explanation and presentation of examples by asking the patient about their triggers for urges. Once again, it is important for the clinician to begin by asking, in an open-ended format, about the patient's understanding of triggers. Triggers can be recorded on the **Coping With Cravings and Discomfort** handout as the patient identifies them. The **New Roads** worksheet, referred to in Session 11 may provide valuable information about triggers, which can be used to supplement this discussion. If information about various types of triggers is not elicited, the clinician may follow with more directive questioning and discuss some of the common triggers listed below.

> It's important to learn how to recognize triggers so you can reduce your exposure to them. Common triggers include:
>
> - Exposure to alcohol, substances, or paraphernalia
> - Seeing other people using substances
> - Contact with people, places, times of day, and situations associated with using (e.g., people you used with, parties, bars, weekends)
> - Particular emotions (e.g., frustration, fatigue, feeling stressed), even positive emotions (e.g., elation, excitement, feelings of accomplishment)
> - Physical feelings (e.g., feeling sick, shaky, tense)
>
> Some triggers are more difficult to recognize. Self-monitoring can help begin to identify them. The easiest way to cope with cravings and urges is to minimize their likelihood of occurring. You can reduce your exposure to triggers by getting rid of alcohol or substances in your home, not going to parties or bars, and limiting contact with friends who use.

Using the common triggers described below, it may be helpful to guide the discussion about internal and external triggers for urges. Primarily, it is important to let the patient know urges can be external (things that happen outside the person) or internal states (e.g., thoughts, feelings, and ideas).

External Situations

- Exposure to alcohol or drugs
- Smell, sight, and sounds of other people drinking or using drugs
- Times during the day when drinking or drug use tended to occur (e.g., getting off work, weekends, payday)
- Stimuli previously associated with drinking or drug use (e.g., wine glasses, bar, crack pipe, medicine bottle, ATM machine)
- Stimuli previously associated with withdrawal (e.g., hospital, aspirin, morning)

Internal States

- Unpleasant emotions (e.g., frustration, depression, anger, feeling "stressed out")
- Pleasant emotions (e.g., elation, excitement)
- Physical feelings (e.g., sick, shaky, tense, pain)
- Thoughts about drinking or drug use (e.g., "I'll feel better if I get high.")
- Beliefs or ideas (e.g., "I will always be an addict.")
- Beliefs about self and others (e.g., "I'm a failure. I'll never be good enough.")

Discuss strategies for coping with triggers

Since it can be expected that the patient will experience triggers for use, the clinician presents several categories and examples of coping strategies found to be helpful.

> **Clinician:** Many times, cravings cannot be avoided, and it becomes necessary to cope with them. The nice part of that is there are many strategies that can be helpful for coping with cravings and urges. I want to talk about some different ways people have learned to cope with them, and we can consider which might be a good fit for you. How does that sound?

The clinician teaches the client four key approaches for managing urges: avoidance, escape, distraction, and embrace.

Necessary Avoidance. Avoidance is a strategy that involves reducing exposure to high-risk situations that trigger urges. Avoidance appears especially important early in recovery.
Examples of avoidance strategies include:

- Getting rid of alcohol or drugs at home
- Avoiding parties or bars where drinking or drug use occurs
- Reducing contact with old friends who drink or get high
- Avoiding circumstances that increase temptation (e.g., cash in pocket, unstructured free time, home alone)

Escape. Escape is a strategy that focuses on finding a safe way out of situations where an urge might occur. This may involve an unexpected situation (e.g., drug dealer shows up at the door) or a situation the patient sees as unavoidable (e.g., wedding). The patient should have a plan for getting out of the situation as quickly as possible if strong urges occur.

The clinician should recommend that the patient consider the following when making their plan for escape:

- Have the means ready; be careful not to get stranded without the means for getting out of a situation if necessary (e.g., transportation).
- Plan what to say or do. Know what to say to people if leaving a risky situation in a hurry.
- Feel good about your choice; using escape is a sign of strength and determination to stick with your goal. Do not be dissuaded by pressure from people to do what you have typically done in the past.

Distraction. Distraction is a strategy involving a shift in attention away from thoughts about using alcohol or drugs. Numerous distracting activities can take a patient's mind off urges to use alcohol or drugs (e.g., going to a movie, calling someone, reading a book, exercising). Urges tend to pass more quickly when a person becomes involved with an alternative activity. The clinician might offer guidance as follows:

Embrace or "Sitting With" the Urge. Sometimes patients may need to face the urge and cope with it directly, and the following embrace strategies may help:

- Talk it through with someone who is supportive and nonjudgmental. Talking can provide you with support when you need it and can help you to get through the urge without using again. Remember the "larger picture," including why you are trying to make this important change. It is important to talk with someone who will not judge or criticize you for having these feelings or urges but will give you permission to express yourself.
- Use meditation or mindfulness activities, which can help you stay present with your experience without the need to act or react; they can also increase awareness generally.
- Wait it out; urges are only temporary.
- Take protection when faced with a high-risk situation.
- Use a reminder card.
- Try urge surfing; delay the decision to use. Most urges to use can be likened to ocean waves: They build to a peak and then dissipate. For many patients, if they choose to wait 15 minutes, the wave will pass. Try imagining you are a surfer riding the wave of craving until it subsides, or use another image that works for you.
- Use imagery. If you feel you are about to be overwhelmed by urges to use, imagine scenes that portray those urges as storms that end with calmness, mountains that you can climb, or waves that you can ride. Everyone can find an image to maintain control until the urge peaks and then dissipates.

> You might envision yourself sitting at the edge of a riverbank and seeing the urge as a boat that is sailing in your direction. You can simply observe the boat from this "distance," note certain qualities or characteristics, but not feel compelled to get on the boat and ride. Just see it come and then pass you by. Images can be made vivid by using relaxation techniques and all the senses (e.g., seeing the thick, green jungle; hearing the blade swishing through the leaves; smelling the tropical plants). Photographs of loved ones can also distract.

Other cognitive, or thinking strategies, can be helpful when managing uncomfortable thoughts and emotions.

Self-talk. People often engage in a running dialogue or commentary with themselves about the events that occur in their day and their actions. These thoughts can strongly influence the way you feel and act. What you tell yourself about your thoughts and feelings affects how you experience and handle them. You can use your self-talk to strengthen or weaken your urges.

Making self-statements is so automatic you may not notice it. For example, a self-statement that is automatic for you may be, "I am a skilled photographer," or, "I'm such a loser." Hidden or automatic self-statements can make them hard to handle (e.g., "I want to get drunk now. I cannot stand this any longer. The urge is going to get stronger and stronger until I use. I will not be able to resist.") Other types of self-statements can make the dealing with difficult feelings easier to handle (e.g., "Even though my mind is made up to stay sober, my body is taking longer to learn this. This urge is uncomfortable, but in 15–20 minutes or so, I'll feel like myself again").

There are basic steps in using self-talk constructively:

- **Use self-talk constructively to challenge the statement.** An effective challenge makes you feel better (i.e., less tense, anxious, or panicky), even though it may not make the feelings disappear entirely. The most effective challenges are ones tailored to specific self-statements. Listed below are some challenges that people find useful:
- **What is the evidence?** What is the evidence that if I do not calm down in the next 10 minutes, I'll die? Has anyone ever died from feeling uncomfortable? What's the evidence that people recovering from an anxiety problem do not have the feelings I'm having? What is the evidence that I'll never improve?
- **What's so awful about that?** What's so awful about feeling bad? Of course I can survive it. Who said that change would be easy? What's so terrible about experiencing discomfort? I can get through it. I've gotten through other difficult feelings and experiences and can live to tell about them.
- **I'm a human being and have a right to make mistakes.** Maybe I worry about not getting everything done that I hope to or not being as patient as I should be. What's so bad about that? We all make mistakes, and, in a situation that's complicated, there may not be a clear "right" or "perfect" way to handle things.

Some of these strategies will be necessary or helpful only initially to distract yourself from persistent urges; in the long run, you'll have an easier time if you replace the thoughts with other activities. After a while, abstinence will feel more natural. The urges will diminish in intensity and will come less often. You will also know how to cope with them.

In the example below, the clinician and patient discuss triggers and self-talk strategies.

> **Clinician (C):** You identified one of your strongest triggers as seeing other people with whom you have had conflict, especially family members. Let us try to pinpoint exactly what's going on.

> ***Shirley (S):*** *I feel that if I do not want to be with some family members, they might think I'm acting like I'm better than them. They already make fun of me, calling me the college girl, and all I really l want is to fit in.*
> ***C:*** *You're sensitive to your family members and concerned they'll think you are trying to be better than they are. What is the evidence this will happen?*
> ***S:*** *Well, I guess it's more a fear than a fact. I really do love them and know they love me. But I do not know how they would respond.*
> ***C:*** *What thoughts have you had about telling them these feelings?*
> ***S:*** *I almost told my uncle the other day, and I just could not.*
> ***C:*** *What are some other ways you might let them know?*

Lead Demonstration/Role Play

The clinician gives the patient the **Urge Surfing** handout and orients them to the activity by summarizing the rationale; much of this will have already been discussed in the session. The clinician then walks the patient through a brief demonstration of how to implement the urge surfing strategy by describing each step in the activity and by modeling how to apply the technique. A useful strategy when modeling this is to share out loud your experiences, step by step, as if you were engaging in the strategy in that moment.

Facilitate Patient-led Practice/Assess Skills Transfer

To prepare the patient to practice urge surfing, the clinician asks them to (1) identify a recent situation in which they felt a strong craving or urge to use and (2) describe the trigger(s) and their experience of the craving or urge with enough detail to stimulate some degree of craving in that moment. Then, the clinician supports the patient in practicing urge surfing. They walk the patient through the activity, step by step, reading the instructions and prompts aloud and checking in with the patient, as needed, throughout the activity. When the practice is complete, the clinician affirms the patient's skill application and offers follow-up questions to encourage them to explore their physical, emotional, and cognitive experiences throughout the urge surfing activity.

Identify Real-world Application

The clinician helps the patient to think through opportunities for how they might continue strengthening their skills in managing cravings and urges (i.e., upcoming situations in which the patient anticipates encountering a craving trigger). Ideally, the patient would initiate practice of new skills for managing cravings when they are experiencing mild-to-moderate intensity cravings. This intensity level is heightened enough to provide the patient with an opportunity to practice skill application outside of a high-risk situation. As the patient's skills strengthen, they will become more adept at using these coping strategies and more prepared for managing high-intensity cravings. At the same time, the clinician also supports the patient in planning response strategies for high-intensity cravings or urges by identifying a combination of strategies they can deploy if needed.

The clinician introduces the following exercises to support the patient in identifying potentially triggering situations and a plan for responding to those triggers. Using the **Coping With Cravings and Discomfort** handout, the clinician asks the patient to generate a list of any additional triggers they encounter in daily life. They then ask the patient to circle any triggers they can more easily avoid or reduce their exposure to (e.g., having alcohol or substances in the home). The clinician then supports the patient in generating a craving plan. They ask the patient to select two or three of the general coping strategies discussed and think through how they will put them into practice when experiencing an urge. For example, if the patient seemed to gravitate toward distracting activities, ask them to identify which specific activities would be most helpful? Encourage the patient to consider: Which strategies are available? Which take preparation? If one does not work, what will they try next?

Negotiate and Prepare Between-session Challenge
The exploration of real-world skill application is a natural transition into negotiation of a between-session challenge. The clinician encourages the patient to continue reviewing the materials handed out at this and previous sessions. They ask the patient where and when the patient can commit to using avoidance, escape, distraction, and embrace coping skills to manage urges and cravings. The patient is encouraged to continue practice of urge surfing, along with other strategies, as relevant to their identified triggers and craving plan.

For any identified between-session challenges, the clinician works with the patient to ensure that they know what they will do, when they will do it, and how often it will be done, mentally rehearsing its application in their daily life. Most patients benefit from writing down this plan somewhere accessible to also serve as an ongoing reminder. For this session, the clinician also introduces and encourages the patient to use the **Daily Record of Urges to Use** handout to track their urge experiences and coping responses throughout the week.

Elicit Commitment
The clinician explores the patient's commitment for completing the between-session challenge (e.g., at least two times) and uses MI strategies, as needed, to assess and strengthen commitment. The clinician also asks the patient to think through any potential obstacles to their skills practice and works with them to identify solutions and activate resources, as needed, to support their skill application.

Summarize and Conclude
The clinician reviews the content of the session, solicits feedback from the patient, responds empathically to their comments, and troubleshoots any difficulties. They ask that the patient report back on their efforts to complete the between-session exercise at the next session. The clinician prepares the patient for the next session by introducing the topic and by explaining how it will be helpful on the path toward wellness.

Session 7 Handouts: Handling Urges, Cravings, and Discomfort

Coping with Cravings and Discomfort

About urges and cravings
- Urges are common in the recovery process. Do not regard them as signs of failure. Instead, use your urges to help you understand what triggers your cravings.
- Urges are like ocean waves. They get stronger only to a point; then they start to subside.
- You win every time you defeat an urge to use. Urges get stronger the next time if you give in and "feed" them. However, if you do not feed it, an urge eventually will weaken and die.

My triggers
Make a list of craving triggers. Circle the triggers you can more easily avoid or reduce your exposure to, such as removing alcohol or substances in your home.

1.	2.
3.	4.
5.	6.
7.	8.
9.	10.
11.	12.
13.	14.

My plan
Select two or three of the general strategies discussed, and plan how to put them into practice if you experience an urge.

I will use these strategies if I experience an urge or trigger:

1) _____

2) _____

3) _____

Between-session challenge
For the next week, make a daily record of urges to use alcohol or substances, the intensity of those urges, and the coping behaviors you used.

Fill out the **Daily Record of Urges to Use** handout:

- Date
- Situation: Include anything about the situation and your thoughts or feelings that seemed to trigger the urge to use.
- Intensity of Cravings: Rate your craving: **1 = none at all, 100 = worst ever**.
- Coping Behaviors Used: Note how you attempted to cope with the urge to use alcohol or substances. If it helps, note the effectiveness of your coping technique.

Daily Record of Urges to Use

Date	Situation (Include Thoughts and Feelings)	Intensity of Cravings (1–100)[a]	Coping Behaviors Used

[a] Intensity of Cravings Scale: 1 = none at all, 100 = worst ever.

Urge Surfing

Many people try to cope with their urges by gritting their teeth and toughing it out. Some urges, especially when you first return to your old using environment, are too strong to ignore. When this happens, it can be useful to stay with your urge to use until it passes. This technique is called urge surfing.

Urges are like ocean waves. They are small when they start, grow in size, and then break up and dissipate. You can imagine yourself as a surfer who will ride the wave, staying on top of it until it crests; breaks; and turns into less powerful, foamy surf. The basis of urge surfing is similar to that of many martial arts. In judo, one overpowers an opponent by first going with the force of the attack. By joining with the opponent's force, one can take control of it and redirect it to one's advantage. This type of technique of gaining control by first going with the opponent allows one to take control while expending a minimum of energy. Urge surfing is similar. You can join with an urge (rather than meet it with a strong opposing force) as a way of taking control of your urge to use. After you have read and become familiar with the instructions for urge surfing, you may find this a useful technique when you have a strong urge to use.

Urge surfing has three basic steps:

1) **Take an inventory of how you experience the craving.** Do this by sitting in a comfortable chair with your feet flat on the floor and your hands in a comfortable position. Take a few deep breaths and focus inward. Allow your attention to wander through your body. Notice where in your body you experience the craving and what the sensations are like. Notice each area where you experience the urge, and tell yourself what you are experiencing. For example, "Let me see. My craving is in my mouth and nose and in my stomach."
2) **Focus on one area where you are experiencing the urge.** Notice the exact sensations in that area. For example, do you feel hot, cold, tingly, or numb? Are your muscles tense or relaxed? How large an area is involved? Notice the sensations and describe them to yourself. Notice the changes that occur in the sensation. "Well, my mouth feels dry and parched. There is tension in my lips and tongue. I keep swallowing. As I exhale, I can imagine the smell and taste of [_____]."
3) **Refocus on each part of your body that experiences the craving.** Do not try to escape from or avoid the experience of craving. Accept its presence. Pay attention to and describe to yourself the changes that occur in the sensations. Notice how the urge comes and goes.

Many people notice that after a few minutes of urge surfing, the craving vanishes. The purpose of this exercise, however, is not to make the craving go away but to experience the craving in a new way. If you practice urge surfing, you will become familiar with your cravings and learn how to ride them out until they go away easily.

Session 8. Working with Thoughts: Part 1

Introduction

In this session, our first task is to educate the patient and to help them recognize the brain as a "word-generating machine" and that these words are thoughts, and thoughts are not reality. To the extent that patients buy in to these automatic thoughts as reality, the thoughts control behavior and emotion. This can happen in a couple of ways. Either the patient believes the thoughts are reality, and they taint their view of the world, like a distorted lens through which the patient sees their experiences, or the patient can go to war with the thoughts, trying to change them. This is a sort of Chinese finger trap toy, where the more the patient fights the thought, the more it persists. In both instances, your patient is fused to the thought, emotions, and connected behaviors.

> Avoidance of pain and discomfort can be viewed as a self-limiting problem-solving approach that often perpetuates suffering.

Gaining an understanding of how their problematic thoughts are affecting them is a crucial first step. Once this understanding is established, the clinician introduces skills to disrupt this pattern and to give the patient a chance to try out new strategies to address the problematic thoughts so that the patient is neither buying into nor fighting with them. This action works to provide psychological space for the patient to create a change by choosing their actions based on what they value, as opposed to a self-limiting thought to which they have been fused.

The objective of this session is for the clinician to provide the patient with information about the evolutionary role of different types of emotions and the relationships between thoughts and emotions, particularly as they relate to their substance use, depression, or other self-limiting behaviors. This information, along with discussion about the patient's unique experiences and handling of various emotional states, provides a rationale for trying to gain a new perspective on our thoughts and to cultivate certain emotions while reducing the impact of others. The clinician may find it beneficial to cover this material in more than one session, depending on its relevance for the patient and the patient's ability to incorporate the information into their daily life.

According to the CBT approach, emotions do not simply rise out of nowhere, and they are not necessarily directly related to events that take place. They are, however, intricately linked with our thoughts, interpretations, and perceptions about the things that happen. Therefore, it is possible to change the way one feels about oneself or a situation by altering the way one is thinking and by engaging in purposeful activities that produce positive or healing emotions.

The Patient's Experience

In this session, the patient is encouraged to recognize when they are fused to their thinking. Fusion refers to the act of confusing thinking with actual experience. The clinician provides examples of when fusion can be helpful, and when it is not, and teaches the patient different strategies to defuse from thoughts. The interventions the clinician employs are largely experiential and used to help the patient recognize thoughts as internal dialogue. When the patient is fused to problematic thoughts, these thoughts can steer the patient away from the value-driven life they are seeking. They may have some "aha" moments as they view thinking in this different way. They will also leave the session with additional skills to overcome the effects of fusion in their lives. As with other sessions, the patient should always experience the clinician as nonjudgmental. There may be a sense of lightness and humor when examining certain thoughts that are clearly irrational or not in the patient's best interests, given what they are trying to achieve in treatment.

Clinician Preparation

Session 8. Working With Thoughts	
Materials • *Clinician's Quick Reference* • *Gaining Distance and Perspective on Troubling Thoughts* • *Managing Thoughts About Substance Use* handout • *Problems and Values* handout	**Total Time** One hour **Delivery Method** CBT-focused individual or group therapy
Strategies • Follow OARS. • Demonstrate skill and role play. • Follow CBT skills session reminders.	
Goals for This Session • Help the patient identify and learn to accept automatic thoughts without becoming fused to them.	

Session 8 Outline and Overview

1) Maintain rapport and review.
2) Normalize fusion as helpful in some circumstances, and express the importance of choosing to defuse from thinking when it is not.
3) Identify situations in which fusion to thinking can lead to problematic behavior.
4) Discuss thought fusion and strategies to defuse:
   - Describe situations likely to trigger automatic thoughts.
   - Explore how fusion to these thoughts leads to lapse or relapse.
   - Provide in-session examples of fusion and defusion.
5) Explore conceptual difficulties:
   - Review material, and probe for the patient's understanding of basic concepts.
   - Use language that reflects thinking as separate from the thinker; provide metaphorical examples to further clarify fusion/defusion.
   - Walk the patient through a stressful episode to understand how fusion contributed to the situation and how defusion can be employed.
6) Develop skills for coping with automatic thoughts:
   - Explain general principles of defusing from problematic thoughts.
   - Describe specific strategies for defusing from problematic thoughts; review Managing Thoughts About Substance Use handout.
7) Practice skills for defusion from problematic thoughts:
   - Demonstrate the thoughts-as-passengers metaphor.
   - Help patient experience Mind Watching and Naming the Brain.
   - Demonstrate Challenging Reason Giving
8) Assign between-session exercises.
9) Review and conclude session.

Session 8 Protocol

Maintain Rapport and Review

The clinician welcomes the patient and enquires about the patient's thoughts and feelings since the last session, use of information covered in earlier meetings, and engagement in practice efforts. They provide an overview of the session that will help identify times when the patient is fused with problematic thoughts. The clinician will teach one or more defusion exercises and encourage the patient to try the exercises on some of their own thoughts, both in session and between now and the next session.

Normalize Fusion with Thoughts

The clinician discusses thought-fusion problematic language to separate thinking from the thinker.

> *The brains of people that have used substances for a long time often generate lots of thoughts about using. When you come into contact with situations where you previously used, the brain will generate thoughts about using. Sometimes it may not even be clear what happened that caused these thoughts to arise. This is normal; almost anyone who stops using has thoughts about starting up again pop up. The thought about using is not a problem to be solved; it is a passing, internal experience that we can choose to buy into or not. This skill topic will help you learn new ways to interact with those thoughts before you slip back into using behavior.*
>
> *Or*
>
> *Similarly, the brain of a person who has experienced significant trauma may have an inner narrative: "Am I safe here? If I must flee, what is the way out?"*

Identify fusion with thoughts associated with problematic behavior

The clinician explains how thought fusion relates to the problematic behavior, using the "Having, holding, and buying a thought" exercise.

> *As any person goes through a normal day, their brain generates hundreds, if not thousands, of thoughts. Most of these thoughts pass right on through our awareness, and we do not dwell on them. This is just "having a thought." However, when we develop behavioral habits, like using drugs or being anxious, particular thoughts catch our attention. For example, we may have the thought that "I am not going to have fun unless I get high," or "People are saying bad things about me." Oftentimes, we buy into thoughts like this because this is the pattern we have developed in our behavior, and the thought seems like reality. This is what we call "buying a thought." When we do, we often follow it with behavior (e.g., in this case, using drugs or avoiding social settings). What we want to talk about today is how to hold a thought. We aren't trying to fight it, make it go away, or challenge it. Instead, we want to recognize it as a thought...not a reality, not an inevitability, just a string of words that our brain generated that we get to choose to buy or not.*

Discuss fusion with problematic behavior—Thoughts by using the passengers on a bus metaphor
The clinician describes the passengers on a bus metaphor.

> So, I want you to imagine yourself as a bus driver. You have a route you have to drive, and you are doing that. You make a stop and pick up a rough-looking rider; he is kind of scary, has a knife on his belt, an angry look, and scowls at you when you get him on the bus. You keep driving, and, as you are about to make a turn to follow your route, the mean-looking passenger yells, "Do not you dare turn here, or I will make you sorry!" Imagine you pick up three or four more passengers. All of them are angry, a little scary, tell you what to do, and threaten you. Eventually you just do what they say. Then you realize you know what they are going to say, and you do it without even being asked to avoid the conflict.
>
> Imagine that your life is this bus, and the route is how you want to live your life based on what is valuable to you. For example, you may see being a parent as very valuable, and you want to live your life in ways that make you a better one. The angry passengers are thoughts your brain produces (i.e., using thoughts), and, eventually, these thoughts drive your decisions instead of your values. What is a thought that you have had in the past that you bought, and it led to using? What is another one? How about one more?
>
> So, what do you do? You could turn around and tell the passenger to sit down. If they do not sit down, you could stop the bus and go back there and try to make them stop or kick them off the bus. When you do that, you are no longer driving your bus or leading your life the way you want. Instead, you are caught up with your mind and still not leading the value-driven life you want. You have already tried obeying the passengers; that may even help you have a little peace, but it still keeps you from the life you want. Fighting the thoughts and giving in to the thoughts are both examples of being fused to thoughts, and both stand in the way of living the life you want to live.
>
> You need another option, and that is to hold your thoughts. Holding your thoughts is when you recognize them for what they are: a string of words that your brain has generated. They are not reality; they are not inevitable to happening; they are just words. When you have been anxious, depressed, or using drugs for a long period of time, your brain may generate a lot of these thoughts.

Some examples that people share oftentimes include some of the ones are described below.

Attachment. Sometimes our brains form nostalgic attachments to persons and events, remembering the good times and minimizing the not good times. Similarly, our brains can form negative attachments: "I was beaten and robbed when I visited Boston. I hate that place. I will never return there, ever!"

Testing Control. After a period of abstinence, people in recovery may become overconfident. For example, they may think "I bet I can use tonight and go back on the wagon tomorrow morning." Curiosity also can be a problem: "I wonder what it would be like to get high again?"

Crisis. A person may respond to stress by saying, "I can handle this only if I'm high," or "I went through so much, I deserve to get high," or "When this is over, I'll stop using again."

Feeling Irritable. Some people find new problems arise after they become abstinent or make other life changes (e.g., divorce, separation). They believe these problems will resolve if they get into a new relationship. For example, they may think, "I'm short-tempered and irritable around my family. Maybe it's more important for me to be a good-natured parent and spouse than it is to stop using right now."

Escape. Individuals want to avoid unpleasant situations, feelings, conflicts, or memories. The tendency to want to avoid or to try to escape from emotional pain is common and contributes to mistaken beliefs that one is incapable of dealing with the situation or feeling.

> Often avoidance and waiting for things to get better takes us away from what is most important to us: the person we want to be and the life we want to live.

Negative Feelings and Experiences. Failure, rejection, disappointment, fear, anger, hurt, humiliation, embarrassment, and sadness tend to demand relief. People find they want to be able to stop these negative feelings or to have greater control over their impact. They may want to anesthetize or numb themselves from the emotional pain they feel they cannot control or prevent. They may seek an absence of feeling rather than dealing with the experiences they are having and become disconnected from themselves and their true needs. Or they may seek a kind of pleasure to erase the negative feelings.

Relaxation. Thoughts of wanting to unwind are normal, but sometimes people look for a shortcut, trying to unwind without doing something relaxing. An individual may choose the more immediate route through alcohol or other substances.

Socialization. This overlaps with relaxation but is confined to social situations. Individuals who are shy or uncomfortable in social settings may feel they need something in social situations to decrease awkwardness and anxiety.

Improved Self-image. This situation involves a pervasive negative view of oneself and associated low self-esteem. When individuals become unhappy with themselves, feel inferior to others, regard themselves as lacking essential qualities, feel unattractive or deficient, or doubt their ability to succeed, they seek relief from these painful feelings.

No Control. The attitude of being unable to control how we feel or think ensures recurrence. Individuals who give up the fight, conceding defeat before attempting to change, may feel out of control in other aspects of their lives as well. This attitude differs from the "to-hell-with-it" attitude in which individuals do not necessarily feel powerless, they just do not want to continue doing the work of change because the work is hard.

Explore conceptual difficulties

Some patients may have difficulty understanding this concept. It is important to take your time here; if the concept is not understood, it compromises the benefits of defusion. This may be particularly true for patients who are overly concrete in their thinking (e.g., those with some cognitive limitations due to trauma, developmental, or physiological issues). When this happens, a more behaviorally focused skills training tends to yield better outcomes. A key concept to defusion is recognizing that thoughts are only language, sentences that the brain produces that we then accept as reality. One way to express this concept in more concrete terms is through the exercise below involving imagining water.

> **Clinician (C):** Imagine for a second a glass of water. Can you see it in your mind? What does it look like?
> **Patient (P):** Well, it's cold, it's clear.
> **C:** OK, cold, clear. Are there little beads of water outside the glass? Is there ice in it? Can you kind of remember what a cold glass of water feels like in your mouth? Can you remember the taste?
> **P:** Yeah, like when you are really thirsty, and you take a drink, and you can feel it run all the way down to your stomach almost. Or when you drink it too fast, and you get that headache.

> **C:** Right! I know that feeling, super refreshing. OK, so now take a drink.
> **P:** I do not know what you mean; there is no water?
> **C:** Exactly! Your brain is super powerful. It can almost reproduce the feeling of taking a drink; it can create a picture in your mind of the glass of water, but no matter how much your brain generates these images, it never really can make water. So, replace water with that thought you mentioned that your brain likes to put out there for you, that "I will not have any fun unless I get high." It's the same; it seems true when your brain spits that out, right? But it is no different than the water your brain was just imagining. Try to think of your brain as a word generator. Some of those words can be helpful, some may not be, but all of them are just words. What we want to do here is help you develop the ability to choose what things your brain puts out that you want to buy into or fuse with.

Being overwhelmed by thoughts and buying them as reality is what leads to taking actions on those thoughts. To help the patient gain an understanding of thinking as an ongoing action over which they have little control, we want to use language deliberately to separate the patient from the thoughts the brain generates. Understanding thinking in this way gives the patient room to decide what thoughts they want to buy based on what they want from their lives.

When the patient is clear on what thought fusion and defusion are, then we can go into teaching skills to defuse. A few examples of exercises that can help with this are described below. It is very important to continue to be consistent in how you describe thoughts as you teach the defusion skills. For example, as opposed to saying things like "your thoughts," replace with "thoughts that pop up," "thoughts you are having," or "thoughts your brain put out." This will further drive home the concepts addressed above.

Develop skills for thought defusion

The clinician helps the patient identify automatic thoughts and reviews some of the techniques used in previous sessions. Then they teach up to three of the skills described below to defuse them from their thoughts.

Mind Watching

If you have used drugs or alcohol for a while and decide to quit, it is likely that your brain will produce some thoughts about using. As we discussed, the thought is not the problem; it's what we do with it. If you learn to slow down and recognize these thoughts, you can give yourself the option to hold or buy those thoughts.

Similarly, persons who have ended highly problematic relationships may have thoughts of reuniting with their former partner, despite neither the person nor the partner having made any changes.

One way to hold a thought is by Mind Watching. You can work through a Mind Watching exercise with the client to impart the skill. You can tailor several examples to fit your client (e.g., Leaves on a Stream or Watching Clouds exercises). Dialogue with a client regarding these exercises is described below.

> **Clinician (C):** I want to do a simple exercise with you. It requires closing your eyes or lowering your gaze if closing your eyes feels uncomfortable and just watching your mind for a bit. Would that be OK?
> **Patient:** Sure.

> **C:** Great. The purpose is to help you recognize when you are fused with your thoughts. Imagine that you are lying in some comfortable grass looking up at the sky, and you are just watching. Now imagine each cloud has a little sign on it, and what is written on the sign is the thought your brain is having at that moment. You may see some of these thoughts as pictures. That is fine; just see that little picture printed on the cloud. So go ahead and close your eyes. Your task is just to watch the clouds pass; let them float on by. At some point, you will notice that the clouds are gone, and you have been captured by a thought. When that happens, I want you to back up a bit and try to identify what thought you bought that took you out of mind watching.

At this point, the clinician helps the patient center and observes the exercise. Try not to talk much. Offer encouragement like "[J]ust watch the clouds float by, and notice when they stop." If you notice any changes in the client's face or body posture, note it to yourself, and let it trigger a gentle reminder to the patient to "just watch the clouds."

> **Clinician (C):** OK, let the last couple of clouds go by, and then come back to this room. What did you notice?
> **Patient (P):** Well, at one point, the clouds stopped, and when I looked back, I realized that I was stressing about going to this meeting where this woman will be there who I really, really like and then I think, "There is no way she will ever care about you. You are not in her league."
> **C:** Oh, so what was the last thought you noticed before the clouds stopped? Did it start out being printed on the card?
> **P:** Yeah, the cloud said, "Get real! You are not in her league!" Then 10 or 15 seconds went by, and I realized the clouds were gone.
> **C:** So that little moment was when you bought the thought! You were no longer watching your brain generate thoughts; you were in your thoughts. Remember how we said thoughts can be like a lens when we are fused with them? When this happens, we stop recognizing thoughts as just words our brains spit out and start experiencing the thought as something real that you have to do something about. The beauty of this exercise is you can do it any time and recognize that when the clouds stop, you can put the thought back on a cloud, and just watch more of them go by. This is what we mean by holding a thought.

Naming the Brain

When the patient understands that the brain is a constant word generator and not a reflection of who they are, we can then separate the person from the brain and even pit their interests against one another. One way to do this is through the Naming the Brain exercise. Some patients may want to give the brain human names; others may be uncomfortable with this and more inclined to name a particular mode of thinking after the effect (e.g., "the judgy mind," "the using brain"). This name can then be used in dialogue with the patient and as a means for the patient not to buy into thoughts on their own. To reinforce this, the clinician may say things like "[I]t sounds like your judgy brain was having a field day with this."

Challenging Reason Giving

Reasons are explanations for behavior (e.g., "I got drunk because I was so upset with my husband"). People give reasons for behavior all the time, and these reasons are often connected to some understanding they have about themselves. Giving a reason for behavior is connected to particular behaviors, but this does not mean one caused the other. This is the heart of this exercise: not to challenge the actual thought but to challenge the whole idea of giving reasons for behaviors. An example dialogue of Challenging Reason Giving is provided below. Like the previous exercise examples, we are not going to challenge the form of the thought but rather how the thought works in the patient's life.

> *Clinician (C):* You said you wound up drinking last Wednesday. Can we talk about that a bit?
> *Patient (P):* Sure.
> *C:* Why did you drink last Wednesday?
> *P:* I do not know. I guess I drank because I just do not feel like my life is improving, and I am stuck in this crummy relationship.
> *C:* So you drank because your life is not improving?
> *P:* Yeah.
> *C:* Is that the first time you ever felt like your life is not improving?
> *P:* No, I feel like that all the time!
> *C:* Well, it's interesting that you feel like this all the time, but you only drank on Wednesday. I mean, if feeling this lack of progress causes drinking, I would think you would be drinking every day.
> *P:* Yeah, but I also have reasons not to drink. I mean, I want my relationship and kid to get back on track.
> *C:* Right, so there are reasons not to drink, too. Those reasons were also there when you drank Wednesday. I bet if you thought about it, you could come up with more reasons not to drink, and you could probably come up with more reasons to drink as well. It sounds like there is an unending number of reasons to drink or not drink that we could come up with, but, in the end, we choose a behavior or do not, and the reasons are still there.
> *P:* So are you saying reasons do not matter?
> *C:* I am saying that there are plenty of reasons to drink or not drink, but that none of those reasons make you drink. You already uncovered that you avoid drinking even when the reason you provided is there. In fact, you did not drink for six of seven days last week, and you noticed you had that thought about your life not improving the whole time. So maybe the reasons your using brain produces do not cause the drinking.

Assign Between-session Practice
Problems and values

At the end of the session, the clinician explains the between-session practice on **Problems and Values**. They should ask the patient to recap what they learned about defusion and address any misunderstanding. The clinician should then note that the patient has some ways to hold thoughts, and, this week, we want the patient to identify times when their brain generates using thoughts. When that happens, the patient can use the handout to identify:

- Column 1: Thoughts and feelings they have that they get caught up with
- Column 2: Actions they have taken that make their life worse in the long run
- Column 3: Values that they have for themselves.
- Column 4: Goals and actions that are aligned with the values they want to develop.

The patient uses this information to identify courses of action consistent with what is valuable to them, while holding the thoughts and feelings that could lead back to using.

Review and Conclude

The clinician reviews the content of the session, asks the patient for feedback, responds empathically to their comments, and troubleshoots any difficulties. They explain that the patient will report back on their efforts to complete the between-session exercises at the next session. The clinician also prepares the patient for the next session by introducing the topic and by explaining how it will be helpful on the path toward wellness.

Session 8 Handouts: Working with Thoughts

Clinician's Quick Reference to Session 8

1) Maintain rapport and review.
2) Normalize fusion as helpful in some circumstances, and express the importance of choosing to defuse from thinking when it is not.
3) Identify situations in which fusion to thinking can lead to substance use.
4) Discuss thought fusion and strategies to defuse:
    - Describe situations likely to trigger automatic thoughts.
    - Explore how fusion to these thoughts leads to lapse or relapse.
    - Provide in-session examples of fusion and defusion.
5) Explore conceptual difficulties:
    - Review material, and probe for the patient's understanding of basic concepts.
    - Use language that reflects thinking as separate from the thinker; provide metaphorical examples to further clarify fusion/defusion.
    - Walk patient through a using episode to understand how fusion contributed to use and of how defusion can be employed.
6) Develop skills for coping with automatic thoughts:
    - Explain general principles of defusing from using thoughts.
    - Describe specific strategies for defusing from using thoughts; review **Managing Thoughts About Alcohol or Substances** handout.
7) Practice skills for coping with automatic thoughts:
    - Demonstrate the thoughts-as-passengers metaphor.
    - Help patient experience Mind Watching and Naming the Brain.
    - Demonstrate Challenging Reason Giving.
8) Assign between-session exercises.
9) Review and conclude.

Managing Thoughts About Substance Use

When trying to stop using alcohol or other substances, it is common for your brain to generate lots of using thoughts and for these thoughts to act as triggers for potential lapses. A variety of approaches may be helpful to you as you face these thoughts.

- Recognize that thoughts are just words generated by your brain.
  - Having a thought does not mean you have to "buy it;" you can simply recognize you are having a thought without acting on it.
  - One thought does not have to take on more significance or have more salience than any other thought; that is, one need not become "fused" to a particular thought or story.
- Use mindfulness or meditation practice to work with challenging thoughts.
  - See the thought as "separate" from you; step back from it.
  - Name the type of thinking you are challenged by, for example, "using mind."
  - Observe thoughts as they pass through your mind; recognize when you get caught up or fused with a thought.
  - Imagine the thought is just passing through, as if stopping temporarily at a hotel, and is not "owned" by you.
- Use creative visualization or imagery to work with challenging thoughts.
  - Imagine you are lying in a comfortable place watching clouds pass, and each of the thoughts you have are printed on a cloud. Let the clouds pass.
  - If/when you notice the clouds stop, notice the thought that you stopped on, and go back to letting the thoughts pass.
- Remind yourself of what is valuable to you, and ask if the thoughts your brain is producing are getting you closer to or further away from those values.
  - Make a list of what is truly valuable to you. The list should include the qualities you want in yourself, your relationships, your work, etc.
  - When the using mind starts producing thoughts, ask yourself if the thoughts are in line with living the life you want to live.
  - Ask yourself what action(s) would be consistent with your values.

Problems and Values

Struggling, Suffering, and Fusion		Value-driven Life	
Problematic Thoughts and Feelings: What thoughts and memories do you get "fused" to? What emotions, cravings, and feelings do you struggle with?	**Problem Actions:** What are you doing that makes your life worse in the long term, wastes your time and money, or negatively affects your relationships or goals?	**Values:** What really matters to you? What characteristics do you want to have in yourself? What qualities do you want in your relationships? How about in your work life?	**Goals and Actions:** What are you doing that makes your life better in the long term? What would you like to do more of? What life-enhancing actions do you want to take?

Source: Russ Harris (2009); www.actmadesimple.com

Gaining Distance and Perspective on Troubling Thoughts

This is a relatively simple and useful exercise that enables your patient to step back from difficult or troubling thoughts and to view them in a broader and more compassionate context.

1) Take a few minutes for deep breathing relaxation.
2) Ask your patient to explore and identify self-limiting thoughts with you that interfere with their progress and well-being.
3) Summarize using compassionate and nonjudgmental reflections.
4) Ask your patient to summarize those thoughts, each in just a few words (three or less), such as "I'm a loser."
5) Use 3 × 5 cards or small, separate pieces of paper, and have your patient write down those thoughts.
6) Once complete, have your patient place those cards on their lap or on the table in front of them.
7) Process that these thoughts are just words.
8) Explore how it feels having these words at a distance. Use compassionate, nonjudgmental reflections to model self-compassion for the patient.
9) Summarize that these thoughts never entirely go away, but their power and influence can be diminished, and, with time, we gain a new perspective on those thoughts and our actions.

Session 9. Working with Emotions

Introduction

In Session 8, the clinician provides the patient with information about the evolutionary role of different types of emotions and the relationships among thoughts, emotions, and behaviors (e.g., alcohol use, depression, other self-limiting behaviors). This information, along with discussion about the patient's unique experiences and handling of various emotional states, provides a rationale for trying to cultivate certain emotions while reducing the impact of others. As stated earlier, you may find it beneficial to cover this material in more than one session, depending on its relevance for the patient.

The Importance of Positive Emotions

Fredrickson (2000), in her article "Cultivating Positive Emotions for Optimizing Health and Well-Being," refers to her "broaden-and-build model of emotions" (p. 6) and the role of different types of emotions with regard to their evolutionary value. Positive emotions, sometimes called "approach emotions" because they lead people toward affiliative activities (e.g., joy, interest, contentment, sociability), have the benefit of helping individuals to experience a broader perspective and capacity to deal with challenges. They are the feelings that facilitate a sense of expansiveness, creativity, hope, persistence, and resilience.

Goleman (2003) also highlights the value and benefit of positive emotions for their "healing properties" (p. 33). This idea of positive emotions having healing potential is of great interest to those working in health and related fields. Increasing the amount of time spent in positive emotions can be beneficial on many levels. From a psychological standpoint, it can increase problem-solving capacity by helping someone access multiple pathways for addressing a particular challenge. It may create a kind of "stress inoculation" (Meichenbaum, 2007, p. 499) whereby individuals will have greater ability to tolerate and respond constructively to stressors. Positive emotions can counteract the negative effects of stress (e.g., suppressed or weakened immune function).

In contrast, negative emotions, which can be referred to as "withdrawal emotions" (e.g., fear, sadness, anger, self-loathing), tend to be narrowing or constricting because they reduce our "momentary thought-action" repertoire. This makes sense from an evolutionary standpoint because when we are faced with life-threatening danger, it is better to hold a narrow focus and scan the environment quickly to determine how to achieve or regain a sense of safety. The problem occurs when negative emotions become chronic or automatic, even in situations where there is no objective danger present. The example becomes clear in thinking about PTSD. An individual with PTSD becomes hypervigilant to signs of danger and may be triggered by things not objectively a threat in the present, although they may certainly have signaled danger at another time and place (e.g., an adult who was physically abused as a child having a heightened sensitivity to signs of disapproval or anger in others).

Positive emotions have the ability to "undo" or reduce the hold that negative emotions can have on a person. Therefore, helping people cultivate or foster more positive feelings and experiences can reduce their experience of negative emotions. This is similar to the theory that forms the basis and rationale for using relaxation training for anxiety and phobias. It may be difficult or impossible to experience both tension and relaxation simultaneously, and, therefore, increasing relaxation will have the effect of competing with anxiety and ultimately winning.

Patients who come to treatment are likely to be struggling with their handling of different emotional states. They will report that the alcohol or other substance helps them feel better. However, using substances to treat difficult or painful emotional states (i.e., as an "affective" or "emotional regulator") often results in more problems and does not address the primary issue of feeling bad. In fact, when substances become a routine escape from negative states, this cycle tends to create even more negative feelings because now the person has to cope with the consequences (e.g., health, relationships, legal, occupational) associated with excessive use.

In this session, the clinician also explores the patient's experience with depression and other negative states. The patient learns to recognize and cope with negative affective states. The clinician addresses the possibility of negative moods, explaining that anxiety, irritability, and depression are common among people overcoming an alcohol or substance use problem.

Some theories about the etiology and maintenance of substance use suggest that substances are used to regulate negative emotional states when one has not developed other, more constructive methods of self-regulation. Helping individuals reduce their experience of negative emotions may remove an important trigger for substance use. The reduction of negative emotional states also may create opportunities for more creative, expansive states and increase problem-solving and feelings of self-efficacy.

CBT views the experience of negative emotional states as being affected strongly by one's thoughts or interpretations of events, while also recognizing the role of neurobiological factors. That is, an experience may be felt as highly negative when one makes personal attributions (e.g., blaming oneself entirely for a negative event or outcome: ["It was all my fault our soccer team lost the game"]). This amplifies the extent of a negative effect (e.g., "This is terrible. I will never be able to achieve my goal of quitting smoking"). The individual may engage in other thought processes that serve to heighten a sense of negativity, futility, and disaster. CBT describes a number of commonly employed cognitive distortions that tend to foster and intensify negative emotions.

The Patient's Experience

This session is intended to increase the patient's understanding of the role of different emotional states and of how the emotions involved in discovering, exploring, and practicing pleasurable activities can engender positive feelings. Many times, patients who have developed risky use of substances have come to think of the substance use as fun and enjoyable. Over time, the substance use takes the place of other important activities and relationships and replaces activities that were once enjoyable. The focus of this session is on helping the patient reconnect with activities, hobbies, and other experiences that have been pleasurable in the past or seem they would be enjoyable if the person has never tried them.

Clinician Preparation

Session 9. Working with Emotions	
Materials • *Clinician's Quick Reference* • *Focus on Emotion: Roles of Positive and Negative Emotions* handout • *Focus on Emotion: Pleasant Activities* handout (uses the same activities as *Increasing Pleasant Activities* handout in Session 5) • *Cognitive Fusion That Dampens One's Mood and Restricts Behavior* handout • *Managing Negative Moods and Depression* handout • *Patient Health Questionnaire-9 (PHQ-9)* handout • *Generalized Anxiety Disorder-7 Item Scale (GAD-7)* handout	**Total Time** One hour **Delivery Method** CBT-focused individual or group therapy
Strategies • Follow OARS. • Demonstrate skill and role play. • Follow CBT skills session reminders.	
Goals for This Session • Educate the patient about the role of different emotional states. • Elicit discussion and reflection about the patient's emotional experiences and methods of handling different emotions. • Increase patient's awareness about the value of positive and healing emotions and methods for increasing these states. • Become aware of different experiences of negative moods and their role. • Discuss the constricting and sometimes-damaging effects of certain negative emotions. • Become more aware of how moods affect alcohol or substance use. • Learn strategies to recognize, process, and cope with these emotions.	

Session 9 Outline and Overview

1) Maintain rapport and review previous week.
2) Introduce the concept of working with emotions.
3) Discuss the evolutionary value and/or role of various emotions in day-to-day life.
4) Explore the patient's experience with different emotions, connection with alcohol or other drug use, and typical ways of regulating their emotional state.
5) Provide a rationale for fostering positive emotions, which can be constructive and healing.
6) Review a list of pleasant activities and develop a plan for increasing opportunities for positive emotion.
7) Provide a rationale for decreasing or dissolving the effects of negative emotions.
8) Discuss thinking patterns or cognitive distortions that tend to dampen or depress one's mood:
   - Review Cognitive Fusion That Dampens One's Mood and Restricts Behavior.
   - Explain cognitive distortions.
   - Explore automatic thought patterns that appear to lead to negative mood states.
   - Ask the patient to identify which automatic negative thoughts in which they may engage before or during depressed, anxious, or irritable moods.
9) Build internal resources for handling automatic thoughts:
   - Discuss with the patient guidelines for evaluating these thoughts.
   - Give the patient the Managing Negative Moods and Depression handout.
   - Engage the patient in problem solving to address problems contributing to their negative moods.
10) Link negative moods with alcohol or substance use:
    - Explore the relationship between the patient's alcohol or substance use and their experience of negative moods.
    - Explore methods of changing the patient's automatic thoughts that can lead to alcohol or substance use.
11) Assign practice exercises involving pleasant activities.
12) Review and conclude.

Session 9 Protocol

Maintain Rapport and Review
Welcome the patient, and review events from the previous week. Inquire about between-session exercises if they were given. Discuss the patient's current status regarding substance use, readiness to change, and progress with goals.

Introduce the Concept of Working with Emotions
Introduce the topic of emotions and their role in our lives. Share with patient the handout *Focus on Emotion: Role of Positive and Negative Emotions*.

> *Hi. Today I want us to talk some about emotions and the role they play in our lives. I know you told me you had been feeling pretty sad a lot, and you think that is related to your using alcohol the way you have been. I am hoping that, through our discussion today, you will have a better understanding about emotions in general and, more specifically, how you experience and cope with different emotional states. I want to share some information with you about different emotions and how they all have some value.*

Discuss the Evolutionary Value and/or Role of Various Emotions in Day-to-day Life

> *For example, it's important for us to feel sad when we have some kind of loss or disappointment. Or to feel scared when there is a threat to our safety. And even to feel angry when we have been treated unfairly. Those negative emotions are important because they help us to figure out what we need to be safe or to take care of ourselves. However, those feelings can also make us feel kind of disconnected from people, withdrawn, and as though there aren't a lot of things we can do to feel better. For example, you seem to have come to believe that when you are feeling sad, drinking is the only thing you can do to feel better. There are actually many things you can do that have the potential for lifting your mood. And the really interesting thing is that when you start doing things that make you feel more positive (e.g., joyful, engaged, hopeful), you will not be feeling as negative because it's difficult to feel both good and bad at the same time.*
>
> *It's not that we should never have negative feelings, but we might want to step back and see whether we can have some greater control or role in the way we feel. If we can put effort into doing things that are likely to make us feel more positive, this will help us in other ways, too. When we are feeling positive, we are more likely to be creative and able to work toward goals we have. We can think of different solutions to a difficult problem, rather than feeling as though there is only one way. Does that fit with your experience? Do you notice that when you are in a good mood, you feel more capable of handling challenges? Or your problems do not seem as big and unmanageable? Whereas when you are feeling down or negative, everything seems so hard and like too much work? And no one can really seem to understand or help you?*

Explore the Patient's Experience with Different Emotions, Their Connection with Alcohol and Other Drug Use, and How They Tend to Regulate Their Emotional State

> *Can you tell me a little about how your mood is in general? What kinds of things seem to make you feel more positive? What makes you feel more discouraged or negative? How do you deal with negative feelings? How do you suppose your use of drugs or alcohol might or might not relate to different feelings you have?*

Provide a Rationale for Fostering Positive Emotions, Which Can be Constructive and Healing

> *Scientists and those interested in studying the role and value of different emotions have found that it is possible and desirable to increase our experience of positive emotions and that this is very helpful to our overall health and well-being. For example, when we are in a positive state of mind, we tend to be more creative in our thinking and problem solving. We can see many possibilities open to us in dealing with challenges. We feel confident in our ability to accomplish goals. We feel hopeful about the future. We experience joy and a sense of well-being. It is even good for our heart as our blood pressure may be lowered when we are feeling positive. Trying to cultivate positive emotions is helpful not only in the present moment for feeling better, but may have some longer-term benefits, as we may be able build a store of capability and resources that we can access in the future as needed. Does this make sense to you? Any questions?*

Review a List of Pleasant Activities and Develop a Plan for Increasing Opportunities for Positive Emotion

> *One thing we can do together is to figure out some other activities you could get involved with that would be pleasant for you. You may think you do not know what would be pleasant anymore, but I am going to help you. Let us start by talking about the kinds of things you like to do (or used to like to do), or you could imagine liking to do. For example, I have not gone cross-country skiing, but I really think I would like it. What kinds of things do you like to do? Do you have, or have you had, any hobbies? When did you do that? Why did you stop?.*

After a period of discussion about emotions, the patient's current strategies for handling negative emotions and positive activities the patient generates, take out the **Focus on Emotion: Pleasant** Activities sheet, which uses the same activities as **Increasing Pleasant Activities** handout in Session 5, and review it with the patient. Ask the patient to indicate which of the activities would seem enjoyable. Indicate there are no right or wrong answers, and they may check as many as preferred. If the patient has difficulty, use probes such as asking which activities they have enjoyed in the past, even if they does not engage in them now. Then, ask if there are any other things not on the list that would be pleasant to do. Next, have the patient review the items checked and indicate how difficult or easy it would be to start doing some of them. Finally, ask the patient to select several activities from the list that they would be willing to try over the next week and journal or record what they did and how it went. Ask if the patient has any questions.

> *I'd like to spend some time today talking about different emotions and how your negative feelings might be related to your thoughts. We need to be able to experience and express a lot of different feelings, both positive and negative. It's important to be able to experience grief, for example, when we have had a significant loss. The problem happens when we get stuck in negative emotions, beyond the point where they are helping us to heal or move forward. Do you know what I mean? Because although all emotions are important, negative feelings, like anger, fear, and sadness, can be triggers for depression or substance use. Have you noticed that you are more likely to reach for [____] when you are feeling down or upset? Many people say they tend to use alcohol to help them feel better when they are feeling unhappy. A problem with doing this is that it can become a habit, and people may not develop other, healthier ways of dealing with these difficult feelings.*
>
> *Another problem with staying for long periods in negative emotions is that they tend to take over, and we may forget that we have had times where we felt really well or believed we could accomplish our most important goals. Negative emotions can keep us from being creative in how we approach our life and our struggles. For example, in a negative state, it's hard to see there are usually many different solutions or ways we can approach problems and challenges. Have you heard this saying, "When all you have is a hammer, everything looks like a nail?"*
>
> *Discuss this analogy and its relevance for the patient.*
>
> *So, you may be able to gather that I am building a case here for us to try to reduce your experience of negative emotions and feelings. I think it could be helpful if you could learn how to move more quickly out of negative feelings when they are no longer useful to you, and to recognize the ways your own thinking about things might be contributing to your feeling negative at times.*

The clinician summarizes the links between negative moods and substance use and enquires about the patient's experience with negative states.

> Moods may relate to the effects of stopping substance use or to the losses in one's life (e.g., family, job, finances). Difficulties with negative mood states (e.g., depression) may have started before substance use and may serve as a trigger for continued use. Abstinence from substances usually leads to improved mood, especially as patients start to cope effectively with other problems, but some individuals experience depression or other moods even after being abstinent for weeks. Because negative moods often pose a risk for relapse, we should address this possibility directly during treatment.

Link Negative Moods and Substance Use Through Examples

The clinician explores the relationships among substance use, the experience of negative moods, and the role of automatic thoughts.

> **Sanaa (S):** I miss drinking when I'm overwhelmed by bad feelings. I felt better after drinking.
> **Clinician (C):** Drinking helped you cope with your negative mood.
> **S:** Yeah, but I would get depressed again after drinking for a while or when the buzz wore off.
> **C:** What works for you in the short term causes other problems later.
> **S:** Yeah.
> **C:** Today we have reviewed ways to cope with negative thoughts. You said getting up and moving around helps. Researchers have found that often the negative feelings do not just happen. That is, they do not come from nowhere. In fact, negative feelings may be related to the way we think about things or to the way we interpret situations.

Focus on Reducing Negative and Constricting Emotions

The clinician focuses on negative moods through problem solving and increasing pleasant activities (may use the Increasing Pleasant Activities handout from Session 5). If during the course of this session, the clinician suspects the patient can benefit from continued counseling or psychotropic medications, they should explore these possibilities with the patient, particularly with one who is significantly depressed, has an anxiety disorder, or has a personal or family history of mental disorders (e.g., major depression, suicidality, aggression). Preview Session 14 on the use of medication to support treatment and recovery. The clinician may wish to complete a specific depression or anxiety screen (e.g., the PHQ-9 or GAD-7, copies of which are in the handout section). Clinicians should be aware that the PHQ-9 includes a recommended intervention algorithm based upon the screening score. The clinician discusses the following strategies to help a patient with mild-to-moderate levels of depression identify negative feelings by:

- Increasing awareness of negative moods and overly negative thinking
- Challenging negative thoughts
- Solving problems
- Changing the patient's activity level
- Decreasing negative activities

The clinician asks the patient whether they experience mood swings, low energy level, changes in appetite and sleep, and suicidality. If indicated (e.g., in the case of suicidality), the clinician should refer the patient for assessment by a mental health professional. The clinician encourages the patient to be aware of possible distorted perceptions that may precede or coincide with negative moods. They encourage them to pay attention to the context associated with mood changes and to watch for times when confidence level changes.

Reintroduce the Concept of Cognitive Fusion

As previously described, cognitive fusion is a thought process that involves rigidly attaching a thought and interpretation to an experience. Share with the patient this theory suggesting our feelings and thoughts are often closely linked. The clinician reviews the handout ***Cognitive Fusion That Dampens One's Mood and Restricts Behavior***. Either have the patient read it first, or review it together, with one of you reading aloud. After each item, inquire whether the patient relates to it and if it is something they typically do. Explain how these automatic thought processes or distortions are likely to contribute to feeling negative. The clinician explains that a connection exists among how the patient thinks, feels, and behaves and that they can experience fewer negative moods if they think in realistic, balanced ways rather than in overly negative, self-defeating ways.

> *Clinician:* One way to reduce our experience of negative feelings is to examine and then change some of our thought patterns that may be contributing to these feelings. Our feelings are often closely linked to how we are thinking about ourselves and the events in our lives. I want to talk with you about something called a "cognitive distortion," which some people think can really make us feel bad or worse than we would feel otherwise. Here is an example: You make an attempt to stop using cocaine and are able to remain abstinent for three months, but then you have a slip when a friend offers you some alcohol, which then leads to using cocaine for two days. You tell yourself you are a failure and will never be able to stop using cocaine because you just do not have what it takes.
>
> This is an example of a cognitive distortion called "all-or-nothing thinking." This means that situations are evaluated in terms of extremes, and there is no middle ground. Something is either great or terrible. You view yourself as both completely successful and disciplined or a loser and failure because you had a lapse with cocaine.

The patient identifies which automatic negative thoughts in which they engage. If the patient has difficulty identifying these thoughts, the clinician tells them to slow down the action (as if watching a movie in slow motion) or to look at what the situation means. Sometimes writing down the most distressing thoughts helps a patient remember their thoughts. Once the patient identifies their automatic negative thoughts, the clinician gives the patient the handout *Managing Negative Moods and Depression*. The clinician asks the patient to fill out the form thinking about distressing situations to avoid and recognizing that an event often can be interpreted in more than one way (Hellekson-Emery, 1981).

The clinician helps the patient address fused thoughts and feelings through a process of challenging these assumptions and their premises and asking questions such as:

- What is the evidence?
- Are you certain about this?
- Are there other possible explanations/interpretations?
- So what if that were true?
- How would your life be different if it were not true?
- What's the worst part about that?
- What is the likelihood this (fear of something terrible happening) will actually take place?

The clinician encourages the patient to develop a practice of distancing from and questioning their automatic negative thoughts and assumptions. The clinician asks them to pay attention to automatic thoughts that arise during the next week and to write them down in a journal or thought record, along with other information about the situation.

Review and Conclude

Review and summarize the session. Praise the patient's efforts to stay engaged in the process and to make changes. Provide the handouts on *Focus on Emotion: Pleasant Activities, Cognitive Fusion That Dampens One's Mood and Restricts Behavior,* and *Managing Negative Moods and Depression*. Elicit a between-session commitment from the patient (i.e., that they will review the handouts, practice challenging automatic thoughts, and engage in at least two pleasant activities over the next week). Prepare the patient for the next session by introducing the topic and by explaining how it will be helpful in the path toward wellness. Schedule and confirm the next appointment.

Session 9 Handouts: Working with Emotions

Clinician's Quick Reference to Session 9

1) Maintain rapport and review.
   - Check in on past week.
   - Follow up on between-session challenges.
2) Introduce the concept of working with emotions.
3) Discuss the evolutionary value and/or the role of various emotions in day-to-day life.
4) Explore the patient's experience with different emotions, their connection with alcohol or other drug use, and how the patient tends to regulate their emotional state.
5) Provide a rationale for fostering positive emotions, which can be constructive and healing.
6) Review a list of pleasant activities and develop a plan for increasing opportunities for positive emotion.
7) Assign practice exercises involving pleasant activities.
8) Provide a rationale for decreasing or dissolving the effects of negative emotions.
9) Discuss thinking patterns or cognitive distortions that tend to dampen or depress one's mood.
   - Review Cognitive Fusion That Dampens One's Mood and Restricts Behavior.
   - Explain cognitive distortions.
   - Explore automatic thought patterns that appear to lead to negative mood states.
   - Ask the patient to identify which automatic negative thoughts they may engage in before or during depressed, anxious, or irritable moods.
10) Build internal resources for handling automatic thoughts.
    - Discuss with the patient guidelines for evaluating these thoughts.
    - Give the patient the Managing Negative Moods and Depression handout.
    - Engage the patient in problem-solving to address problems contributing to their negative moods.
11) Link negative moods with alcohol or substance use.
    - Explore the relationship between the patient's alcohol or substance use and their experience of negative moods.
    - Explore methods of changing the patient's automatic thoughts that can lead to alcohol or substance use.
12) Review and conclude.

Focus on Emotion: Role of Positive and Negative Emotions

All emotions have some role or function and an evolutionary value.

Negative or "withdrawal" emotions tend to narrow our thinking and constrict our ability when approaching new situations and challenges. Examples include fear, grief, and anger. These emotions can be helpful when we are facing an acute threat and need to act quickly.

Positive or "approach" emotions tend to help us feel more capable, creative, optimistic, and connected with others. Examples include joy, contentment, curiosity, empathy, and enthusiasm. Positive emotions can be healing, have positive effects on our immune system, and counteract the effects of stress. Engaging in activities which promote positive feelings and experiences can have both immediate and far-reaching benefits through building internal resources. Increasing positive emotions may have the benefit of undermining or diminishing negative emotions.

Emotion and substance use

Many people who use alcohol or other substances experience negative emotions both as triggers for, and consequences of, excessive use. Substances become a way of "regulating" emotional states. Increasing positive emotions through activities and experiences that enhance well-being may remove emotional triggers for substance use.

Describe a recent situation where you felt negative, discouraged, angry, fearful, or sad. How did you cope with the situation and/or the feelings you had? In retrospect, could you have handled things differently? How might you rewrite or replay events if you could?

_____
_____
_____

Describe a time when you felt really positive, content, or hopeful. What happened, or what were you doing? What contributed to your positive feelings or outlook? Could you recreate this experience through your thoughts or actions?

_____
_____
_____

What types of experiences are likely to result in positive emotions for you?

_____
_____
_____

Can any of these experiences serve as replacements for alcohol or substance use?

_____
_____
_____

Focus on Emotion: Pleasant Activities

The following is a list of activities that people find pleasurable to engage in. Please check those that seem appealing to you, either because you know you like them, or you imagine you would like them if you tried. Also, check any items you are not sure about but might be willing to consider if you had some support or encouragement to try them out. There are no grades for this exercise. Check as many as you wish. If there are things not listed that you want to include, please add them.

❏ Reading a book	❏ Going to the movies	❏ Going out to a meal
❏ Exercising	❏ Listening to music	❏ Writing or journaling
❏ Dancing	❏ Singing	❏ Computer/Internet
❏ Photography	❏ Drawing	❏ Writing/calling a friend
❏ Yoga	❏ Baking/cooking	❏ Shopping
❏ Painting	❏ Swimming	❏ Boating
❏ Ice skating	❏ Knitting/crocheting	❏ Taking a bath
❏ Gardening/lawn	❏ Fixing things	❏ Refinishing furniture
❏ Going to live theater	❏ Library	❏ Visiting a park or garden
❏ Skydiving	❏ Running	❏ Organizing
❏ Party/social event	❏ Hiking	❏ Fishing
❏ Skiing	❏ Playing competitive sports	❏ Yard sales
❏ Spending time with friends/family		

Other activities:

_____

_____

Cognitive Fusion That Dampens One's Mood and Restricts Behavior

Types	Example
Personalizing	Thinking all situations and events revolve around you "Everyone was looking at me."
Magnifying	Blowing negative events out of proportion "This is the worst thing that could happen to me."
Minimizing	Downplaying the positives "I got the job, but probably no one else applied."
Either/or Thinking	Not taking into account the full continuum "I'm either a loser or a winner."
Taking Events Out of Context	After a successful experience, focusing on one or two rough points "I may have gotten the job, but I blew that one question in the interview."
Jumping to conclusion	Making a premature conclusion without enough data "I have a swollen gland. It must be cancer."
Overgeneralizing	Making a sweeping judgment based on one event "I failed this time; I fail at everything I ever try."
Self-blame	Blaming oneself rather than specific behaviors that can be changed "I'm no good."
Mindreading	Believing you know what everyone else is thinking "Everyone there thought I was fat and ugly."
Comparing	Comparing yourself unfavorably with someone else "That supermodel has a better figure than I do."
Catastrophizing	Focusing on the worst possible outcome or explanation. "He did not call, and I know something terrible has happened to him."

Managing Negative Moods and Depression

Use the **"three As"** to overcome negative feelings:

1) Be aware of signs of depression and negative states.
   - Reflect on your moods and situations that influence them.
   - Notice automatic negative thoughts that increase negative emotions.
   - Observe experiences and situations that narrow or constrict your overall outlook.
2) Answer or respond to the automatic thoughts OR observe them with mild disinterest.
   - Practice mindfulness and put distance on thoughts. Thoughts are thoughts.
   - Transform negative thoughts and feelings into constructive actions.
3) Act differently.
   - Increase activities that promote positive emotions.
   - Engage in pleasant activities.
   - Reduce involvement with unpleasant and unnecessary activities and with people who have a negative effect on your outlook.
   - Reward yourself for positive steps along the way and the process of change.

In the space below, take notes for each of the three areas above as they relate to your own struggles with negative moods.

_____

_____

_____

_____

_____

_____

_____

_____

Patient Health Questionnaire-9 (PHQ-9)

Nine-symptom checklist

Patient Name _____   **Date** _____

1) Over the last two weeks, how often have you been bothered by any of the following problems?

Not at all	Several days	More than half the days	Nearly every day
0	1	2	3

   a) Little interest or pleasure in doing things
   b) Feeling down, depressed, or hopeless
   c) Trouble falling/staying asleep, sleeping too much
   d) Feeling tired or having little energy
   e) Poor appetite or overeating
   f) Feeling bad about yourself or that you are a failure or have let yourself or your family down
   g) Trouble concentrating on things, such as reading the newspaper or watching television
   h) Moving or speaking so slowly that other people have noticed or the opposite—being so fidgety or restless that you have been moving around a lot more than usual
   i) Thoughts that you would be better off dead or of hurting yourself in some way

2) If you checked off any problem on this questionnaire so far, how difficult have these problems made it for you to do your work, take care of things at home, or get along with other people?

Total Score Depression Severity
1–4   Minimal depression
5–9   Mild depression
10–14   Moderate depression
15–19   Moderately severe depression
20–27   Severe depression

Not difficult at all   Somewhat difficult   Very difficult   Extremely difficult
1   14   27

Developed by Drs. Robert L. Spitzer, Janet B.W. Williams, Kurt Kroenke and colleagues, with an educational grant from Pfizer Inc. No permission required to reproduce, translate, display, or distribute.

Generalized Anxiety Disorder 7-item Scale (GAD-7)

Patient Name _____   Date _____

Choose the one description for each item that best describes how many days you have been bothered by the following over the past two weeks:

	None	Several	Seven or More	Nearly Every Day
Feeling nervous, anxious, or on edge				
Unable to stop worrying				
Worrying too much about different things				
Problems relaxing				
Feeling restless or unable to sit still				
Feeling irritable or easily annoyed				
Being afraid something awful might happen				

Scoring

Sum scores from each question:
None = 0
Several = 1
Seven or more = 2
Nearly every day = 3
Total score: _____
A total score of 5–9 suggests mild anxiety.
A total score of ≥10 suggests moderate to severe anxiety.

Source

Spitzer, R. L., Kroenke, K., Williams, J. B. W., & Lowe B. (2006). Generalized Anxiety Disorder 7 (GAD-7) [Database record]. *APA PsycTests*. doi: 10.1037/t02591-000.

Session 10. Making Important Life Decisions

Introduction

There are many paths to recovery, and the path the patient may take may differ from what science may suggest. The right path for the patient is what works for them.

So many people experiencing substance use, depression, or other life challenges live their lives by habit and circumstances. They often hope things will get better when circumstances change, not fully recognizing that we bring who we are wherever we go. And waiting for things to get better is often to consign ourselves to be the observer and not the architects of our own lives. Often this waiting for things to get better takes us away from what is most important to us: our values and beliefs of the person we want to be and of the life we want to live.

One of the things we have learned from people in long-term recovery is they strive to live and act each day grounded in their chosen values and acting with intention. This is the spiritual core often spoken of in fellowships.

Our purpose in this session is to support the patient to become aware of and to own those values and to make decisions for living and acting in accord with that which they hold most important.

So, what do we mean by values? "Values are freely chosen ways that we understand our place in the world. They are patterns of behavior that evolve over time based on our actions and the satisfaction we feel doing those things for their own sake. Acting in accord with our chosen values is intrinsically rewarding" (Hayes et al., 2013).

Session 10 expands on previous motivational activities and is applicable to anyone making an important life choice. We can normalize ambivalence and the real, normal angst that is healthy in making a change in line with that which is most important in the life your patient wants to live. Yes, change is not without risk, and so is staying the same. The clinician supports the patient to identify and embrace areas where decisions need to be made. In Session 1, the *Life Movie*, and Session 2, the *Awareness Record* (functional analysis), the clinician and patient have a growing awareness of those values and in what way the patient is living and acting. The first part of this session is a reflective discussion where the clinician clarifies and brings to light (again) the patient's chosen values and determines if they are acting in alignment with or disconnected from those values. This conversation about disconnection from valued living can be uncomfortable (e.g., "I feel like such a failure that I have not been here for my kids the way they need me"). The clinician facilitates agreement in those life areas where the patient seeks to make change.

When the patient is ready, the clinician can provide them with a consistent decision-making method designed to provide clarity while increasing readiness and action. Handouts for this session include a values clarifying tool, readiness rulers, and decisional balance. The primary discussion strategies include scaling (using readiness-to-change ruler), double-sided reflections, pros and cons of change (using a decisional balance sheet), looking ahead, looking back, clarification of values using compassionate reflections, and imagining extremes.

A supportive other person may be invited to join Session 10 to provide additional statements about the benefits of making a decision to stop using (or another important prosocial change) and, if necessary, an accurate recollection of negative events associated with continued use. It is important for the clinician to monitor and prevent this from becoming a negative or overwhelming experience for the patient (e.g., the supporter is angry or frustrated with the patient over past use and threatens dire consequences).

Session 10 focuses on the following:

- Identifying key decisions that need to be made
- Exploring and clarifying core values that could inform decision making

- Using the decisional balance to tip the scales in favor of change
- Using Readiness-to-Change Ruler and Decision-Making Guide.
- Affirming the patient's ability to take action on a decision
- Using double-sided reflection to showcase where the patient is and where they want to be
- Affirming that change can feel uncomfortable and so can staying the same

The Patient's Experience

The patient:

- Experiences a nonjudgmental conversation about ambivalence and decisions regarding continued use or other important life decisions
- Learns a process for making decisions intentionally, with comprehension and clarity
- Develops a thorough understanding of current reasons for staying the same and current reasons for making a different choice

Clinician Preparation

Session 10. Making Important Life Decisions	
Materials • *Clinician's Quick Reference* • *MI Skills and Strategies* • *Values Exploration* handout • *Readiness-to-Change Ruler (Pre and Post)* explanation • *My Values* handout • *Decision-Making Guide* handout	**Total Time** 45–60 minutes **Delivery Method** MET-focused individual therapy

Strategies
- Follow OARS.
- Use EDARS.
- Identify stage of change.
- Incorporate MI eliciting change talk; current motivation (*Readiness-to-Change Ruler*); elaboration; looking back, looking forward; pros and cons (decisional balance); and imagining extremes.
- Develop a "real-life practice challenge" (e.g., sampling sobriety).

Goals for This Session
- Further explore the patient's attitudes and values.
- Elicit ambivalence and increase verbalized discrepancies in favor of change.
- Use MI to strengthen change talk strategies and tools to enable visual record of the patient's values and goals.
- Provide the patient with a clear set of strategies for making important life decisions.
- Elicit commitment from the patient to take one action step to reinforce a decision made during the session.

Session 10 Outline and Overview

1) Engage and assess the patient's readiness to proceed.
   - Welcome the patient and continue to build rapport; address any obstacles to the therapeutic alliance.
   - Share the session agenda.
   - Ask whether any changes have occurred since the last meeting.
   - Discuss the decision to continue use, the benefits, and any consequences.
   - Review the between-session challenge(s).
2) Introduce the motivational strategy involving readiness for change.
   - Introduce an important life decision of concern for patient (e.g., being the person that I want to be; achieving abstinence from substances; being a good father, mother, or parent; leaving or remaining in uniformed service; marriage or divorce; disclosure of sensitive information to an important other). Explore through compassionate reflections the patient's core values.
   - Introduce the Readiness-to-Change Ruler and Decision-Making Guide.
   - Elicit the patient's readiness score.
   - Use double-sided reflection to bring into the conversation where your patient is and where they want to be. Reflect on alignment or disconnect with their values.
   - Discuss real and potential future for the patient without and with change.

Note to clinician: When exploring with patients where there is a disconnect in values, this is often accompanied by strong effect of shame and guilt ("I'm not being the father I want to be").

3) Introduce and teach decision-making steps.
   - Discuss the concept of decision making, normalizing ambivalence as part of the process.
   - Provide a rationale for focusing on decision making.
   - Introduce the idea that certain steps can make the decision-making process less overwhelming and potentially clearer.
   - Emphasize that while these steps can be used for any decision, today's session focus will be on the decision as to whether to continue use of substances or ____.
   - Give patient the **Decision-Making Guide**, and review steps 1 through 5.
4) Complete steps 1 through 3 of the **Decision-Making Guide** for the patient's decision regarding use.
   - Elicit the decision topic from the patient and options they can choose.
   - Using the **Decision-Making Guide**, explore pros and cons of each choice, including how the choice relates to the patient's short- and long-term goals and the feelings each decision evokes.
   - Discuss the history of the patient's life prior to use.
   - Discuss real and potential future for the patient without and with change.
   - Elicit the patient's top three statements in each category; end with the benefits of changing.
5) Use the **Readiness-to-Change Ruler** in the **Decision-Making Guide**; ask the patient to rate their readiness.
6) Summarize the change talk discussions, emphasizing any change in readiness:
   - Illustrate any increased readiness or continued ambivalence.
7) Have the patient complete step 5 of the Decision-Making Guide.
8) If appropriate, assign a between-session challenge, and elicit a specific commitment to complete the challenge.

- If the patient is not ready to make changes but is willing to engage in continued exploration, suggest committing to accurately monitoring use to identify any possibility of change or reduction.
- If/when the patient has decided to end treatment, affirm the patient's efforts to date and end in a positive fashion. It may be possible to ask the patient to think it over, talk about it with a significant other, and then call with a final decision in a day or two.

9) Review and conclude the session.

Session 10 Protocol

Strengthen Rapport

The clinician welcomes the patient, asks about the week in general, and proceeds to focus on use behaviors. They use rapport-building strategies to understand and nonjudgmentally reflect the patient's reasons and decision to continue using.

> *Clinician (C):* Thanks for sharing the highlights of your week with me. You paint the picture of how busy you are at work and how much you need to find quick, easy ways to relax when you get home.
> *Michael (M):* That's right. My time feels so limited, and my energy is pretty low by the time I get home, and I just look forward to a couple of cold beers and a few hits off my pipe. Then I can settle into being with my wife and family for dinner or whatever else is on the schedule.
> *C:* You've identified an efficient and nice way of taking care of yourself to ease the transition from work to home life.
> *M:* Right, and so when my doctor asked me to see you, I was a bit annoyed and wondered why, in the scope of all the possible problems, she figured I needed to address this first. Anyway, I'm still not convinced I need to change, even though the assessment and our first discussions make it clear that my regular and long-term use of alcohol and weed, combined with my lack of exercise, is contributing to my risks for heart trouble.
> *C:* That makes sense because your habit of relaxing works well, and why bother changing if there is no immediately obvious sign of damage to your health but rather a risk in the future.
> *M:* You said that perfectly. There's just not enough reason for me to change right now.

Engage and Assess the Patient's Readiness to Proceed

The clinician takes out the **Readiness-to-Change Ruler** and **Decision-Making Guide** and asks the patient to respond to the first ruler by marking the appropriate level of "readiness." The clinician explains this will also be reviewed after talking today. (The delivery of the pre-readiness ruler can be adjusted in any way that is appropriate for the patient; it can be handed out in the second session as part of the between-session challenge and then discussed at the beginning of Session 3 as a way to get into the conversation about readiness.)

> *Clinician:* All right, you sound pretty definite about your position here. And it can be helpful to actually state a number on where you stand now with regard to changing your use, a baseline marker (similar to a cholesterol test), so if for any reason you decide to make changes, we can see where you started. Here is a ruler, and I'd like you to score where you believe you stand right now.
> *Michael:* That's easy. I'm like 10% on this. I know there are a few important health reasons to do something, but, like I said, it's just not enough now.

The clinician refers to the **Decision-Making Guide** and **Readiness-to-Change Ruler** handouts and introduces the idea of learning a decision-making process. They could say something like:

> I get it. While you care about your health, being able to use is really important to you. Given that you are not really in a place to want to make a big change right now, would you be willing to talk with me just a little bit more today? I'd like to talk to you about a few strategies that can help you

> *make and commit to important life decisions. Many individuals wrestle with making important life decisions: a soldier telling his commander that he has an alcohol problem, partners deciding whether to stay in or leave a relationship, and stopping drinking or drug use are a few examples. Sometimes, when we feel overwhelmed or unsure of what direction to go, being able to go through a set of steps can slow things down, help us to think logically, and remind us of our goals and how our choices can affect our ability to reach our goals. While these steps can be used for any type of decision, I thought it might be helpful if we use them to go through your choices around your use. How does that sound to you?*

The clinician reviews steps 1 through 5 generally on the **Decision-Making Guide**. After briefly teaching the patient about the five steps, the clinician then begins to engage them in a decision-making discussion about use using the five-step process.

The clinician may use strategies to elicit change talk but clearly realize the patient is on the low end of desire and perceived reasons for needing to change. They ask the patient to think back to a time when they did not regularly use to relax and to discuss the differences. The clinician probes for other strategies the patient used in the past to feel good after a busy day. Then they ask the patient to look ahead, assuming there are no changes, to predict what life and health will feel like. The clinician reflects and illuminates the differences between the two descriptions: (1) when not using but doing other activities and (2) when use is continued into the future. The patient is asked to look at the **Decision-Making Guide** and to list the pros and cons.

- Accept all answers (do not argue with answers given by patient).
- Explore answers.
- Be sure to note both the benefits and costs of current behavior and change.
- Explore the costs and benefits with respect to patient's goals and values.
- Summarize the costs and benefits.

After the patient completes a few statements for each category, the clinician asks them to read them aloud, finishing with the benefits of changing use. The clinician summarizes the benefits and returns to the **Learning New Coping Strategies** handout (from Session 1), describing a few potential replacements for the patient's stated benefits of use. Next, they switch gears and ask the patient to imagine some possible extremes in a real future without change.

> **Clinician (C):** What will it be like in a few years if you continue using and go back to your doctor for a cardiac wellness visit? What's the worst news you can imagine getting?
> **Michael (M):** I never really like to think about that. Like I said, I just live day to day, and that kind of thought is above my pay grade, but since you are asking... I guess I could find out my cholesterol is too high and be told to take Lipitor or some pill like that. My doc might also tell me that he strongly recommends I quit substances to avoid some kind of stroke or heart attack or something. (My dad had a heart attack at 54. That was really scary.)
> **C:** The risks get worse until you are forced to take medication and live with the chances of a serious heart condition.
> **M:** Yeah, but we all take risks every day. This is one my doc, my family, and now you care to talk about it.

The clinician summarizes the **Decision-Making Guide** discussion. The clinician then reassesses the patient's readiness to stop using the **Readiness-to-Change Ruler**. If a shift occurs, the clinician should evoke from the patient their thoughts and feelings about the shift. The clinician can then shift the discussion by asking the patient in an open-ended manner what they intend to do around their use. If interest in any degree of change is stated, negotiate a plan for reduction of use or for stopping altogether.

Review and Conclude

There are several possible outcomes after this motivational-enhancement change discussion. If remaining undecided, the patient may be encouraged to continue exploration and to remain in treatment until reaching a clear decision. The clinician might ask them to try "sampling a sobriety period" or suggest continuing to raise self-awareness and committing to accurately monitoring use to identify any easy targets of change or places to make reductions in use. If the patient commits to stopping use of substances, the clinician can introduce change plan tools from Sessions 1 and 2.

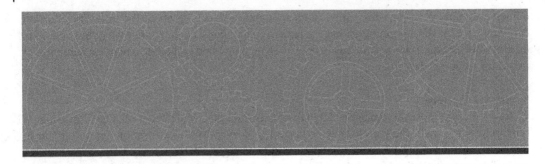

Session 10 Handouts: Making Important Life Decisions

Clinician's Quick Reference to Session 10

1) Welcome the patient and continue to build rapport.
   - Review the past week.
   - Follow up on the between-session challenge.
2) Share the session agenda and rationale.
   - Discuss the decision of concern, benefits, and any consequences.
3) Introduce a motivational strategy involving readiness for change.
   - Introduce the Readiness-to-Change Ruler.
   - Elicit the patient's readiness score regarding a specific concern.
   - Seek elaboration and outcomes.
   - Discuss the history of the patient's life prior to use or in relationship to a current concern.
   - Discuss real and potential futures for the patient without and with change.
4) Introduce and teach decision-making steps.
   - Discuss the concept of decision making, normalizing ambivalence as part of the process.
   - Provide a rationale for focusing on decision making.
   - Introduce the idea that certain steps can make the decision-making process less overwhelming and potentially clearer.
   - Introduce how clarity of personal values helps guide decision making.
   - Emphasize that while these steps can be used for any decision, today's session focus will be on the decision whether to continue to use.
   - Give the patient the ***Decision-Making Guide,*** and review steps 1 through 5.
5) Complete steps 1 through 3 of the ***Decision-Making Guide*** for decision regarding use.
   - Elicit from the patient what the decision topic is and from which options the patient can choose.
   - Using the ***Decision-Making Guide***, explore pros and cons of each choice, including how the choice relates to the patient's short- and long-term goals and what feelings each decision evokes.
   - Review relevant history of the patient's life.
   - Discuss real and potential futures for the patient with change and without change.
   - Elicit the patient's top three statements in each category; end with the benefits of changing.
6) Use the ***Readiness-to-Change Ruler*** in the ***Decision-Making Guide*** to ask the patient to reassess their readiness.
   - Summarize the change talk discussions, emphasizing any change in readiness. Illustrate any increased readiness or continued ambivalence.
   - Have the patient complete step 5 of the ***Decision-Making Guide***.
   - If appropriate, assign a between-session challenge, and elicit a specific commitment to complete it.
   - If appropriate, discuss and help the patient develop a specific plan (e.g., reduction target, "sampling sobriety period," or stop date, if the patient has not already stopped using).
   - If the patient is not ready to make changes but willing to engage in continued exploration, if the change is substance specific, suggest committing to accurately monitoring use to identify any possibility of change or reduction.
   - If the patient has made a decision, affirm their efforts to date, and end in a positive fashion. It may be useful to ask the patient to think it over, talk about it with a significant other, and then call with a final decision in a day or two.
7) Review and conclude.

MI Skills and Strategies

MI Spirit • Interviewing • Collaboration • Guiding **MI Principles** • Express empathy • Develop discrepancy • Roll with resistance • Support self-efficacy **Fundamental Skills** • Open-ended questions • Affirmations • Reflections • Summarizations **Change Talk** • Desire to change • Ability • Reason • Need • Commitment **Eliciting Change Talk** • Importance/confidence ruler • Querying extremes • Looking back, looking forward • Evocative questions • Decisional balance • Goals/values exploration • Elaboration	**Responding to Change Talk** • Reflection • Elaboration questions • Summary • Affirmation **Elicit-Provide-Elicit** **Menu of Options** **Dealing With Resistance** • Simple reflections • Amplified reflections • Double-sided reflections and shifting focus • Agreement with a twist • Coming alongside • Reframing • Emphasizing personal control • Disclosing feelings **Traps** • Premature focus • Labeling • Question/answer • Confrontation/denial • Expert • Blaming

Readiness-to-Change Ruler Explanation

The **Readiness-to-Change Ruler**, with the **Decision-Making Guide**, is used to assess the patient's willingness or readiness to change, determine where they are on the continuum between "not prepared to change" and "already changing," and promote identification and discussion of perceived barriers to change. The ruler represents a continuum from "not prepared to change" on the left to "already changing" on the right.

The **Readiness-to-Change Ruler** may be used as a quick assessment of their present motivational state relative to changing a specific behavior and serves as the basis for motivation-based interventions to elicit behavior change. Readiness to change should be assessed regarding a specific activity (e.g., reducing use of alcohol), since patients may differ in their stages of readiness to change for different behaviors.

Administration

1) Indicate the specific behavior to be assessed on the **Readiness-To-Change Ruler** form. Ask the patient to mark on a linear scale from 0 to 10 their current position in the change process. A 0 on the left side of the scale indicates "not prepared for change," and a 10 on the right side of the scale indicates "already changing."
2) Question the patient about why they did not place the mark farther to the left, which elicits motivational statements.
3) Question them about why they did not place the mark farther to the right, which elicits perceived barriers.
4) Ask the patient for suggestions about ways to overcome identified barriers and actions that might be taken.

Interview questions

"Could we talk for a few minutes about your interest in making a change?"
"On a scale from 1 to 10, with 1 being not ready at all and 10 being completely ready, how ready are you to make any changes in your alcohol use?"
"You marked (or said) [____]. That's great. That means you are [____]% ready to make a change."
"Why did you choose that number and not a lower one, such as a 1 or a 2? Sounds like you have some important reasons for change."

Values Exploration

In this simple exercise, have your patient place the ***My Values*** sheet in front of them and take a minute to review the list of values. Without major deliberation, have the patient write five or six values that they hold most important **today** in the center. Note: Today is important. In successive rings, add five more and five more. Reflect and explore with the patient on each of the values at the center. Ask them, "Why are these of greatest importance? How aligned with these are you today? Where might you choose to make a change and why?" This exploration will better prepare the patient and clinician for decision making and action planning.

List of values
- Acceptance
- Achievement
- Adventure
- Helping Others
- Attentiveness
- Balance
- Beauty
- Caring
- Charity
- Courage
- Connection (Connecting w/Others)
- Competence
- Creativity
- Curiosity
- Determination
- Discipline
- Friendliness
- Friendship
- Fun
- Generosity
- Grace
- Gratitude
- Honesty
- Hopefulness
- Humility
- Humor
- Independence
- Integrity
- Introspection
- Joy
- Justice
- Kindness
- Knowledge
- Leadership
- Learning and Growth
- Love
- Loyalty

- Nature (Appreciation of)
- Open-Mindedness
- Openness w/Others
- Optimism/Being Positive
- Peace
- Philanthropy
- Play/Playfulness
- Reason/Logic
- Reliability
- Respect
- Responsibility/Keeping Promises
- Self-control
- Spirituality/Faith
- Stability/Security Support
- Teamwork
- Thoughtfulness
- Trustworthiness
- Wisdom
- Wonder
- Work
- Other

My Values

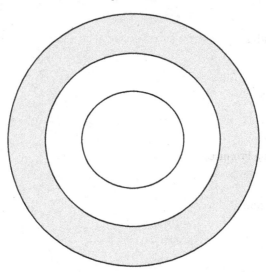

Instructions: This is a direct way to better understand your values. In the center, include five or six values **most** important to you today, your true north. In the next ring, include values that are important. In the third ring, include those that have some importance in your life.

It's important to remember that values can and will shift in priority over time.

Decision-Making Guide

Why create this decision-making guide?

This will help you think about the choices you are being presented with so you can calmly and logically identify and consider the **good things** and the **not-so-good things** about each choice. While you are being asked to complete this sheet around your choice as to whether to continue using or to abstain, it can be a helpful strategy when making other important life decisions. Weighing the **good things** and the **not-so-good things** helps people make decisions. For example, while drinking may sometimes help people relax, it could also cause problems with family or work. Ask yourself, "What are the good things and the not-so-good things about my current use? What are the good things and the not-so-good things about changing my use?"

STEP 1: Define what decision you have to make, including options.	Decision Topic:
STEP 2: Brainstorm the good and not-so-good things about continuing the behavior. Reflect on core values.	Option 1 (continuing behavior):
STEP 3: Brainstorm the good and not-so-good things about changing the behavior. Reflect on values.	Option 2 (changing behavior):

Continuing Behavior		Changing Behavior	
Cost	Benefits	Cost	Benefits
1.	1.	1.	1.
2.	2.	2.	2.
3.	3.	3.	3.
4.	4.	4.	4.

Consider....

How will continuing the behavior help me act in accord with my values and reach my goals?	How will changing the behavior help me help me act in accord with my values and reach my goals?

STEP 4: Assess how ready you are to make a change in your behavior, using the readiness ruler below.

Not at all 0cm 1 2 3 4 5 6 7 8 9 10 Very

Section 2　Clinician Guidance for 16 Sessions of Integrated Cognitive Behavioral Therapy

STEP 5: Write down your decision below, including how you are going to act on your decision and when you want to look back and consider how well it is working.
I intend to:
I will do this by:
I will evaluate my decision and how it is working in *(time frame)*:

Decision-Making Guide Example

Why create this decision-making guide?

This will help you think about the choices you are being presented with so you can calmly and logically identify and consider the **good things** and the **not-so-good things** about each choice. While you are being asked to complete this sheet around your choice as to whether to continue using or to abstain, it can be a helpful strategy when making other important life decisions. Weighing the **good things** and the **not-so-good things** helps people make decisions. For example, while drinking may sometimes help people relax, it could also cause problems with family or work. Ask yourself, "What are the good things and the not-so-good things about my current use? What are the good things and the not-so-good things about changing my use?"

STEP 1: Define what decision you have to make, including options.	Decision Topic: My getting angry with my partner over little things
STEP 2: Brainstorm the good and not-so-good things about continuing the behavior. Reflect on core values.	Option 1 (continuing behavior): Keep doing what I am doing
STEP 3: Brainstorm the good and not-so-good things about changing the behavior. Reflect on values.	Option 2 (changing behavior): Better understand how I get so angry so easily. Take a 5-minute step back and cool down. Communicate without blaming.

Continuing Behavior		**Changing Behavior**	
Cost	Benefits	Cost	Benefits
1.	1.	1.	1.
2.	2.	2.	2.
3.	3.	3.	3.
4.	4.	4.	4.

Consider....

How will continuing the behavior help me act in accord with my values and reach my goals?	How will changing the behavior help me help me act in accord with my values and reach my goals?
Helps me handle my problems in the moment so I can keep going and get through the day,	Maybe my problems will get better, so I will not feel so stressed out and down all the time. I will have more money and do better at work and school, which will help me to stay independent.

STEP 4: Assess how ready you are to make a change in your behavior, using the readiness ruler below.

Not at all 0cm 1 2 3 4 5 6 7 8 9 10 Very

STEP 5: Write down your decision below, including how you are going to act on your decision and when you want to look back and consider how well it is working.
I intend to: Do a better job with my temper.
I will do this by: When I get frustrated, I will take a 5-minute timeout to cool down and get clear about what am I really frustrated about.
I will evaluate my decision and how it is working in *(time frame)*: I will evaluate my decision and how it is working in one week.

Session 11. Enhancing Self-awareness of Substance Use

Introduction

Session 11 focuses on helping the patient to build self-awareness. Patients often view themselves and their behavior as somewhat of a mystery. They may feel puzzled and confused by what they do and why they do it. By helping a patient take greater notice of how things are happening in life, with specific focus on alcohol and substances or mood, the clinician provides a powerful tool and builds the important capacities for reflection and self-awareness.

There are many ways to increase self-awareness. The ICBT approach makes use of "functional analysis" as a way to carefully examine the patterns of substance use or other concerning behaviors. Even if a patient has been involved with certain behavior for a long time and sees themself as highly self-aware, the person may be surprised by what is revealed during an in-depth inquiry.

The clinician is encouraged to discuss with the patient many aspects of patterns. It is helpful to learn about the conditions where the patient is more and less likely to use. Conditions may be external (e.g., being with particular people or in certain places), and they may be internal (e.g., feelings, thoughts, general states of mind, associations).

The Patient's Experience

In Session 11, the patient is able to explore patterns of use in a nonjudgmental atmosphere. They are encouraged to share many aspects of their inner experience. The patient is also supported in discussing the positive and negative impacts of use to develop better self-knowledge and a fuller picture for the clinician. The patient may begin to identify potentially useful coping strategies to reach goals in relation to substance use.

Clinician Preparation

Session 11. Enhancing Self-Awareness	
Materials • *Clinician's Quick Reference* • *Review the Progress* handout • *Awareness Record* handout (from Session 2) • *Learning New Coping Strategies* (from Session 1)	**Total Time** One hour **Delivery Method** CBT-focused individual or group therapy
Strategies • Follow OARS. • Support self-efficacy. • Demonstrate skill and role play. • Follow CBT skills session reminders.	
Goals for This Session • Help the patient begin to learn and practice skills that enhance self-awareness. • Re-introduce the patient to the rationale for coping skills training. • Examine the patient's high-risk situations, triggers, and coping strategies.	

Session 11 Outline and Overview

1) Build rapport and review:
   - Welcome the patient; check in about the week in general.
   - Review the patient's cravings, recent use experiences, and successes.
   - Review the between-session challenge.
   - Attend to the therapeutic alliance, and address any obstacles, concerns.
   - Assess motivational factors and change readiness.
2) Explore the development of SUD patterns:
   - Provide the rationale (e.g., the learned or associative nature of addiction), pairing with alterations in thinking and feeling.
   - Use the patient's own experiences to illustrate how using alcohol or other substances can change one's feelings; if the patient has not stated any examples, provide examples that are appropriate to their situation.
   - From the patient's stated use situations, identify examples of environmental triggers for use; ask the patient for other triggers they have experienced.
   - Elicit examples of feelings, beliefs, or automatic thoughts people may have about substances. Use examples provided by the patient, and ask the patient for more examples.
   - Suggest that the patient start the process of change by understanding their behavior; ask, "Does this make sense to you?"
3) Empower though self-knowledge; understand high-risk situations and triggers. Explore with the patient:
   - Typical use situations (e.g., places, people, activities, time, days)
   - Triggers for use
   - Recent use situation
   - Thoughts and feelings at use times (tense, bored, stressed, etc.)
   - Have the patient complete the **Awareness Record**, and summarize the list
4) Put the pieces together. Help the patient draw connections, consider new roads, and build coping strategies.
   - Emphasize the importance of coping strategies.
   - Reintroduce Learning New Coping Strategies (from Session 1).
   - Introduce a drawing-connection exercise, and identify new pathways toward desired outcomes.
   - Ask the patient to identify strategies they have tried and those that might work best.
5) Develop or elicit a specific between-session challenge that incorporates material from the session.
6) Review and conclude.

Session 11 Protocol

The clinician welcomes the patient and provides an overview of the session. In this session, they draw on information from previous sessions to increase the patient's understanding about use patterns.

Build Rapport and Review

To continue building rapport with the patient, begin the session by eliciting information about life during the past week. Initially, try to focus on nonproblem areas. This is an opportunity to learn about the patient's interests and strengths. Such information can be used later to develop strategies for addressing the patient's substance use. The clinician continues to use MI skills to do this and always expresses genuine curiosity about the patient's life.

> *How have things been since we last met?* or *Tell me about something enjoyable you did during the past week?*

If the patient cannot think of anything enjoyable during the past week, ask about interests and activities they are likely to engage in, even if not during the past week.

> *Tell me about some of your interests or hobbies?* or *What kinds of things do you like to do in your free time?*

Continue by asking the patient how they have been doing over the past week regarding alcohol and/or drug use.

> *Tell me about your [drug(s) of choice] use during the past week?* or *What has your use been like since we last met?* or *What thoughts have you had about your use since we last spoke?*

Guidelines

Listen for possible changes in the patient's behaviors, thoughts, and feelings regarding use. Try to refrain from asking many questions. Let the patient tell you how they have been doing regarding their use or abstinence. Respond with reflective comments, and attempt to elicit the patient's own motivation-enhancing statements. Affirm any efforts made to reduce use and look for opportunities to support the patient's sense of self-efficacy. If there has been little or no change in the patient's use, look for opportunities to develop discrepancy through the use of double-sided reflections, exploring pros and cons, and seeking elaboration.

Explore the Development of SUD Patterns

The clinician asks the patient to look closely at their behavior, environment, and beliefs to identify patterns of SUD. See the sample language provided.

> *We think of repeated substance use as learned behavior. When people start to use alcohol or other substances a lot, they learn that it changes the way they feel. For example, some people use it like a tranquilizer to help them cope with stressful situations. Some use it when they feel blue. Others expect it to enhance positive feelings. Some think it makes them more confident. And some use it to avoid thinking about troublesome things. How does that fit with your experience? [Waits for answer.]*
>
> *After a while, things in the environment can trigger use, sometimes without your even realizing it. The environment can trigger cravings. Things in the environment that can trigger use include seeing or smelling alcohol or other substances, being around people who are using, or being in stressful situations. During the assessment session, we talked about the connection you have noticed between getting paid on Fridays and buying alcohol. Are there other connections like that for you?*
>
> *People often develop beliefs about substances they are using. These are ideas or "automatic thoughts" you have come to believe about you and your substance use. I've heard you say things in previous sessions like, "I cannot be creative or work effectively without it," "I cannot take the way I feel when I've tried to quit," and "I need to change, but it's not worth the effort." What other beliefs do you have about you and [____]?*
>
> *Substances can change the way a person feels, acts, and thinks. To help you avoid or cope with the situations in which you smoke and to help you find things you can do instead of using, let us start by working on understanding your behavior. Does this make sense to you?*

Explore High-risk Situations and Triggers, and Build Patient Empowerment Through Self-knowledge

The clinician explains that substance use behavior is learned over time. The patient's understanding of their use patterns can help them change those patterns. Understanding high-risk situations can help the patient avoid or cope with those situations. See the sample language provided.

> *If using alcohol or other substances changes the way a person acts, thinks, and feels, it's helpful to begin by identifying use patterns and habits. Once your patterns are identified, you may find it easier to change your behavior. You can find ways to cope with your high-risk situations without using. Change involves learning specific skills and strategies. Once you know about the situations and problems that contribute to your using, you can look for other ways to handle those situations. What do you think about that?*

The clinician focuses on the patient's behaviors and high-risk situations. See the sample language provided.

> *In what situations do you use alcohol and/or other substances (e.g., places, people, activities, specific times, days)?*
>
> *What are your triggers for using (e.g., when you are in a social situation, when you have had a tense day, when you are faced with a difficult problem, when you want to feel relaxed)?*
>
> *Can you describe a recent situation when you used (e.g., a relapse story)?*
>
> *Can you remember your thoughts and feelings at the time you used (e.g., tense, bored, depressed, stressed, overwhelmed, angry)?*
>
> *What were the consequences of using?*

Guidelines

Knowing what affects someone's own use gives more personal awareness (power) to decide whether to use or not use. Looking at the pros and cons of what happens after use also increases understanding and helps the individual make the decision about use in the future.

Provide the patient with the ***Awareness Record*** handout, which was introduced in Session 2. Walk through the form again as the patient fills it out regarding their personal use from the previous week or a recent use episode.

> Can you describe in detail the last time you used or had an opportunity to use? As you recall the incident, see if you can identify the triggers, thoughts and feelings, decision to use, and pros and cons of your use.

Ask the patient to read the columns in the ***Awareness Record*** handout and follow up with a series of questions to help generate statements for each required column. Get the patient to verbalize responses to each section of the handout before writing it down. This enables offering feedback/suggestions before anything is put on paper. The patient is less likely to feel criticized this way.

For example: "Many people report that a common trigger is a negative situation, such as a fight with others and the bad feelings that arise as a result." Has this happened to you recently? Generate a discussion with the patient regarding personal triggers. Then, have the patient fill in the ***Awareness Record*** handout.

> Now that we have filled in your ***Awareness Record*** worksheet, I'd like you to read it aloud.

To emphasize nonuse decisions, it is also good to ask:

> Can you give me an example of a time when the same trigger did not result in your using?

Indicate that this situational analysis—via the ***Awareness Record*** worksheet—is something you hope the patient will continue using between sessions to help support decisions and steps toward reducing use and improving future wellness.

For example:

> We think self-awareness and self-knowledge are essential to breaking the cycle of negative habits (e.g., automatically drinking) that some people get into. Instead, using the ***Awareness Report*** worksheet makes us take a moment to think about all the elements prior to and after our actions. This will help us understand how to avoid, replace, and cope with the thoughts, feelings, and situations in new ways.

The clinician asks the patient about alcohol and substance use behavior using MI techniques (e.g., reflection, expressing empathy). while learning important information about the patient's use environment. See the sample language provided.

> **Clinician (C):** In what situations do you find yourself using?
> **Doug (D):** When things get hectic at home. Between my wife and my son, it seems as if everyone is out to get me. When I smoke, I can cope with them.
> **C:** Using helps you cope with stress at home. Are there other situations when you smoke?
> **D:** Not right now. When I go home, I should be able to relax, but with all the nagging, I end up using to escape.
> **C:** You want your home to be peaceful, but conflicts over your using push you to smoke.
> **D:** Yeah; sounds crazy, does not it?
> **C:** Your situation is difficult. Things you identify that lead you to smoke are called triggers. You've said that conflicts at home trigger you to smoke. What are your thoughts and feelings during times of conflict at your house, right before you light up?
> **D:** I'm thinking that if everyone would get off my back, I might be able to quit using. But they do not, and it's the only way I know how to relax.
> **C:** You find yourself in a bind. Let us use the **Awareness Record** [presents it] to list the things we are talking about. You said using [____] helps you relax. What else does it do for you?
> **D:** It helps me sleep. When I do not get high, it's hard getting to sleep. I used to enjoy the high a lot more than I do now. I keep using, but I do not even get that high anymore.
> **C:** Sounds as if you are listing the negative parts of using. Are there others?

Together the clinician and patient fill out the ***Awareness Record***. Complete for two recent experiences (one internal, one external, if possible) or for one use and one nonuse example.

Put the Pieces Together: Draw Connections, Consider New Roads, and Build Coping Strategies

Identify the positive effects

The patient will likely have discussed some positive effects in the course of identifying triggers and listing consequences. Summarize these, and ask the patient to identify other desired effects of substance use.

> I have already learned about some affects you look forward to when you drink, like feeling some relief from stress and forgetting about the day. I am wondering what other effects of drinking you enjoy?

Use of evocative questions can be helpful for eliciting multiple effects. Both the positive (e.g., euphoria, drug effects) and the negative reinforcement (e.g., numb feelings, stop worrying) that may result from substance use should be considered as factors that maintain substance use.

Section 2 Clinician Guidance for 16 Sessions of Integrated Cognitive Behavioral Therapy

> *What else?*
> *If you stopped using alcohol today, what would you miss most?*
> *Does drinking make some things in your life more tolerable?*
> *What is the feeling you are looking for when you have your first drink of the night?*

Directive questions can also be used as needed.

> *You mentioned drinking in some social circumstances. What do you think alcohol does for you in that type of situation?*

Summarize the effects

> *It sounds like we have gotten most of these. Let me read back what we have come up with so far. Some of the desirable effects of drinking that you see include reducing stress, forgetting about the day, feeling more socially confident, being able to stand up for yourself, feeling some excitement, feeling rewarded, and relieving boredom. Does that sound about right? This probably accounts for most of the effects you are looking for when you drink but perhaps not all. If you think of something else, we can always add it later.*

Draw connections

The clinician should help the patient make a connection between the triggers and the effects on the ***New Roads*** worksheet (see Figure 2).

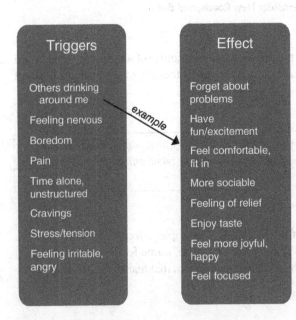

Figure 2 New Roads Worksheet

Discuss psychological dependence

The relationship between triggers and effects is a good representation of how the patient has come to rely on substances to achieve a desired effect or to cope with some unpleasant circumstances. Attempting to cut back on or quit using substances often causes an increase in discomfort for the patient, and without other options to manage the distress, continued substance use is more probable. This psychological dependence on substances will persist until the patient has addressed the deficit in coping skills and found more adaptive means for achieving these effects.

> *You have mapped this out well. One thing I noticed right away is that almost every trigger leads to this effect of "feeling relaxed." It is clear that feeling relaxed is an important effect for you, and drinking is how you get there most of the time.*
>
> *What we have here is a map of how you have come to depend on alcohol in your life. If alcohol dependence were just a physical problem, you could get a 3-day detox and come out never wanting to use again. In some way, this is a map of what keeps you using alcohol, even when you may not want to. This is psychological dependence. Over time, you have come to depend on alcohol to achieve these positive effects. When you stop drinking, you may begin to feel uncomfortable, not because of any physical withdrawal, but because you are not finding a way to get from this side (point to triggers) to this side (point to effects). Breaking the psychological dependence involves finding another way to get from the trigger to the effect that does not involve alcohol. If you can find ways to achieve some of these effects without drinking, I think you are going to have a lot less desire for alcohol. What do you think?"*

Consider new roads

Introduce the idea of finding a new road or path for achieving desirable outcomes in each trigger situation.

> *So, I am curious. As you look at all these triggers and the desired effects, can you think of any way you could get a similar effect you are looking for without alcohol as a new road or path?*

If the patient has trouble identifying any alternative coping strategies, reminding them of alternative strategies that they talked about in previous sessions may be helpful for moving the discussion forward.

> *Earlier you told me that watching TV is a good escape from reality for the moment. This is one way to get this effect of forgetting about problems. Can you think of any other ways?*

As the patient discusses current coping strategies and possible new means for achieving the desired effects, reflect and affirm as needed.

> *Exercise has worked for you in the past when you are feeling stressed, and it may be something that could help you again now. These are great ideas you are coming up with. What else can you imagine would help you get from any of these triggers to the desired effects without drinking?*

The clinician keeps a detailed account of the new roads the patient identifies over the course of this discussion, and, when the patient has run out of ideas, the clinician summarizes the patient's strategies.

> You have really done a great job coming up with other ways to achieve these effects without needing to drink to get there. You have things you have been using for a while that work in some of these situations. You also have some ideas about new strategies you could try for a few of these trigger situations, such as exercise, distracting yourself, and leaving your house when you are bored. These are all great ideas.

The clinician emphasizes the importance of coping strategies. See the sample language provided.

> We've talked about your high-risk situations and triggers, and we have started to make connections between several important things. This is important because many people are unaware of how they put themselves at risk for using. Now we'll focus on coping with these situations in ways that will help you resist the urge to use. You've already read the **Learning New Coping Strategies** (presents Session 2 handout again). Let us take a few moments to go through it and identify the strategies you have tried and others that might work. Remember, some strategies involve things you can do or specific actions you can take, some involve ways of thinking, and some involve other people or your surroundings.

Assign a Between-session Challenge

The clinician gives the patient a blank copy of *Awareness Record* and asks the patient to document episodes of craving or desire for substances between this session and the next. The clinician chooses an appropriate assignment from among the following and reviews the instructions with the patient:

- Future Self Letter
- Relaxation Practice Exercise

Review and Conclude

The clinician reviews the content of the session, asks the patient for feedback, responds empathically to their comments, and troubleshoots any difficulties. They explain that the patient will report back on their efforts to complete the between-session exercises at the next session. The clinician prepares the patient for the upcoming session by briefly describing the topic and how the skill addressed will support the patient's needs. This emphasizes and builds a positive expectation for the upcoming work.

Session 11 Handouts: Enhancing Self-awareness

Clinician's Quick Reference to Session 11

1) Build rapport and review.
   - Welcome the patient; check in about the week in general.
   - Review the patient's cravings, recent use experiences, and successes.
   - Review the between-session challenge.
2) Explore the development of addictive patterns.
   - Provide rationale (e.g., the learned or associative nature of addiction, pairing with alterations in thinking and feeling).
   - Use the patient's own experiences to illustrate how using alcohol or other substances can change one's feelings; if the patient has not stated any examples, provide examples that are appropriate to their situation.
   - From the patient's stated use situations, identify examples of environmental triggers for use; ask the patient for other triggers they have experienced.
   - Elicit examples of feelings, beliefs, or automatic thoughts people may have about substances. Use examples provided by the patient, and ask the patient for more examples.
   - Suggest that the patient start the process of change by understanding their behavior; ask, "Does this make sense to you?"
3) Build empowerment though self-knowledge by understanding high-risk situations and triggers.
   - Explore with the patient:
     - Typical use situations (e.g., places, people, activities, time, days)
     - Triggers for use
     - Recent use situation
     - Thoughts and feelings at use times (e.g., tense, bored, stressed)
   - Complete **Awareness Record** and summarize the list.
4) Put the pieces together: Draw connections, consider new roads, and build coping strategies.
   - Emphasize the importance of coping strategies.
   - Reintroduce learning new coping strategies.
   - Introduce a drawing connection exercise, and identify new pathways toward desired outcomes.
   - Ask the patient to identify strategies they have tried and those that might work best.
5) Develop or elicit a specific between-session challenge that incorporates material from the session.
6) Review and conclude.

Awareness Record

As a way to increase awareness about your patterns of use, we'll use this form to identify the kinds of situations, thoughts, feelings, and consequences that are associated with your alcohol/substance use. It may be difficult initially, but once you get accustomed to paying more attention, you will become skilled at discovering the ways in which you typically use alcohol/substances.

Trigger. What types of events tend to make you want to use? For example, an argument, disappointment, loss, or frustration; spending time with friends who use; having alcohol/substances easily available to you; recalling positive memories of past use.

1. _____
2. _____

Thoughts, Feelings, and Beliefs. What were you thinking or how were you feeling in relation to the triggers you have identified? For example, thinking you were incompetent or stupid or that you could never achieve a particular goal; feeling angry, sad, frightened, or glad.

1. _____
2. _____

Behavior. What did you actually do when you were thinking and feeling in these ways? For example, used [____], went out to dinner, isolated yourself from people.

1. _____
2. _____

Positive Consequences. What good came out of your response to the situation? For example, I felt much better for a short period.

1. _____
2. _____

Negative Consequences. What negative things happened as a result of your response? For example, I felt bad about myself for using; I could not complete the work I needed to finish.

1. _____
2. _____

Awareness Record

As a way to increase awareness about your patterns of use, use this form to identify the kinds of situations, thoughts, feelings, and consequences that are associated with your alcohol/substance use.

Describe incident:

Trigger	Thoughts, Feelings, and Beliefs	Intensity of Feeling	Behavior	Positive Results	Negative Results
(What set me up to be more likely to use alcohol or drugs?) or (to feel heightened depression or anxiety?)	(What was I thinking? What was I feeling? What did I tell myself?)	Low–high, 1–10	(What did I do then?)	(What good things happened?)	(What bad things happened?)

Date and Time: _____

Awareness Record Example

As a way to increase awareness about your patterns of use, use this form to identify the kinds of situations, thoughts, feelings, and consequences that are associated with your alcohol/substance use.

Describe incident: Spent evening with my friend smoking weed and drinking beer.

Trigger	Thoughts, Feelings, and Beliefs	Intensity of Feeling	Behavior	Positive Results	Negative Results
(What set me up to be more likely to use alcohol or drugs?) or (to feel heightened depression or anxiety?)	(What was I thinking? What was I feeling? What did I tell myself?)	Low–high, 1–10	(What did I do then?)	(What good things happened?)	(What bad things happened?)
Friend called and invited me to get high with him. Nothing else to do.	"I want to reward myself." "I'm bored." "Felt good about going 15 days without using, so felt OK about getting high today."	It was a 6.	Went out with friend and used.	Had fun. Felt good to get high, having gone 15 days without.	Broke the 15-day abstinence (although was not too worried about this). Did not get as much done. Did not feel as healthy.

Future Self Letter

Sometime during the next week, imagine that a year has passed and that you have not used alcohol or substances for a year. Making believe that it's next year, and write a letter to yourself (the old you). Write about your life as it has become. Include the reasons why you stopped a year earlier, what your lifestyle is like in the new year, and the benefits you enjoy from not using. Mention in your letter any problems you faced during the past year in giving up alcohol or substance use. Describe yourself without alcohol or substances as clearly as you can. As you visualize yourself in the future without alcohol or substances, it may help to think about friendships, self-esteem, health, employment, recreational activities, and general lifestyle satisfaction. If you prefer, draw, sketch, or paint a picture of this image of yourself in the future, rather than depicting it in writing. Choose a medium that will allow you to see another possibility for yourself.

This exercise is extremely useful. It helps you visualize your journey and your goal. Having a clear picture of where you are going, why, and how you are going to get there will be useful in the months ahead. At our next session, we'll talk about the future you foresee for yourself.

Relaxation Practice Exercise

Arrange to spend some quiet time in a room where you will not be interrupted. Try to practice this relaxation technique at least three times during the next week. Proceed through the 8 groups of muscles in the list below, first tensing each for 5 seconds and then relaxing each for 15–20 seconds. Settle back as comfortably as you can, take a deep breath, and exhale very slowly. You may feel most comfortable if you close your eyes. Notice the sensations in your body; you will soon be able to control those sensations. Begin by focusing your attention on your hands and forearms.

- Squeeze both hands into fists, with arms straight. Then relax hands.
- Flex both arms at the elbows. Then relax arms.
- Shrug shoulders toward head. Tilt chin toward chest. Then relax shoulders and neck.
- Clench jaw, gritting your teeth together. Then relax jaw.
- Close your eyes tightly. Then relax eyes.
- Wrinkle up your forehead and brow. Then relax these muscles.
- Harden your stomach muscles, as if expecting someone to punch you there (continue to breathe slowly as you tense your stomach). Then relax stomach.
- Stretch out both legs, point your toes toward your head, and press your legs together. Then relax legs.

Self-rating task

Each day that you engage in this exercise, rate your relaxation level before and after, using the following guide: *0 = highly tense; 100 = fully relaxed*.

Day	Time	Before	After

Session 12. Using Mindfulness, Meditation, and Stepping Back

Introduction

Session 12 re-introduces the patient to the practice of mindfulness, which has been found effective in the treatment of substance abuse, depression, anxiety, and other health and psychological difficulties (Witkiewitz et al., 2005) and existed within the wisdom traditions for thousands of years.

Meditation

Meditation is a well-established practice and part of many religious philosophies, particularly in the East. Western world has incorporated it as a therapeutic and health strategy because of its broad appeal, relative accessibility, demonstrated efficacy, and lack of adverse consequences. ICBT incorporates medication because it is a highly accessible, easily learned (though not necessarily easily practiced) strategy and has been used successfully in the treatment of many physical and emotional health conditions (e.g., substance use, depression).

While the learning and practice of meditation could itself be the subject of an entire treatment guide, we include it here as one of the skills-building sessions in hopes the information will encourage the patient to engage in further study and practice beyond the time involved with ICBT. Many different types of meditation are available, from very formal to informal. Given the brevity of the clinician's contact with each patient, an informal approach to teaching meditation is encouraged, rather than one tied to the tenets of a particular religious practice. The clinician offers meditation as one strategy that may be helpful in reducing or stopping use of alcohol and other substances. Patients can also look into classes in the community as a way to learn more and as a strategy for prosocial connections. They can also check online for free resources related to both meditation and mindfulness. Websites, apps, and social media platforms (e.g., YouTube) have dozens of examples.

Mindfulness

Mindfulness refers to the practice of increasing one's capacity to remain in the present moment and accept experience without judgment. The practice recognizes our minds are busy; distracted; and reactive to events, situation, thoughts, and feelings. Building a capacity for mindfulness involves becoming increasingly aware of one's moment-to-moment experience and approaching the present moment with acceptance. The intended outcome is a move toward "present-centeredness," which creates greater clarity about the nature of one's struggles, builds capability for accepting situations and feelings as they are, and sheds light on new pathways for recovery and growth.

There are numerous ways to increase mindfulness or the ability to stay in the present moment, and it is easy to recognize how often one becomes "non-mindful." Meditation is one method, which can involve sitting (or lying down) and focusing on a single point of concentration (e.g., the breath or a mantra, word or phrase, or nonword). Other ways also exist (e.g., engaging in daily activities like walking or driving to work) but with extra attention on staying present, self-aware, and connected to the here and now.

Explore How Increasing Mindfulness Can be Helpful for Change

One important reason mindfulness can be useful in addressing substance use problems is because individuals tend to use substances to escape from difficult emotions or experiences. Alcohol and other substances can serve as "affective regulators," and the patient may have few other tools or options when faced with overwhelming sadness, fear, anger, etc.

> Mindfulness strengthens our observing self so that without the lens of our restless brain, we can look at our thoughts, feelings, beliefs, and perceptions.

Building a capacity for mindfulness (e.g., through meditation) can help patients learn how to withstand and "stay with" difficult internal states, rather than automatically opting for substances.

When conducting the session on enhancing awareness during Session 11, the clinician may have learned about high-risk situations for the patient, such as feeling a certain way (e.g., powerless, discouraged). The information from the functional analysis can be helpful in teaching the patient about mindfulness and meditation. The clinician might remind the patient about certain high-risk or trigger emotions and suggest how mindfulness could help handle the feelings differently. For example, when meditating for any length of time, one becomes acutely aware of the transient nature of internal states, and, yet, most people are likely to feel "attached" to these states. We feel as though our thoughts and feelings are ours and that they belong to us. If one can approach a particularly disturbing thought and note, "Oh, it's just a thought," this can change the way one feels and reacts.

Similarly, if one can step back from an intense emotional experience and observe, "Oh, that's dissatisfaction," or, "That's just longing," this ability can be tremendously empowering because one no longer has to act or do something about a particular thought or feeling. It is also not necessary to continue to feel bad about a certain kind of thought because thoughts are not necessarily true. The patient comes to see themself as more than, or at least separate from, any particular emotional state, thought, or idea.

The Patient's Experience

In this session, the patient is re-introduced to the concept of mindfulness and the practice of meditation as strategies for achieving a state of nonjudgmental acceptance of the present moment. They are encouraged to develop an attitude of curiosity and interest in moment-to-moment experiences. A mechanism for achieving important goals related to alcohol or other substance use, mindfulness is seen as consistent with the overall objectives of cultivating self-awareness and self-acceptance. The exercises during this session may be novel and seem strange to the patient, and it is important for the clinician to both normalize this reaction and to encourage the patient to give them a try. The patient should have the experience of feeling more present and connected and more aware of the feelings and thoughts that occupy consciousness. They may become aware of difficult or unpleasant emotions that tend to distract, and this information can be useful to the clinician in building coping skills during this and later sessions.

Clinician Preparation

Session 12. Using Mindfulness, Meditation, and Stepping Back	
Materials • *Clinician's Quick Reference* • *Mindfulness Meditation Instructions* handout • *Meditation Exercise* handout • *Meditation Exercise: On the Riverbank* handout	**Total Time** One hour **Delivery Method** CBT-focused individual or group therapy
Strategies • Follow OARS. • Support self-efficacy. • Demonstrate skill and role play. • Follow CBT skills session reminders.	
Goals for This Session • Re-introduce the patient to the concept of mindfulness. • Teach the patient about meditation and different approaches for focusing awareness. • Provide several experiential exercises demonstrating mindfulness and meditation.	

Session 12 Outline and Overview

1) Build rapport and review:
   - Check in with the patient on recent experiences.
   - Attend to the therapeutic alliance, and address any obstacles or concerns.
   - Assess motivational factors and change readiness.
2) Introduce the concept of mindfulness:
   - Awareness and acceptance of present moment
   - Connection to alcohol/substance use
   - Role of mindfulness in regulating internal states
3) Conduct experiential exercises demonstrating mindfulness:
   - Conduct a mindfulness exercise (e.g., eating a raisin)
   - Process patient's experience and reaction
4) Discuss meditation as a(n):
   - Part of religious practice but also as part of nonreligious health practices
   - Strategy for increasing mindfulness
   - Strategy for managing difficult emotions and thoughts
   - Approach for coping with alcohol or other substance use
5) Conduct experiential meditation exercise:
   - Do a breathing meditation
   - Process the patient's experience
6) Provide the following to the patient:
   - Mindfulness Meditation Instructions
   - Alternate meditation exercise (**On the Riverbank**)
   - Encouragement for daily practice
7) Review and conclude.

Session 12 Protocol

The clinician greets the patient and elicits information about life during the previous week. They ask about any between-session exercises (e.g., journaling, thought records, awareness records) and enquire about the patient's current feelings, change readiness, and progress on goals. The clinician continues to use MI skills, always expressing genuine curiosity. Following are some examples of how to initiate such interaction with the patient.

> How have things been since we last met? or Tell me about something enjoyable you did during the past week.

If the patient cannot think of anything enjoyable during the past week, ask about interests and activities, even if they did not engage in them during the past week. Continue by asking how they have been doing over the past week regarding alcohol or drug use.

> What have your emotions been like since we last met? or What concerning thoughts have you had since we last spoke?

Listen for possible changes in the patient's behaviors, thoughts, and feelings regarding use, anxiety, or depression. Try to refrain from asking too many questions. Let the patient tell you how they have been doing. Respond with reflective comments and attempt to elicit the patient's own motivation-enhancing statements. Affirm any efforts made to reduce use, and look for opportunities to support the patient's sense of self-efficacy. If there has been little or no change in the patient's use, look for opportunities to develop discrepancy through the use of double-sided reflections, exploring pros and cons, and seeking elaboration.

Provide an Overview of Session and Description of Mindfulness

Introduce the topic with brief descriptions of mindfulness and meditation. It might be helpful to begin by asking whether the patient has heard of or been exposed to these ideas and what the experience has been.

> Well, I am pleased to talk to you today about an important practice called mindfulness. Have you ever heard this term before? Mindfulness is simply trying to stay focused on the present moment and on what's happening with you right now. You know how everyone is so busy in this world, between our computers, cell phones, televisions, and rushing here to there. Well, often people do not even have time to enjoy a simple meal. Or they are so distracted by all the things they have to get done that they do not even know how they feel or what they might like to do if they had a free moment. Does this sound familiar to you?
>
> Some people think that using alcohol or substances is a way for them to just slow down, relax, or feel better in the face of all the stress they have. Is that how you tend to think about your substance use? But there are other ways to do this that do not have the harmful consequences that substances can. I want to teach you about mindfulness and some specific ways to increase this ability, which we all have.

> *Mindfulness can be increased in a variety of ways, but the overall purpose is to help you to become more "present," that is, more aware of your experience of the present moment. It is a way to help you feel less distracted and pulled in many directions. It is a way to help you perhaps feel more grounded, focused, and calm. Increasing mindfulness has been found effective for people struggling with mood, anxiety, and substance use problems. I think this could be very helpful as you try to make these important changes in your use of [___]. For example, you told me during our first meeting that you have a hard time "shutting off your busy brain" and that [substances] seems to help you do this. Developing skills related to mindfulness may help you manage when you are feeling uncomfortable without using any substances. Are you willing to give it a try? Great!*

The clinician leads the patient in several experiential exercises involving mindfulness and/or meditation. The focus of these exercises is to help the patient become more aware of how they experience the present moment.

The raisin exercise

Give the patient (or each group member) one raisin, piece of chocolate, or other small item of food. (Ask beforehand if there are any foods that might be problematic.) Have the patient put the food item in the mouth and ask them not to chew or swallow it right away. Then ask them to focus on various aspects (e.g., taste, texture, feeling in the mouth). Ask the patient to notice more complex experiences (e.g., the chocolate seems sweet at first but then slightly salty) and ask about thoughts and feelings experienced while eating this small morsel. Eventually, the patient may finish eating. Then inquire about any interesting observations (e.g., many people are astounded to realize how one small raisin can be quite satisfying when one is fully present in the moment to experience and enjoy it).

> *Okay, here is our first exercise in mindfulness. This may seem a little silly, but just bear with me. I want you to take this raisin. Now, first look at it and notice what you see. Okay, now you can place it in your mouth, but do not eat it right away. I just want you to see what happens when you stay present to eating this one, small raisin, rather than doing the automatic thing we all do of swallowing food and not even paying attention to the experience of eating. So put it in your mouth and just let it sit on your tongue....what do you notice? (You do not have to answer out loud. I'm just going to toss out questions for you to think about if you can.)*
>
> *What sensations are there? What is the flavor? How does it feel to just sit there and not chew it right away? What happens when you think about where this raisin came from and how it got to this place so you could eat it? What is the actual texture? Does it change? How about the flavor? What do you notice about yourself as you are eating this raisin in this much slower way? Is it frustrating? Enjoyable? How does it compare to how you usually eat? Okay, now you can start to chew and swallow the raisin. Pay close attention to this as well. Notice each moment and how you feel as you eat the raisin. Are you feeling more or less hungry after this exercise? More or less satisfied? Anything else you noticed?*

The clinician discusses the patient's experience with this exercise and how it compares to their usual approach toward daily activities. Try to address the following points:

- Is this a significant departure from the way the patient is living?
- Discuss how making efforts to be more mindful—when it comes to eating, working, doing laundry, or spending time with friends or family—could have the effect of reducing the desire for alcohol or substances.

- Some people refer to our being mindful and present as being our authentic self.
- Using substances actually takes one away from the present moment and may contribute to feelings of disconnection or being emotionally numb.
- Disconnecting from feelings, or trying to get past them quickly, does not generally help one to work through difficult emotions in an effective way.
- Mindfulness-based activities such as meditation can teach the patient that they are capable of experiencing and getting through even very painful feelings. It is working through difficulty rather than avoiding difficulty.

These may be new concepts for patients. Acknowledge and explore skepticism or reluctance to consider this new way of approaching lived experience. Indicate that a goal of this treatment is to help patients learn valuable tools that can assist them in making the changes they want for themselves. Not every tool or strategy will be appealing to every patient. They can choose or focus on the ones that seem most credible, helpful, and useful. However, ask that they be open to learning new strategies, even if they seem strange at first or unlikely to be of benefit.

Discuss Meditation

Following the mindfulness exercise, discuss meditation as a technique or practice that can also improve mindfulness or the ability to remain present in the moment. Inquire about the patient's previous experience, understanding, and/or perspective related to meditation approaches. If the patient has little or no background, provide a general introduction. Then conduct a demonstration to practice a short breathing meditation.

The clinician can explain that meditation has been practiced for thousands of years. It is part of many religious traditions (e.g., Christianity, Hinduism, Buddhism), particularly in the Eastern part of the world. Many view meditation as a viable path to enlightenment or a heightened state of being. The Western world has also adopted meditation because it is seen to have many health benefits. For example, there is evidence that people who meditate can reduce their blood pressure, require less anesthesia for surgery, and improve their sleep, among other things. Meditation also seems to be beneficial in reducing depression and anxiety and in helping with substance-related problems. While it may seem very simple, and learning it is simple, it is the consistent practice of meditation that can be challenging. It can also be difficult for some people to "just sit" or "do nothing" because this runs counter to our societal value that we should also be productive and engaged in some kind of activity. The idea of "stopping" or sitting with one's thoughts and feelings without acting on them may be quite novel. Some sample language follows.

> I'd like you to give this a try because I think it has great potential value in relation to your goals for this treatment. You will not be graded on how well you do meditation. I'd just like you to try it. Many times, people who develop alcohol or drug difficulties become accustomed to reacting to difficult emotional states by using. It seems in the moment that this will help them solve the problem or get them past the feeling they do not want to experience. However, it is this kind of avoidance of painful states that can lead to harmful patterns and habits and contribute to beliefs about ourselves that are not constructive (for example, thinking that alcohol or drug use is the only way to deal with a particular problem or feeling). Among the benefits of meditation is the developing awareness that our thoughts and feelings are actually quite transitory. There is a sense of impermanence in that everything changes in a dynamic state of flux. This can be unsettling for those of us who are seeking "ground" or a sense of permanence and security. However, if we accept that things are in fact changing all the time, including us, that makes it possible to fashion our own future, at least in the next moment. It can help us to be hopeful in seeing that we are capable of many, many things, despite what we may have come to believe through some unfortunate conditioning.

Meditation involving the breath

> Meditation can mean many things. In this exercise, we want to teach you a simple and straightforward meditation technique that involves sitting and focusing on your breathing for a specific period of time. You can sit in the chair or on the floor [if there's carpet, not hard floor] and cross your legs. With either position, try and keep your back straight. It's better not to lie down or become overly relaxed. This is not a relaxation exercise, although we will learn about those later. What I'd like you to do is simply turn your attention to the in and out of your breath. You do not need to change your breathing in any way. Just pay attention to it. You can close your eyes or keep them open with a "soft focus" (for example, on the carpet a few feet in front of you).
>
> I'm going to signal the start of our meditation with this sound [e.g., bell, tap, other gentle sound]. We will sit for 10 minutes. If you have never done this before, this will feel like a very long time. All I ask you to do is try to focus your attention on your breathing. Just noticing it. The in and out of it. It is inevitable your mind will wander. It will be difficult to stay focused on your breathing for this entire time. You may become aware of things you have to do; things you are happy or upset about; different sensations in your body, such as hunger, discomfort, or feelings of boredom or anxiety. This is totally normal. It does not mean you are doing it wrong, not trying, or that it cannot help you to do this. When you notice your mind has gone astray, just gently bring your attention back to the breath. You can also make an observation to yourself such as, "Oh, thinking," and come back to focusing on your breath. At the end of the 10 minutes, I will make a signal for us to stop. Do you have any questions before we start?

The clinician conducts the 10-minute meditation. When it's complete, inquire about the patient's experiences. It is typical for someone who has never tried meditation to be astonished at how long the 10 minutes seem. The patient may report becoming sleepy or physically uncomfortable (especially if sitting cross-legged) or being unable to focus on breathing. They may report not feeling any better or different after the exercise. Reassure the patient that all these feelings are normal and typical of what most others say after meditating for the first time. Indicate that one generally does not feel better immediately after a meditation session. It is something that accrues benefits over time with repeated practice. Just like any other skill, it is something that takes some discipline and willingness to invest energy in to become proficient or to notice clear benefit. Explain there are many benefits from meditation for those who practice regularly. If it seems appropriate, give examples (e.g., lowering blood pressure, reducing cardiovascular risk, reducing anxiety and depression, improving focus and attention, changing use of substances). Ask the patient to try over the next week to find a time of day to practice this new skill. They may want to designate a space at home with less likelihood of distraction and a time of day that can be built into practice most comfortably. For example, some find first thing in the morning a good time to meditate. Ask if there are any questions or concerns.

Review and Conclude

Thank the patient for being open to hearing about these concepts and for trying the exercises, especially if there was some disinclination initially. Provide the session handouts on meditation, mindfulness, and instructions for practice. Ask the patient to try the skills over the next week each day at a convenient time and to record the experience in a journal (e.g., day, length of sitting, overall experience). Discuss the next session planned for the patient and how the topic chosen and skills learned will be valuable on the path toward wellness.

Session 12 Handouts: Using Mindfulness, Meditation, and Stepping Back

Clinician's Quick Reference to Session 10

1) Build rapport and review.
   - Check in on past week.
   - Follow up on between-session challenges.
2) Introduce mindfulness, and provide a rationale.
   - Build awareness and acceptance of present moment.
   - Make the connection to alcohol and substance use.
   - Introduce the role of mindfulness in regulating internal states.
3) Conduct experiential exercises to demonstrate mindfulness.
   - Engage in a mindfulness exercise (e.g., eating a raisin).
   - Process the patient's experience and reaction.
4) Discuss meditation.
   - Used as part of religious practice but also incorporated into nonreligious health practices
   - Employed as a strategy for increasing mindfulness
   - Employed as a strategy for managing difficult emotions and thoughts
   - Used as an approach for coping with alcohol and substance use
5) Conduct experiential meditation exercise.
   - Do breathing meditation.
   - Process the patient's experience.
6) Provide the following to the patient:
   - Meditation instructions
   - Alternate meditation exercise (**On the Riverbank**)
   - Encouragement for daily practice
7) Review and conclude.

Mindfulness Meditation Instructions

Source: Jacob Lund/Adobe Stock Photos

1) Find a quiet, comfortable location, with few distractions.
2) Choose a time of day that increases the chance you will be able to sit quietly with few distractions.
3) Sit on a cushion (cross-legged, if not difficult) or chair. Try to keep you back straight, but do not hold tension there to do this (i.e., do not try too hard).
4) Maintain a soft gaze.
5) Have a timer and signal for starting and stopping.
6) Choose a single point of focus (e.g., the breath or a word or phrase, nonmeaningful word, image or picture).
7) Sit quietly for 10 minutes, and maintain focus.
8) Observe distracting sounds, thoughts, and feelings with mild disinterest, and attempt to return to focus. This may happen many times during one sitting. Try not to be discouraged but, rather, recognize this is how our minds work.
9) Try to practice this daily, and journal or record the experience in a journal or log.

Meditation Exercise: On the Riverbank

For this variation on a standard meditation, find a quiet place with few distractions. Begin by focusing on your breathing and trying to slow it down to increase a sense of peace and relaxation. Count slowly with each inhalation and exhalation, from 1 to 10, so your breathing rate slows considerably. Imagine yourself sitting on a riverbank on a beautiful, sunny day, watching the water flow by. You may notice fish, stream currents, or a small boat sailing by from time to time. Imagine that as you sit on the bank, observing what is happening, these objects passing by are your thoughts, feelings, and sensations that arise in the course of your meditation. Consider that with each object, each representing an experience of yours, you may choose how to relate to it.

For each thought, feeling, or interpretation that threatens to derail or take you off track, recognize that you have the capacity to swim, sail, or sit back and watch it come and go. After all, they are all "just thoughts" or "just feelings." They are not necessarily true, good, or bad. They just are. Perhaps they do not even belong to you but are merely finding a host, temporarily, to attach to. You can become attached to them and their "stories," own them, hide from them, and live in fear of them. Or you can simply take notice as you might a sailboat passing by on a summer's day but not go for a ride. And simply wait for the next interesting entity to pass your way. Keep your focus...

Session 13. Addressing Suicidality

Introduction

In recent years suicidality, as indicated by the number of incidents of suicide attempts and persons considering suicide, has exponentially increased, in part due to the COVID-19 pandemic. According to the KFF analysis of the U.S. Census Bureau's Household Pulse Survey (Kaiser Family Foundation (KFF), n.d.), 9% of adults have experienced suicidal thought in the previous month. As the developers of this clinical guide, we felt it important to provide this session on suicidality for clinicians, as many have only received cursory instruction on this important issue.

This is not a clinical session like the others. Rather, it is a primer to better prepare you if or when a patient of yours is describing suicidality (also known as suicidal ideation). We will define suicidality and suicide risk stratification, identify care management strategies, and summarize treatment interventions. We encourage clinicians to do a deeper exploration of this content and recommend readings, including *The Clinical Manual for Assessing and Treating Suicidal Patients* (Chiles et al., 2018) or "Dialectical Behavior Therapy for Patients With Borderline Personality Disorder and Drug-Dependence" (Linehan et al., 1999).

The Patient's Experience

As defined by Crosby et al. (2011, pp. 21, 23) and Centers for Disease Control and Prevention (2022), "Suicide is death caused by injuring oneself with the intent to die. A suicide attempt is when someone harms themselves with any intent to end their life, but they do not die as a result of their actions." Anecdotally, from patient perspectives, suicide is:

- Not about wanting to die but, rather, about not wanting to live
- An escape from unbearable suffering
- A means to end a situation in which one feels trapped and experiences no hope
- A feeling of hopelessness (the most common emotion in suicide)

This loss of hope is viewed as a critical dimension in suicide risk, as beautifully captured in a Reddit comment from 2022: "A loss of hope is the lowest place to where our mind, heart, and soul may travel. It goes beyond depression, suffering, pain, and leaves you at a place where even being sad has no purpose. It is a dangerous point to fall to, and anyone in that place for long will eventually succumb." Chiles et al. (2018) describe suicidality as intolerable pain, interminable pain that is always there, and inescapable pain that will never go away. From this perspective, suicide is escape.

No single explanation can account for all suicidal behavior, but approximately 50% of suicidal men and women also experience major depression. Suicidality exists near equally among women and men. However, 80% of deaths by suicide are men (see text box).

> **Male Suicide**
>
> - Evidence has been collected worldwide that indicates men are far less likely to seek help for mental health challenges, irrespective of age, nationality, or ethnic or racial background (Wang et al., 2007).
> - They are half as likely as women to seek services for depression and anxiety (Wang et al., 2007).
> - Normative masculine characteristics contribute to male reluctance to seek care (Addis & Mahalik, 2003).

- Men are more likely to seek care to address externalizing issues (e.g., alcohol misuse, anger management) (Addis & Mahalik, 2003).
- Mental health issues among men often remain hidden, overlooked, or underdiagnosed.

Triage screening, described later, can offer a strategy for early identification. Evidence indicates that a larger percentage of patients attempting suicide will visit a primary care provider within several months of the actual attempt (Oliffe et al., 2019).

Redefining Understanding of Suicide

According to Hayes, Linehan, and Chiles previously mentioned, the clinician should understand suicidality as a unique behavioral issue. More than a manifestation of an underlying condition, the drivers of suicidal thoughts and intentions seem to arise from a cascade of individual, social, and contextual factors:

- **Individual Factors.** Hopelessness, previous suicidal behavior, gender (male), mental illness, chronic pain or illness, immobility, alcohol or other substance misuse, low self-esteem, low sense of control over life circumstances, lack of meaning and purpose in life, poor coping skills, guilt and shame, and feeling like a burden to others.
- **Social Factors.** Lack of social support, abuse and violence, social isolation, family dispute, conflict and dysfunction, separation/divorce, bereavement, other significant loss, peer rejection, and incarceration.
- **Contextual Factors.** Access to lethal means, unemployment, economic insecurity, financial stress, neighborhood violence and crime, poverty, school or work failure, social or cultural discrimination, and homelessness.

Care Management for a Suicidal Patient

With any suicidal patient, care management is important. We suggest that you or your clinic staff consider training and adopting the Collaborative Assessment and Management of Suicidality (CAMS) model. CAMS is the most widely used suicide-risk-management model and is perhaps best understood as a therapeutic framework for managing the care of suicidal patients. We provide this reference as an informational resource (Tyndal et al., 2022).

Factors for Formulating Risk Stratification

As part of your clinical interview, clinicians are advised to consider predictors of imminent danger. Table 1 identifies common predictors and levels of risk.

Section 2 Clinician Guidance for 16 Sessions of Integrated Cognitive Behavioral Therapy

Table 1 Common Predictors and Levels of Suicide Risk

Immediate Predictors	Low Risk	Moderate Risk	High Risk
Method	Undecided	Decided	Decided
Means	Not Present	Easy Access	In Possession
Time & Place	Not Chosen	Tentative	Chosen
Lethality	Low	Moderate	High
Preparation	None Made	Some Planning	Steps Taken
Prior Attempts	No	Yes	Yes
Life Events or Conditions			
Trauma	None or Mild	One or Moderate Stress	Several or Severe Trauma

Identification and Early Intervention Matters

Colleagues from the federally funded Screening, Brief Intervention, referral to treatment (SBIRT) initiatives brought forward a true innovation. When triage screening, most programs use a tool, such as the PHQ-9, and will conduct a brief triage screen using the PHQ-2, which includes the first two questions of the PHQ-9. While adequate as a triage screen for depression, it misses the opportunity to screen for suicidality. Developers of this manual added to the PHQ-2 a single question, #9 of the PHQ-9, which addresses self-harm and suicidality. This simple enhancement has enabled the early identification of hundreds of adults with suicidal ideation who otherwise would have not been identified. Any suicidal ideation indicates the need for a more complete psychosocial assessment and a suicidality risk assessment (e.g., the Columbia-Suicide Severity Rating Scale) to guide clinical decision making. This innovation supports early intervention. This innovation is the phq-3.

Introducing the PHQ-3 INNOVATION

The introduction to the PHQ-9 is: Over the last two weeks, how often have you been bothered by any of the following problems?

PHQ-2 Questions 1 and 2

- Item 1. Little interest or pleasure in doing things?
- Item 2. Feeling down, depressed, or hopeless?

PHQ-9, Question 9

- Item 3. Thoughts that you would be better off dead or of hurting yourself in some way?

Any affirmative response to Item 3 should result in a referral to a behavioral health provider for further assessment and intervention.

Clinical Objectives for Addressing Suicidality

- Keep your patient alive. Although hospitalizing someone, especially someone not wanting to go, can be highly stressful for both the clinician and patient, sometimes this is necessary.
- Use your MI spirit and skills to support engagement and rapport building in order to reinforce hope and hopefulness.

- Identify the individual, social, and contextual factors that feed your patient's suicidal intent.
- Create and implement a treatment plan that addresses hopelessness, as well as the individual, social, and contextual factors.
- Characterize suicidal thoughts as cognitive fusion, and mobilize strategies previously described to address and support defusion.
- Embrace MI spirit and skills to affirm and reinforce hopefulness and to align hopefulness with patient values.
- Mobilize specific ICBT sessions to address these targeted issues by using skills and strategies such as the following: ***Eliciting the Life Movie***, ***Awareness Record***, dropping anchor, working with thought and feelings, problem solving, and/or enhancing social support.

Clinician Preparation

Session 13. Addressing Suicidality	
Materials • *PHQ-9* handout • *Columbia-Suicide Severity Rating Scale* • Other handouts, as indicated	**Total Time** One hour **Delivery Method** CBT-focused individual or group therapy

Strategies
- Develop a written suicide safety plan and treatment plan.
- Follow OARS.
- Use MI skills supporting self-efficacy and treatment engagement.
- Target use of ICBT sessions based on situational awareness of identified needs.
- Consider a psychiatric consultation.
- Engage in consultation with peers or a supervisor for your own affective needs and to process what may feel like values or ethical challenges.

Session 13 Protocol

Important note to clinician: With a patient demonstrating any degree of suicidality, you should carefully document and discuss patient care with your supervisor and (if available) your medical/psychiatric director or consultant. Patients at high risk should be evaluated for possible hospitalization.

For the Clinician to Do

- Be in the moment with a patient
- Reinforce connection
- Offer reassurance (hope) that things can get better.
- If the patient is at higher risk, do not leave them alone.

Several Things for the Clinician Not to Do

- Do not engage in philosophical discussions about suicide.
- Do not describe suicidal ideation as attention-seeking behavior.
- Do not try and talk patients out of thinking the way they are thinking.
- Never promise to keep someone's suicidal feelings a secret.

Recommended Elements of a Suicide Safety Plan

- **Knowing the Warning Signs.** Ask, "How will you know when this safety plan should be used?" and "What do you experience when you start to think about suicide?"
- **Using Coping Strategies.** Ask, "What can you do if/when thought and feelings begin to escalate?" Use MI skills and problem solving to help your patient self-define coping strategies.
- **Leveraging Social Support.** Identify family or friends who would offer help. Ask, "Who among your family or friends do you think you could contact for help during this difficult time? Who do you feel you can talk to when under stress?" Ask for several people and their contact information. Ask "May I call them now with you to be sure they feel they can do this?"
- **Identifying Helpful Social Contacts and Settings.** If steps 2 or 3 do not work, help the patient identify helpful social contacts and settings that may distract them from crisis. Ask, "Who or what social setting helps you take your mind off your problems? Who helps you feel better when you are with them?" Help them identify potential safe places they can go to be around people (e.g., peer support center, coffee shop), hotlines, or other resources. The goal is to distract the client from suicidal thoughts.
- **Identifying Professionals and Agencies.** List the names and contact information of professionals and agencies available during the daytime and after hours, including the mental health crisis response unit and other supports (e.g., the suicide lifeline). Ask, "Who should be on the safety plan?" Provide increased support within the organization.
- **Making the Environment Safe.** Ask about the availability of lethal means, and ensure that a plan is in place to restrict access, including involving family and significant others who can assure removal of lethal means. Check with your local law enforcement contact to see if gun locks are provided. If at all possible, provide information to the family about what to look for and what to do.

Session 13 Handouts: Addressing Suicidality

Columbia Suicide Severity Rating Scale

SUICIDE IDEATION DEFINITIONS AND PROMPTS	Past month	
Ask questions that are bolded and <u>underlined</u>.	YES	NO
Ask Questions 1 and 2		
1) *<u>Have you wished you were dead or wished you could go to sleep and not wake up?</u>*		
2) *<u>Have you actually had any thoughts of killing yourself?</u>*		
If YES to 2, ask questions 3, 4, 5, and 6. If NO to 2, go directly to question 6.		
3) *<u>Have you been thinking about how you might do this?</u>* E.g. "*I thought about taking an overdose but I never made a specific plan as to when where or how I would actually do it....and I would never go through with it.*"		
4) *<u>Have you had these thoughts and had some intention of acting on them?</u>* As opposed to "*I have the thoughts but I definitely will not do anything about them.*"		
5) *<u>Have you started to work out or worked out the details of how to kill yourself? Do you intend to carry out this plan?</u>*		

6) *<u>Have you ever done anything, started to do anything, or prepared to do anything to end your life?</u>*	YES	NO
Examples: Collected pills, obtained a gun, gave away valuables, wrote a will or suicide note, took out pills but didn't swallow any, held a gun but changed your mind or it was grabbed from your hand, went to the roof but didn't jump; or actually took pills, tried to shoot yourself, cut yourself, tried to hang yourself, etc. **If YES, ask:** *<u>Was this within the past three months?</u>*		

☐ Low Risk
▨ Moderate Risk
■ High Risk

Patient Health Questionnaire-9 (PHQ-9)

Over the last two weeks, how often have you been bothered by any of the following problems? (Use "√" to indicate your answer)

	Not at all	Several days	More than half the days	Nearly every day
Little interest or pleasure in doing things	0	1	2	3
Feeling down, depressed, or hopeless	0	1	2	3
Trouble falling or staying asleep, or sleeping too much	0	1	2	3
Feeling tired or having little energy	0	1	2	3
Poor appetite or overeating	0	1	2	3
Feeling bad about yourself—or that you are a failure or have let yourself or your family down	0	1	2	3
Trouble concentrating on things, such as reading the newspaper or watching television	0	1	2	3
Moving or speaking so slowly that other people could have noticed? Or the opposite—being so fidgety or restless that you have been moving around a lot more than usual	0	1	2	3
Thoughts that you would be better off dead or hurting yourself in some way	0	1	2	3
Subtotals for office coding	0			
			Total Score	

If you checked off any problems, how difficult have these problems made it for you to do your work, take care of things at home, or get along with other people?

Not difficult at all	Somewhat difficult	Very difficult	Extremely difficult
❑	❑	❑	❑

Developed by Drs. Robert L. Spitzer, Janet B.W. Williams, Kurt Kroenke, and colleagues, with an educational grant from Pfizer Inc. No permission required to reproduce, translate, display or distribute.

Session 14. Using Medication in Support of Treatment and Recovery

Introduction

Significant research over the past 2½ decades has greatly increased our understanding of the biological mechanisms associated with substance use, misuse, and dependence and the biological underpinnings of certain mental disorders. This knowledge has helped to advance the appropriate use of medications in the treatment of substance use and mental disorders. Despite these advances, many disorders are not routinely treated with medications because of insufficient information provided to patients, stigma associated with the use of medications, or a lack of routinely available medication to treat the disorder.

The focus of this session is to facilitate a conversation with the patient regarding the benefits and potential risks associated with taking a prescribed medication to support treatment and recovery. While not all patients may need this support, there is evidence that a significant percentage of them benefit from medication. Medication can be used to address an SUD and/or the symptoms of a COD. The clinician is encouraged to maintain an approach that supports patient autonomy in making these decisions. Often what results from a conversation of this sort is not a full commitment to take a prescribed medication but at least a willingness to meet with a prescriber as part of a medication evaluation. This enables the patient to fully understand the potential benefits of medication use.

The Patient's Experience

In this session, the patient will participate in a respectful conversation about the possible benefits of medications, while being fully supported in the ability to make this decision on their own. They will learn with what symptoms or issues medication may help (e.g., intense craving or withdrawal symptoms in the case of medications addressing substance use), depressed mood, mood swings, problems with sleep, and anxiety or panic. The clinician will provide factual information, including handouts describing types of medications. This information will support the patient in their efforts to make a more informed decision regarding treatment. The clinician addresses the patient's questions and concerns and provide information only within the scope of practice. If the patient decides they are interested in either a medication evaluation or in actively pursuing medication support, the clinician will be actively engaged, advising of available and appropriate prescribing resources. They will offer to provide information to the prescriber in advance of the medication evaluation session but only with the patient's written permission.

Clinician Preparation

Session 14. Using Medication in Support of Treatment and Recovery	
Materials • *Clinician's Quick Reference* • *PHQ-9* (See Sessions 9 and 13 handouts) • *GAD-7* (See Session 9 handouts) • *Medications to Treat Opioid Dependence, Alcohol Dependence, Anxiety Disorders, and Depression* handouts	**Total Time** One hour **Delivery Method** MET-focused individual or group therapy
Strategies • Follow OARS. • Discuss decisional balance. • Disseminate information. • Support decision making and planning. • Coordinate care in support of medication evaluation.	
Goals for This Session • Discuss the patient's thoughts and feelings about the use of medication as an adjunct to treatment services. • Help the patient learn more about medications, their potential benefits, and the risks in the treatment of substance use and other disorders. • Support the patient's decision making regarding the use of medications. • When indicated, actively support referral. Provide follow-up when a medication evaluation is indicated and when medication is prescribed.	

Knowledge of medications and their role in treatment and recovery is viewed as an essential core competency in a clinician's professional development. Their attitudes and beliefs regarding medications should be minimized in these patient discussions. It is important for the clinician to remain focused on what may be of greatest value to this patient, as well as have access to reliable and correct information about medications and local prescribers.

If concerns for a co-occurring mental disorder is prompting these medication discussions, the clinician may choose to use a valid screening tool to gather relevant information. The most common CODs that brief treatment addresses are depression and anxiety. The clinician may choose to use validated screening tools (e.g., the PHQ-9 to screen for depression, the GAD-7 screen for anxiety). These are public domain tools readily available and easy to use (copies appear in the handout section for Session 9). Screening tools do not diagnose, but they help to better identify associated symptoms and inform clinical conversations.

If prescribing resources are available within the clinician's practice, it is important to know how to make an internal referral and shepherd that process. If a referral into the community is required, it is incumbent on the clinician to know of available resources and to be proactive in networking with these prescribers. Within the clinician's practice, it is often necessary to know the patient's insurance status because not all prescribers are on the panels of all insurers.

Session 14 Outline and Overview

1) Enhance rapport; discuss the past week, in general (pros and cons) and in terms of progress toward recovery goals; and review the weekly challenge.
2) Ask permission to discuss treatment options and provide the rationale for medication in support of recovery goals.
3) Explore the patient's thoughts, feelings, and beliefs about and prior experiences (if any) with medications.
4) Provide information as necessary.
5) Address negative perceptions of medications.
6) Facilitate patient reflection on risks and benefits of medications.
7) Facilitate a decisional balance discussion.
8) Negotiate a plan for next steps.
9) Follow up on a decision for a medication evaluation, when indicated.
10) Review and conclude.

Session 14 Protocol

If a patient has some awareness of medications that can support recovery, they may be actively seeking further information and referral. In other circumstances, where they appear to have limited knowledge about medications and, in the clinician's judgment, medications may be a useful adjunct, a more detailed discussion and feedback process may be indicated to explore this option.

Setting the Agenda

Patients have a wide range of knowledge, beliefs, and experiences associated with the use of medications. Discussion should be tailored to the individual. If the patient has no previous experience related to medication, the clinician may wish to initiate the conversation using characteristic MI approaches. They may simply ask at the beginning of the conversation to spend a few minutes discussing treatment options to provide some information and feedback.

> *We have talked about ways we can work together to address your [drinking or substance use]. One of the options we have not yet considered is for you to take one of the medications approved for treating substance use problems. There are no "magic pills" out there that will make recovery easy, but we do have some good medicines that help people who are motivated to make some changes. If you would like, we can talk about what some of these options are and consider them if this is something you want to pursue.*

When a patient has some experience with medications, they may be the person raising the issue. If this is the case, the initial work of the clinician is much easier. The clinician can ask open-ended questions. For example, they might explore whether previous experience with medication was helpful. Were there issues or problems taking medications? How long was the patient taking medications, and what led to stopping? The reason a patient discontinued medications is important to understand and discuss.

Through this process, the clinician can elicit beliefs about the acceptability and effectiveness of the use of medications. It is important to recognize any negative perceptions the patient may have. It may be possible to address any negative perceptions by providing more accurate information. Suggesting a reevaluation with a competent prescriber may also be helpful. It is always essential to stress the patient's right to choose and to make sure that the choice is made based on an understanding of the benefits, risks, and limitations of medications.

Asking Permission

> *One of the things you have been interested in is learning more about the options for taking medication that will help you with your treatment and recovery. Would it be OK if we took some time today to talk about this?*

Getting Started

Always begin with the patient, including their needs, knowledge, attitudes, and prior experience, and then talk about what a medication may be able to provide.

> *I would like to begin by getting a better understanding of what you already know about possible options for medication. I can fill you in on some additional details and what you might expect and try to answer questions you might have about these medications. My goal is to provide you with information about options and let you make a choice as to whether this is something you want to pursue further. If it is, I can help you find someone qualified to evaluate you for these medications.*

Addressing Negative Perceptions

There are many common reasons patients may be reluctant to take medications, including side effects, cost, inconvenience of taking pills each day, denial about the condition experienced, sense of shame or stigma about taking psychiatric medications, and negative influence of others. Among all medical conditions, there seems to be the greatest reluctance to take medications for SUD problems because of the negative perception of SUD medication.

When a patient is reluctant to consider medications, it is often helpful to explore their view about medications in SUD treatment. It may help to ask open-ended questions and to use reflective listening to fully understand the patient's perception before attempting to address the negative perceptions. A common negative perception might be: "Medication is not going to help me achieve anything that I could not otherwise achieve through just making up my mind or attending counseling or going to AA meetings."

Patients sometimes question whether there is a benefit to taking medications in addition to, or in place of, other types of treatment or support services. The counselor might explain that evidence suggests medication combined with counseling is often more effective than counseling alone in the treatment of opioid dependence, alcohol dependence, and nicotine dependence. While counseling and AA are both effective, the addition of medications may address certain neurobiological factors that promote substance use, improving the chances of positive outcomes and reducing the likelihood of relapse.

> **Patient (P):** *I'm afraid medication is going to harm my liver or some other part of my body if I do not give my body a rest.*
> **Clinician (C):** *Some medications may adversely affect the health of the liver or other parts the body, but these medications would not be routinely prescribed to patients with significant impairment in liver or other bodily functions. The potential harm that is caused by medications is usually much less than the harm caused by the uncontrolled drinking or use of other drugs. When patients show impaired liver function from medication, dose reduction or discontinuation is usually effective in reducing any of these problems.*
> **P:** *Medication is a crutch; I need to be completely drug free to be truly in recovery.*
> **C:** *Abstinence from drugs of misuse certainly is important. And being 100% drug free is an appealing goal for most people who have suffered through the disease of chemical dependence or other chronic diseases. Many people would choose to recover from the disease without the aid of medicine if there was a clear chance of success. However, our role here is to provide you with the best information we can to support your treatment and recovery. Often people who are active in the 12-step fellowships have strong beliefs about the use of medications. I would encourage you to read the documents prepared by Alcoholics Anonymous regarding the appropriate use of medication in support of treatment and recovery. Their approach is not anti-medication; rather, it is the use of medication appropriately prescribed.*
> **P:** *Some of these medications are addictive. Taking this medication is just trading one addiction for another.*
> **C:** *None of the medications approved for alcohol dependence are physically addictive.*

Agonist and Partial Agonist Medications

For patients concerned about the dependence potential of medications, careful wording is recommended when they consider replacement therapies (e.g., methadone, buprenorphine). While these medications produce physical dependency, the harm associated with unsuccessful treatment outcomes far exceeds the harm of taking the medication. Replacement therapies have a proven track record of reducing harmful consequences of opioid-dependence-related health problems, overdose, HIV infection, crime, and family and social problems. These therapies are also associated with an increased overall quality of life, along with an increased chance of achieving ultimate, complete abstinence at some point in the future.

Conclusion

Helping the patient resolve their ambivalence about taking medications for SUD treatment may take time within normal counseling sessions. Rushing the patient into a decision may elicit resistance and result in the patient committing to doing something they do not want. If the negative perceptions cannot be resolved, the clinician may choose to leave the topic alone but open to discussion at a later date.

The clinician should take the time to enhance their own knowledge about approved medications for treating SUDs. In the handout section for this session are informational materials on approved medications for the treatment of SUDs. Additional information can be found online at the websites of the National Institute on Drug Abuse, National Institute on Alcohol Abuse and Alcoholism, and SAMHSA.

If a decision has been made to participate in an evaluation process, it is the clinician's role and responsibility to facilitate this process. The passive suggestion of finding a number in the phonebook or on the Web or of handing someone a list of names and referrals is likely to yield little, if any, success. The important aspect of making a referral is actively facilitating the first contact. This scheduling process may often take place in the office with the clinician and over the telephone. After the appointment is set, it is important to follow up with the patient to ensure they have been successful and to troubleshoot when the plan is not a success.

Summarizing the Session

The clinician summarizes the content of the session, highlighting the major points and accomplishments. This may include reviewing the reasons the discussion of medication took place and the potential risks and benefits of medication, identifying any commitments the patient made to think about or pursue a medication referral, reinforcing any patient efforts, and clearly identifying activities the clinician has committed to undertake. When referrals are made, the clinician should promptly take care of any specific tasks needed to ensure the process is expedited.

The clinician lets the patient know that during the next session, they will follow up regarding what has taken place in the intervening time. The clinician reviews any assignments they and the patient need to complete in the days ahead.

Session 14 Handouts: Using Medication in Support of Treatment and Recovery

Clinician's Quick Reference to Session 14

1) Enhance rapport; discuss the past week, in general (pros and cons) and in terms of progress toward recovery goals; review the between-session challenge.
2) Ask permission to discuss treatment options and provide the rationale for medication in support of recovery goals.
3) Explore patient's thoughts, feelings, and beliefs about and prior experiences (if any) with medications.
4) Provide information as necessary about medication.
5) Address negative perceptions of medication.
6) Facilitate patient reflection on risks and benefits.
7) Facilitate decisional balance discussion.
8) Negotiate a plan for next steps.
9) Follow up on a decision for a medication evaluation (when indicated).
10) Review and conclude session.

Medications to Treat Opioid Use Disorder

The Food and Drug Administration (FDA) has approved three medications to treat opioid use disorder (OUD): methadone, buprenorphine, and naltrexone. Cost varies for the different medications, which may need to be considered when weighing treatment options.

Methadone and buprenorphine bind with the brain opioid (Mu) receptor sites (agonist). The person taking the medication feels normal, not high, and withdrawal does not occur. Methadone and buprenorphine also reduce cravings.

Naltrexone helps overcome OUD in a different way (it is also used to treat AUD). It blocks the effect (antagonist) of opioid drugs. This takes away the feeling of getting high if the problem drug is used again. This feature makes naltrexone a good choice to prevent relapse (i.e., falling back into problem drug use).

These three medications have the same positive effect: They reduce substance use. They come in various forms (e.g., as a liquid, tablet, wafer [sublingual], implant, or injectable). Methadone is taken daily, usually in oral form. Buprenorphine is taken either daily (wafer), monthly (injectable), or every six months (implant). The FDA only approved naltrexone to be administered monthly per injection to threat OUD, finding that taking it daily orally did not have the compliance rate needed and, therefore, lacked effectiveness.

Only SAMHSA-certified opioid treatment programs (OTPs) can dispense methadone. Buprenorphine must be prescribed by a health care provider (HCP)who has a regular Drug Enforcement Administration (DEA) license (required for all medical practitioners, pharmacists, dentists, and other health care roles); prior to 2023, HCPs needed a waiver. Pharmacies can dispense its oral forms, but OTPs must dispense the other forms. Any DEA-licensed HCP can prescribe naltrexone, but only the physician or qualified staff can administer it. Some people go to the OTP or doctor's office every time they need to take their medication. People who are stable in recovery may be prescribed a supply of medication to take at home, depending on the medication and their recovery status.

Sources

American College of Emergency Physicians. (2023, January 13). *X-waiver no longer required to great opioid use disorder* [News release]. https://www.acep.org/news/acep-newsroom-articles/x-waiver-no-longer-required-to-treat-opioid-use-disorder.

SAMHSA. (2021). *Medications for opioid use disorder. For healthcare and addiction professionals, policymakers, patients, and families.* Treatment Improvement Protocol 63. https://store.samhsa.gov/sites/default/files/pep21-02-01-002.pdf.

Medications to treat alcohol use disorder

Currently, the Food and Drug Administration has approved three medications to treat AUD:

- Acamprosate
- Oral and injectable naltrexone
- Disulfiram

Research has demonstrated that, including approved medications for the treatment of AUD, in conjunction with treatment, improves treatment outcomes. These medications have been found to:

- Reduce persisting symptoms of withdrawal that can prompt relapse (acamprosate)
- Help minimize alcohol cravings
- Help to avoid relapse
- Prolong intervals between slips or relapses
- Increase the benefits of counseling or other alcohol treatments

Acamprosate (Campral)

Acamprosate helps restore brain function damaged by AUD.

Alcohol causes intense but relatively brief withdrawal symptoms and much longer lasting but milder symptoms of withdrawal. Although milder, these enduring withdrawal symptoms (e.g., difficulty sleeping, irritability, anxiety) can lead to alcohol relapse.

Acamprosate helps motivated patients maintain abstinence by reducing the severity of these longer lasting withdrawal symptoms. Thought to reduce glutamate activity, its exact means of action remains poorly understood.

Advantages of Acamprosate:

- Acamprosate is not metabolized in the liver and so can be used by patients with liver damage or cirrhosis.
- It can be used by patients taking methadone or Suboxone (a combination of buprenorphine and naloxone) and by those requiring opiates for pain control (unlike naltrexone).
- It causes no withdrawal symptoms and can be stopped suddenly, if needed. It can also be taken safely with benzodiazepines.
- It cannot be abused and is not dangerous, even at overdose quantities.
- Side effects are generally minimal, and those that occur are well tolerated.

Acamprosate becomes fully effective between five and eight days after treatment initiation.

Oral Naltrexone (ReVia)

Patients taking oral naltrexone experience reduced cravings for alcohol and, while taking the medication, less pleasure when drinking alcohol. Since drinking does not make people on naltrexone feel as good, people who slip while taking the medication tend to drink lesser amounts.

Oral naltrexone is effective at helping people maintain abstinence or drink less. Studies of oral naltrexone have shown that, compared to people taking a placebo, people taking the medication:

- Have lower rates of relapse
- If they do drink, drink less often and drink less in a sitting

Advantages of oral naltrexone:

- Works well, particularly for people who experience heavy alcohol cravings and are motivated to maintain abstinence.
- Is well tolerated, causing few side effects; the most common side effect is nausea.
- Has no abuse potential and causes no withdrawal symptoms.

Disadvantages of oral naltrexone:

- Cannot be used by some people with liver problems
- Cannot be used by anyone using methadone, Suboxone, or requiring opiate pain medications
- May increase a person's vulnerability to opiate overdose by decreasing opiate tolerance

Injectable Naltrexone (Vivitrol)

Injectable naltrexone works in the same way as oral naltrexone to reduce alcohol cravings and to decrease the pleasures of alcohol consumption. While oral naltrexone needs to be taken daily, intramuscularly injected naltrexone works for a continuous month. With a monthly injectable dose, everyday compliance is not an issue.

Studies that have examined the efficacy of naltrexone as a treatment for AUD have consistently encountered patient noncompliance as a barrier to successful treatment.

The advantages and disadvantages of injectable naltrexone treatment closely mimic those of oral naltrexone treatment. The main benefit of injectable naltrexone is increased patient compliance. Some points of concern include:

- Possibility of an injection-site reaction.
- Duration of effectiveness means any adverse reactions experienced for 30 days.

Disulfiram (Antabuse)

Patients taking disulfiram cannot consume alcohol without becoming ill. Those taking this medication know this and so avoid drinking alcohol while taking it. Normally, alcohol is metabolized by the body into acetaldehyde and then into acetic acid. Disulfiram disrupts the final stage of this process (the metabolization of acetaldehyde into acetic acid), causing a much higher level of acetaldehyde in the body after any alcohol consumption.

High levels of acetaldehyde in the bloodstream lead to very uncomfortable reactions, such as the following:

- Hyperventilation
- Thirst
- Nausea and vomiting
- Chest pains
- Dizziness
- Confusion
- Muscle weakness

At higher doses, the combination of disulfiram and alcohol can lead to serious reactions that can include the following:

- Seizures
- Heart failure
- Respiratory depression
- Death

Does Disulfiram work? Studies have shown that disulfiram helps to reduce drinking days among those actively drinking but does not seem to work better than placebo in supporting abstinence. Patients who are supervised while taking their medication (to ensure compliance) seem to do better than those left unsupervised.

Disulfiram is not an appropriate medication for people with any of the following:

- Mental illness
- Poor impulse control
- Cognitive impairments

Topiramate (Topamax®, Trokendi XR®, Qudexy XR)
While the FDA has not approved topiramate for the treatment of AUD (it was approved to treat seizures and to prevent migraine headaches), some doctors also use it to treat AUD. It helps rebalance chemicals in the brain and correct the electrical activity of brain cells. Several randomized controlled trials found that low-dose topiramate, in conjunction with therapy, is well tolerated and effective in reducing both alcohol craving and symptoms of depression and anxiety present during the early phase of alcohol withdrawal. Studies also found that topiramate considerably helps patients abstain from drinking during the first 16-week post-detoxification period. As with the other medications, side effects occur (e.g., blurred vision, dizziness, drowsiness, confusion).

Sources

Agency for Healthcare Resources and Quality. (2016, February 16). *Medicines to treat alcohol use disorder. A review of the research for adults.* https://effectivehealthcare.ahrq.gov/sites/default/files/pdf/alcohol-misuse-drug-therapy_consumer.pdf.

Mayo Clinic. (n.d.). Topiramate (oral route). *Side effects.* https://www.mayoclinic.org/drugs-supplements/topiramate-oral-route/side-effects/drg-20067047.

Paparrigopoulos, T., Tzavellas, E., Karaiskos, D., Kourlaba, G., & Liappas, I. (2011). Treatment of alcohol dependence with low-dose topiramate: an open-label controlled study. *BMC Psychiatry, 11*(1), 1–7. https://www.ncbi.nlm.nih.gov/pmc/articles/PMC3062593.

SAMHSA. (2015). *Medication for the treatment of alcohol use disorder: A brief guide.* https://store.samhsa.gov/sites/default/files/d7/priv/sma15-4907.pdf.

Medications to Treat Anxiety Disorders and Depression

Anxiety disorders
Antidepressants, antianxiety medications, and beta-blockers are the most common medications used for anxiety disorders.

Anxiety disorders include:

- Obsessive-compulsive disorder (OCD)
- PTSD
- GAD
- Panic disorder
- Social phobia

Please note that new medicines for both anxiety and depression are always being introduced and/or their usage changed. To see the current medications (and their brand names) for these disorders, the National Alliance for Mental Illness regularly updates its list and descriptions of mental health medications. Also see the National Institute of Mental Health's list of mental health medications.

Antidepressants
Antidepressants were developed to treat depression, but they also help people with anxiety disorders. Medical providers commonly prescribe selective serotonin reuptake inhibitors (SSRIs)(e.g., fluoxetine [Prozac]), sertraline [Zoloft], escitalopram [Lexapro], paroxetine [Paxil], citalopram [Celexa]) for panic disorder, OCD, PTSD, and social phobia. The serotonin-norepinephrine reuptake inhibitor (SNRI) venlafaxine (Effexor) is commonly used to treat generalized anxiety disorders (GAD); the antidepressant bupropion (Wellbutrin) is also sometimes used. When treating anxiety disorders, antidepressants are generally initiated at low doses and increased over time.

Some tricyclic antidepressants work well for anxiety. For example, imipramine (Tofranil) is prescribed for panic disorder and GAD. Clomipramine (Anafranil) is used to treat OCD. Tricyclics are also initiated at low doses and increased over time.

Monoamine oxidase inhibitors (MAOIs) are also used for anxiety disorders. Prescribers sometimes prescribe phenelzine (Nardil), tranylcypromine (Parnate), and isocarboxazid (Marplan). People who take MAOIs must avoid certain foods and medicines that can interact with their MAOI and cause dangerous increases in blood pressure. For more information, see the section on medications used to treat depression.

Benzodiazepines and Other Antianxiety Medications
The antianxiety medications called benzodiazepines can start working more quickly than antidepressants. Benzodiazepines used to treat anxiety disorders include:

- **Clonazepam (Klonopin)** is used for social phobia and GAD; Clonazepam is an anticonvulsant medication.
- **Lorazepam (Ativan)** is used for panic disorder.
- **Alprazolam (Xanax)** is used for panic disorder and GAD.
- **Buspirone (Buspar)** is an antianxiety medication used to treat GAD. Unlike benzodiazepines, however, it takes at least two weeks for buspirone to begin working.

Beta Blockers
Beta blockers control some of the physical symptoms of anxiety (e.g., trembling, sweating). Propranolol (Inderal) is a beta-blocker usually used to treat heart conditions and high blood

pressure. Beta blockers also help people who have physical problems related to anxiety. For example, when a person with social phobia must face a stressful situation (e.g., giving a speech, attending an important meeting), a doctor may prescribe a beta blocker. Taking the medicine for a short period of time can help the person keep physical symptoms under control.

What are the side effects?
See the section on antidepressants for a discussion on side effects. The most common side effects for benzodiazepines are drowsiness and dizziness. Other possible side effects include:

- Upset stomach
- Blurred vision
- Headache
- Confusion
- Grogginess
- Nightmares

Possible side effects from buspirone (BuSpar) include:

- Dizziness
- Headache
- Nausea
- Nervousness
- Lightheadedness
- Excitement
- Trouble sleeping

Common side effects from beta blockers include:

- Fatigue
- Cold hands
- Dizziness
- Weakness

In addition, beta blockers generally are not recommended for people with asthma or diabetes because they may worsen symptoms.

Depression
Depression is commonly treated with antidepressant medications, which work to balance some of the natural chemicals in our brains. These chemicals are called neurotransmitters, and they affect our mood and emotional responses. Antidepressants work on neurotransmitters (e.g., serotonin, norepinephrine, dopamine).

The most commonly prescribed types of antidepressants are SSRIs and include:

- Fluoxetine (Prozac)
- Citalopram (Celexa)
- Sertraline (Zoloft)
- Paroxetine (Paxil)
- Escitalopram (Lexapro)

Other types of antidepressants are SNRIs, which are similar to SSRIs and include venlafaxine (Effexor) and duloxetine (Cymbalta). Another antidepressant commonly used is bupropion (Wellbutrin). Bupropion, which works on the neurotransmitter dopamine, is unique in that it does not fit into any specific drug type.

SSRIs and SNRIs are popular because they do not cause as many side effects as older classes of antidepressants. Older antidepressant medications include tricyclics, tetracyclics, and MAOIs. For some people, tricyclics, tetracyclics, or MAOIs may be the best medications.

What are the side effects?
Antidepressants may cause mild side effects that usually do not last long. ***Any unusual reactions or side effects should be reported to a doctor immediately.***

The most common side effects associated with SSRIs and SNRIs include:

- Headache, which usually goes away within a few days
- Nausea, which usually goes away within a few days
- Sleeplessness or drowsiness, which may happen during the first few weeks but then goes away; sometimes the medication dose needs to be reduced, or the time of day it is taken needs to be adjusted to help lessen these side effects.
- Agitation (feeling jittery)
- Sexual problems, which can affect both men and women and may include reduced sex drive and problems having and enjoying sex

Tricyclic antidepressants can cause side effects, including:

- Dry mouth
- Constipation
- Bladder problems; it may be hard to empty the bladder, or the urine stream may not be as strong as usual. Older men with enlarged prostate conditions may be more affected.
- Sexual problems, which can affect both men and women and may include reduced sex drive and problems having and enjoying sex
- Blurred vision, which usually goes away quickly
- Drowsiness; usually, antidepressants that make you drowsy are taken at bedtime.

People taking MAOIs need to be careful about the foods they eat and the medicines they take. Foods and medicines that contain high levels of a chemical called tyramine are dangerous for people taking MAOIs. Tyramine is found in some cheeses, wines, and pickles. The chemical is also in some medications, including decongestants and over-the-counter cold medicine.

Mixing MAOIs and tyramine can cause a sharp increase in blood pressure, which can lead to stroke. People taking MAOIs should ask their doctors for a complete list of foods, medicines, and other substances to avoid. An MAOI skin patch is also available and may help reduce some of these risks. A doctor can help a person figure out if a patch or a pill will work for them.

Sources

National Institute of Mental Health (NIMH). (2012). *Mental health medications.* NIH Publication No. 12-3929. Bethesda, MD: National Institutes of Health, Department of Health and Human Services.

NIMH. (2022, June). *Mental health medications.* https://www.nimh.nih.gov/health/topics/mental-health-medications.

Session 15. Engaging with Self-help

Introduction

Twelve-step programs (e.g., AA, Narcotics Anonymous [NA]) have benefited many lives since the founders of AA, Bill W. and Dr. Bob, first got sober in 1935. Although AA and NA meetings are occasionally depicted in films or on television, nothing is quite the same as the experience of attending a meeting firsthand. For people who are contemplating attending their first meeting, there is often a degree of anxiety. Discussion during a counseling session can reduce this anxiety and help the patient to be realistic about what to expect.

AA meetings can be held anywhere, but frequently they take place in public buildings (e.g., places of worship, schools)—accessible locations that usually have plenty of parking. Approaching the meeting location, one might see people gathered outside, chatting before the meeting starts or smoking, as many AA meetings are now smoke free.

The Patient's Experience

The patient will have the opportunity to learn more about 12-step self-help, as well as to discuss with the clinician the potential benefits of participation and any concerns regarding attendance. The clinician will support the patient's self-efficacy in this process, be knowledgeable about 12-step self-help, and be able to direct the patient to local community resources.

Clinician Preparation

Session 15. Engaging With Self-Help	
Materials • *Clinician's Quick Reference* • *What Happens in an AA (or Other 12-Step) Meeting?* handout • Up-to-date rosters of community self-help meetings (provided by Trainee)	**Total Time** One hour **Delivery Method** MET-focused individual therapy with psychoeducation
Strategies • Follow OARS. • Use EDARS, and identify stage of change • Link self-help involvement with increased social support for recovery. • Support patient decision making and plan to attend self-help. • Develop "real-life" practice challenge, and generate commitment.	
Goals for This Session • Clarify the patient's thoughts and feelings about self-help involvement. • Increase patient understanding of the role of self-help in recovery. • Build patient motivation and commitment to attend or at least sample self-help meetings. • Develop a plan for self-help attendance.	

The clinician should have accurate information regarding 12-step meetings in the community. This information is frequently available through the internet, and every state has a central service committee to assist with providing up-to-date meeting locations and times. Through state central service offices, a liaison to the clinician's organization can often be arranged to assist with aiding new patients and facilitating access to meetings.

If the clinician is unfamiliar with AA and NA, they are encouraged to:

- Read available literature
- Attend open meetings in the community to gain firsthand experience
- Become familiar with the basic tenets of self-help, along with the 12 steps and 12 traditions of AA and other 12-Step programs

Session 15 Outline and Overview

1) Ask permission to discuss this topic.
2) Link attendance in self-help meetings with enhancing patient need for improved social supports.
3) Discuss the patient's previous experience, knowledge, and beliefs regarding AA and NA.
4) Using MI skills, process patient ambivalence regarding participation in self-help.
5) Negotiate an agreement to attend a certain number of meetings to learn more.
6) Agree upon a concrete plan of activity in the coming week regarding patient attendance.
7) Summarize and conclude.

Session 15 Protocol

Following the engagement conversations at the beginning of the session, the clinician has several options to introducing this discussion. A first strategy is to link the discussion with often-needed enhanced social supports. The clinician may wish to introduce the topic by asking permission to discuss options for enhanced social supports. Following patient agreement while discussing this topic, the clinician then begins a discussion of self-help.

The clinician may begin by asking the patient if they have previous experience with AA, NA, or other 12-Step program, either directly or by observation. If the patient has previous experience, it is useful to elicit those thoughts and beliefs. If there have been positive experiences, a discussion using MI skills can support this conversation. If the patient has negative thoughts regarding self-help, the discussion can identify the feelings and help them work through them. The clinician may wish to offer information to the patient about the value of meetings and the different types of meetings.

If the patient is seeing some benefits and experiencing some hesitation, reflecting both sides can be useful, along with use of the **Readiness-to-Change Ruler** (Session 10) to further mobilize patient action. If there is agreement to "check out a meeting," it is best to secure a commitment from the patient to attend a defined number of meetings (i.e., at least four to six). It is also useful to encourage the patient to try several different types of meetings as this broadens exposure. Only after securing a commitment to attend meetings does it make sense to begin discussing dates and times of local resources in the area. It is useful for the clinician to have handouts for local meeting times and locations.

If the patient has agreed to attend self-help meetings by the end of the session, it is best to secure an agreement as to what will take place during the coming week. If the patient remains reluctant, the clinician may provide written information regarding meetings and ask the patient to read and consider it. Always, the clinician reinforces the patient's autonomy in making these decisions.

Session 15 Handouts: Engaging with Self-help

Clinician's Quick Reference to Session 15

1) Rapport building
   - Check in on past week.
   - If used, check review of progress worksheet.
   - Follow up on between-session challenge.
   - Assess progress.
2) Orient the patient to session agenda.
3) Link attendance in self-help meetings with enhancing the patient's need for improved social supports.
4) Discuss the patient's previous experience, knowledge, and beliefs regarding AA, NA, or other 12-Step programs.
5) Using MI skills, process patient ambivalence regarding participation in self-help.
6) Negotiate an agreement to attend a certain number of meetings to learn more.
7) Agree upon a concrete plan of activity in the coming week regarding patient attendance.
8) Summarize and conclude.

What Happens in an AA (or Other 12-step) Meeting?

Much of what this discussion describes has been synthesized from public sources describing participation in 12-Step meeting. For further information, some sources are What to Expect at Twelve-Step Meetings, Alcoholics Anonymous, and Narcotics Anonymous.

Most meetings take place in public buildings with defined dates and times. As a meeting begins, the chair usually asks if anyone is attending AA (or any other 12-Step program) for the first, second, or third time ever. The chair may then ask if there are any out-of-town visitors. The purpose is to welcome guests and newcomers. Individuals who are at their first AA meeting or have less than 30 days of sobriety may be welcomed with a hug and awarded a "keep coming back" coin or chip. The chair may talk for a few minutes and then call on meeting participants to talk or "share," requesting that they limit their comments to three to five minutes and restrict their discussion to issues relating to alcoholism and recovery.

Sometime during the meeting, the chair may open the meeting to anyone who has not been called on who really needs to talk, frequently referred to as a "burning desire to share." People who are called upon to speak usually do so by identifying themselves. For instance, "My name is Michael, and I am an alcoholic." The group usually responds with, "Hi, Michael," and then the individual speaks for a few minutes. If a person is called upon and does not wish to talk, they have only to say, "I think I will just listen today," or, "I'll pass." Another safety feature of the meetings is the absence of crosstalk or interruption. Unlike group therapy, AA members share their own experience, strength, and hope with each other, rather than telling one another what to do.

At some point, the meeting pauses for announcements and to collect funds for AA's Seventh Tradition, which states that AA groups are self-supporting through their own contributions. Cash donations of a dollar or two are usual, although newcomers are not required to contribute until they understand what AA is about.

Most meetings last 1–1½ hours. At the end of the meeting, the group members stand, join hands, and recite the Lord's Prayer or the Serenity Prayer, for those who care to join. With slight variations, this basic meeting format is the same throughout the world, varying only in language. An AA member can walk into a meeting anywhere and feel at home.

If you are interested in attending an AA meeting or any of the other 12-step programs, please call your local central service committee for information about a meeting near you.

At meetings, you may witness a lot of laughter and joking. People in AA are not a glum lot, and they insist on having a good time. The humor shows itself in an AA meeting, and newcomers are frequently surprised to hear members laughing about an incident that might seem grim or unfortunate. Usually, the laughter is based on identification with the speaker, as well as on relief that sober people are no longer getting arrested, crashing automobiles, or engaging in unmanageable drunken behavior.

Some people who have never attended an AA meeting express unease with 12-step programs because of "all the talk about God." In AA, "God" is to be understood as "a higher power"—interpreted in any way that works for you. Therefore, a "Group of Drunks" (GOD) providing "Good, Orderly Direction" (GOD) can be the higher power for the alcoholic if they so decide. AA is a spiritual program, not a religious one, and takes no position on political issues or controversy.

The success enjoyed by AA has been so great that many other groups use the AA model for meetings and the 12-step format. There are Gamblers Anonymous, Overeaters Anonymous, Cocaine Anonymous, Narcotics Anonymous, Sex Addicts Anonymous, Co-Dependents Anonymous, and Adult Children of Alcoholics, just to name a few. Of course, there is Al-Anon for the partners, family members, and friends of alcoholics. For the purpose of simplicity, this article talks about AA, but the word cocaine, sex, emotions, gambling, and so on, can be substituted for the word "alcohol" in the 12 steps of Alcoholics Anonymous, and other 12-step programs follow similar formats. Research also indicates that participation in 12-step programs increases an individual's chances for sustained recovery (Donovan et al., 2013).

The 12 steps
1) Admitted that we were powerless over alcohol (and/or drugs) and that our lives had become unmanageable
2) Came to believe that a power greater than ourselves could restore us to sanity
3) Made a decision to turn our will and our lives over to the care of God as we understood Them
4) Made a searching and fearless moral inventory of ourselves
5) Admitted to God, to ourselves, and to another human being the exact nature of our wrongs
6) Were entirely ready to have God remove all these defects of character
7) Humbly asked Them to remove our shortcomings
8) Made a list of all persons we had harmed and became willing to make amends to them all
9) Made direct amends to such people wherever possible, except when to do so would injure them or others
10) Continued to take personal inventory and, when we were wrong, promptly admitted it
11) Sought through prayer and meditation to improve our conscious contact with God as we understood Them, praying only for knowledge of Their will for us and the power to carry that out
12) Having had a spiritual awakening as a result of the steps, tried to carry this message to alcoholics and practice these principles in all our affairs

The 12 traditions of alcoholics anonymous
1) Our common welfare should come first; personal recovery depends upon AA unity.
2) For our group purpose there is but one ultimate authority—a loving God as They may express Themself in our group conscience. Our leaders are but trusted servants; they do not govern.
3) The only requirement for AA membership is a desire to stop drinking.
4) Each group should be autonomous except in matters affecting other groups or AA as a whole.
5) Each group has but one primary purpose—to carry its message to the alcoholic who still suffers.
6) An AA group ought never endorse, finance, or lend the AA name to any related facility or outside enterprise, lest problems of money, property, and prestige divert us from our primary purpose.
7) Every AA group ought to be fully self-supporting, declining outside contributions.
8) AA should remain forever nonprofessional, but our service centers may employ special workers.
9) AA, as such, ought never be organized, but we may create service boards or committees directly responsible to those they serve.
10) AA has no opinion on outside issues; hence, the AA name ought never be drawn into public controversy.
11) Our public relations policy is based on attraction rather than promotion; we need always maintain personal anonymity at the level of press, radio, and films.
12) Anonymity is the spiritual foundation of all our traditions, ever reminding us to place principles before personalities.
Copyright A.A. World Services, Inc.

Session 16. Using an MI/CBT Approach for Traumatic Stress and Substance Use

Introduction

Session 16 is a cluster of three staged sessions that address PTSD. The sessions may take place any time after ICBT Session 1 has been completed. This protocol is included here because patients screening positive for drug and alcohol use risk are at an elevated risk for having experienced trauma(s), "trauma-type" symptoms, and/or a full diagnosis of PTSD. It is essential for HCPs who are integrating behavioral and medical care to be ready to identify, intervene, and, if necessary, refer patients they suspect might have a history of trauma or stress-related disorder. The clinician should conduct initial and secondary screenings for trauma using the Primary Care PTSD (PC-PTSD) screen and PTSD Checklist (PCL) (handouts include military and civilian versions) as soon they identify the need, and the patient agrees.

The National Center for PTSD is updating PTSD assessment measures (e.g., PC-PTSD, Clinician-Administered PTSD Scale, PCL), to be made available upon validation of the revised instruments. Please see the Assessment section of the Center's website at www.ptsd.va.gov/professional/assessment/overview/index.asp for the latest information.

This guide integrates all MET techniques and CBT skills lessons to reduce the symptoms and interactions of trauma and substance use.

Diagnosis and Symptoms

According to the DSM-5, for a diagnosis of PTSD, the patient must:

- Directly experience a life-threatening event
- Witness, in person, the event(s) as it occurred to others
- Learn that the traumatic event(s) occurred to a close family member or close friend; in cases of actual or threatened death of a family member or friend, the event(s) must have been violent or accidental.
- Experience repeated or extreme exposure to aversive details of the traumatic event(s) (e.g., first responders collecting human remains, police officers repeatedly exposed to details of child abuse). Note: This does not apply to exposure through electronic media, television, movies, or pictures, unless this exposure is work related.

The events commonly associated with PTSD include combat or military experience, sexual or physical assault, serious accident, or natural disaster (e.g., fire, tornado, flood). It is helpful to note that the unexpected death of a family member or close friend from natural causes (i.e., not involving disaster or trauma) cannot cause PTSD. Traumatic events need to be clearly different from the very painful stressors that constitute the normal vicissitudes of life (e.g., divorce, failure, rejection, serious illness, financial losses). Adverse psychological responses to such "ordinary stressors" would, in DSM-5 nomenclature, be characterized as adjustment disorders rather than PTSD. The specific distinction for PTSD diagnosis is that while most individuals can cope with ordinary stress, their adaptive capacities are likely to be overwhelmed when confronted by a traumatic stressor.

DSM-5 symptom criteria fall into four broad categories: (1) intrusion (memories or flashbacks), (2) avoidance (escaping negative cues), (3) negative alterations in cognitions and mood (including numbing, persistent and distorted blame of self or others, and persistent negative emotional state), and (4) alterations in arousal and reactivity (including reckless or destructive behavior).

These symptoms must last concurrently for a month (or more) and be perceived as distressing or cause functional impairment. Regarding general health symptoms, there is evidence to indicate PTSD is related to cardiovascular, gastrointestinal, and musculoskeletal disorders. Several studies have found that self-reported history of circulatory disorders and symptoms of cardiovascular trouble were associated with PTSD in veteran populations, civilians, and male firefighters (Jankowski et al., 2019). Many trauma survivors exhibit symptoms consistent with PTSD immediately after an event; however, these rates drop by almost one-half three months after the event (Allen et al., 2008).

Prevalence and Types of Trauma

Overall Prevalence
According to the National Center for PTSD (U.S. Department of Veterans Affairs (VA), National Center for PTSD (NCPTSD), n.d.):

- Most people who go through a traumatic event will not develop PTSD.
- Approximately 6% of the US population will have PTSD at some point in their lives; many recover and no longer meet diagnostic criteria for PTSD after treatment. This number includes those who have PTSD at any point in their life, even if their symptoms go away.
- About 5% of the US population has PTSD in any given year. In 2020, about 13 million Americans had PTSD.
- Women are more likely to develop PTSD than men, with about 8% of women and 4% of men having PTSD at some point in their life. This difference is due, in part, to the types of traumatic events that women are more likely to experience (e.g., sexual assault), compared to men.
- Veterans are more likely to have PTSD than civilians; those who deployed to a war zone are also more likely to have PTSD than those who did not deploy.

A recent meta-analysis of PTSD studies (Schein et al., 2021) estimated that, in the United States, over 80% of the population will be exposed to a traumatic event at some point (Benjet et al., 2016) and that over 8% of those exposed will subsequently develop PTSD (Koenen et al., 2017). While recognizing that study designs, methodology, and populations differed across all the studies, the data suggest an elevated prevalence of PTSD in certain subpopulations, including women, emergency responders, and American Indians/Alaska Natives (Schein et al., 2021). Additionally, PTSD is often misdiagnosed due to coexisting mental health conditions (e.g. depressive and anxiety disorders) (Schein et al., 2021; Brady et al., 2000).

Racial Trauma
When working with patients of color, the clinician should remember that racial trauma can stem from a variety of causes, and many of these are not represented in typical measures designed to assess PTSD (VA, NCPTSD, 2021). When considering PTSD, clinicians often consider sexual abuse, combat, and life-threatening assaults. Williams et al. (2018) explain that many additional sources of traumatization people of color may experience are a result of racialization (e.g., police violence, racial threats, immigration difficulties, workplace harassment). Additionally, only two validated self-report measures of racial trauma include the Race-Based Traumatic Stress Symptoms Scale and the Trauma Symptoms of Discrimination Scale, with evidence of effectiveness of empirically supported trauma treatments among people of color limited, particularly for Asian and Indigenous peoples (Williams et al., 2018).

Gender and Sexual Identification/Orientation
Kimerling et al. (2021) noted that effective research and treatment of PTSD requires attention to gender issues regarding trauma exposure, traumatic stress reactions, and treatment of

PTSD. Numerous studies show that men and women differ markedly in the patterns of exposure to traumatic stressors, with the prevalence of PTSD among women at least twofold that of men, across a wide range of populations and nationalities (Kimerling et al., 2021; Seedat et al., 2009; Shalev et al., 2019). In addition, studies of LGBTQ+ individuals found that they are at higher risk of developing PTSD; prevalence estimates range up to 48% of LGB individuals and 42% of transgender and gender-diverse individuals meeting criteria for PTSD (Valentine et al., n.d.; Livingston et al., 2020).

Combat Exposure

According to the U.S. Department of Veterans Affairs (VA, NCPTSD, n.d.), between 11% and 20% of veterans who served in Operations Iraqi Freedom and Enduring Freedom have PTSD in a given year. As of this writing, as Russia continues to wage war against Ukraine and more citizens enter combat, researchers anticipate rising cases of PTSD in the coming years (Javanbakht, 2022).

Treatment Integration: The Opportunity of SBIRT

PTSD is often misdiagnosed due to coexisting mental health conditions (e.g., depressive and anxiety disorders) (Michaels et al., 2021; Larsen et al., 2008). In both clinical and community samples, many studies found a high comorbidity of PTSD with SUD (Michaels et al., 2021; Gielen et al., 2012; María-Ríos & Morrow, 2020). Approximately 36% to 50% of those that meet criteria for SUD also meet criteria for lifetime PTSD, and those with PTSD predictably have a history of SUD (Michaels et al., 2021, Brady et al., 2004).

The integration of behavioral and medical health presents an important opportunity to identify and intervene with patients, who may lack motivation to seek treatment. One reason people delay treatment is because "avoidance is the hallmark of PTSD" (i.e., PTSD hardwires people to ignore reminders of trauma) (Blum, 2022).

Treatment Types and Efficacy

Recent studies have examined the effectiveness of three main types of interventions: cognitive processing therapy, prolonged exposure, and eye movement desensitization and reprocessing (considered as a type of exposure), and combinations of these approaches adding MET. All these therapies are included in best practice guidelines for "frontline treatments" (Hamblen et al., 2019.). Previously mentioned in this manual, several of the newer therapeutic models (e.g., trauma-focused acceptance and commitment therapy) have demonstrated positive outcomes (Pohar & Argáez, 2017). When implemented with fidelity, these best practices result in successful outcomes in nearly half the cases.

These trauma-focused ICBT sessions focus on delivering a skills-based MET/CBT approach for the following reasons:

- Evidence to support effectiveness
- Delivery in a health care and/or medical environment
- Brief timeframe
- Similarity and use of several techniques in ICBT already described in this guide

The Patient's Experience

In these sessions, patients suffering from the effects of trauma will benefit from a nonjudgmental, helpful approach to understanding their current coping strategies, including substance use. They will become informed about the severity of their trauma symptoms and learn about the current science on the effects of trauma exposure. Patients will discuss how this "new understanding of the science of trauma" relates to their own experience. They may verbalize their ambivalence and demonstrate the emotional and cognitive barriers to making changes. Patients able to engage and commit to making change will learn how to (1) monitor internal and external triggers, (2) relax with different approaches, and (3) use cognitive coping skills. They will practice between-session challenges, use skills presented, and adopt those chosen as most helpful.

Clinician Preparation

Session 16. USING AN MI/CBT Approach for Traumatic Stress and Substance Use	
Materials • *Clinician's Quick References* for Sessions 16-1, 16-2, and 16-3 • *GAD-7* and *PHQ-9* (Session 9 handouts) • *PC-PTSD* and *PCL* (civilian or military, depending on patient) • *Sample Safety Plan* handout • *Deep-Breathing Relaxation* handout • *PTSD Fact Sheet* • *The Suicide Behaviors Questionnaire—Revised (SBQ-R) Overview* handout	**Session Length** One hour **Delivery Method** MET/CBT
Strategies • Follow OARS. • Provide trauma information. • Monitor situational awareness. • Incorporate cognitive coping/restructuring.	
Goals for This Session • Welcome the patient, and continue to build rapport. • Accurately screen the patient for severity of trauma, using the PCL-C for civilians and the PCL-M for military-based trauma. • Discuss the PCL results in a personalized reflective conversation with patient. Review results from a substance use screen (e.g., Alcohol Use Disorders Identification Test and Drug Abuse Screening Test [AUDIT and DAST-10]) to determine the extent to which the patient's trauma symptoms influence the misuse of substances and vice versa. • Increase the patient's knowledge of the biological, physiological, and psychological effects of trauma exposure. • Provide nonjudgmental understanding when discussing the patient's current coping strategies, including the use of substances; normalize the fact that many trauma survivors struggle to find successful and healthy coping strategies. • Provide hope and build positive expectations that effective treatment now exists, and, by working together, it will be possible to treat and reduce both trauma symptoms and substance misuse. • Reduce the patient's "overreactions" based on past experiences that are not adaptive for coping appropriately with present-day situations. • Reduce the patient's ambivalence to change and increase their willingness to adopt new coping strategies: relaxation and cognitive coping/restructuring. • Enhance the patient's coping skills that are specifically helpful in reducing both trauma and SUD symptoms.	

The clinician can use the ICBT session (s) techniques described below as soon as they identify significant trauma symptoms by appropriate screening. As in all ICBT sessions, no matter where a session ends, the structure of the session follows the law of thirds and incorporates rapport, review of progress, MET activity and/or CBT skills lessons, skill transfer/practice, between-session challenge assignment, and summary.

Sessions 16-1, 16-2, and 16-3 Outline and Overview

Session 16-1: Personalized Reflective Discussion Addressing Trauma and Substance Use
1) Welcome the patient and build rapport.
   - Assess the patient's readiness to proceed.
2) Introduce the topic:
   - Share the session model/approach. Include the main activities of treatment Sessions 1–7
     - Personalized reflective discussion addressing trauma and substance use
     - Safety planning
     - Learning a (de-stressing) relaxation technique (e.g., through deep breathing)
     - Psychoeducation about trauma regarding its effects and treatment options
     - Best pathways toward long-term wellness without substance use
     - Identifying, understanding, and monitoring for internal and external triggers
     - Coping reactions
     - Positive and negative consequences
     - Developing skills for working with feelings/thoughts to influence and realize healthy outcomes.

Note to clinician: If the PTSD screens (i.e., PC-PTSD and/or PC-C or M versions) have not previously been completed in the screening/assessment or in ICBT Sessions 1 or 2, conduct at this time, asking first for permission to do so.

3) Ask the patient for their reactions (feelings and thoughts) to completing the PTSD screens and whether any changes have occurred in their trauma symptoms and/or substance use since the last meeting.
4) Review and summarize results and risk levels of the PRS for substances and of the PC-TSD/PCL as part of a personalized reflective discussion (share and give the patient a copy).

Note to clinician: If the patient's symptom severity is concerning, the clinician is advised to seek further evaluation and consultation with a treatment team to discuss the appropriate level of care, medications, and other supports if indicated.

5) Summarize and elicit a between-session challenge (e.g., finding a pleasurable activity leading to decreased feeling of stress and increased feeling of relaxation not involving substances). Have the patient commit to when, where, and with whom they will complete the activity.

Session 16-2: Safety Planning, Deep Breathing Relaxation, and Psychoeducation
1) Welcome and build rapport. Review substance use and trauma symptoms and possible interactions. Review between-session challenge.
   - Introduce the topic.
   - Provide session rationale.
   - Briefly educate the patient on the effects of trauma (i.e., main symptoms); best treatment(s); and negative, long-term effects of using substances to reduce trauma symptoms (PTSD Fact Sheet).

Note to clinician: The primary goal of educating the patient about trauma is to help them better understand how (1) PTSD and stress-related disorders influence their feelings and behaviors and (2) using substances can interfere with their current and long-term wellness.

- Ask your patients what they know about the effects of trauma experiences in general and how the trauma is affecting them (and others).

- Since they are using substances, how do they believe the use of alcohol and substances is affecting their feelings and behaviors?
- After eliciting a personal discussion, ask the patient to specifically describe the most disturbing symptoms, or feelings and behaviors, they experienced recently.
- Describe ICBT session activities that can address these feelings and behaviors.

2) Introduce and explain the need to create a safety plan (*Sample Safety Plan* handout).
   - Explain the **Safety Plan** rationale: "Upsetting feelings may come up as you discuss daily feelings and stressors or even consider talking about the past trauma experience. I am here to help with this and anything else that makes you feel unsafe while you are involved the ICBT program."
   - Elicit and/or screen for past suicidal history (e.g., thoughts, incidents), and indicate that you will need to know how the patient will alert you if they feel unsafe, threatened, or at risk of harming themself or others (*SBQ-R* handout).
   - Assess the patient's past and current history of suicide, and determine the appropriateness of ICBT as a helpful intervention, as well as if there is risk of suicide based on past or current ideations or if intentions appear minimal.
   - Determine if it is clinically appropriate to continue and to introduce the *Safety Plan*. If the risk appears to be great, based on past or current suicidal or homicidal ideations or intentions, seek the involvement of a medical/psychiatric/crisis team for evaluation (prior to the patient's leaving the health care facility, if indicated).
   - Complete the patient the safety plan document specific to self-harming, suicidal, aggressive, and/or violent reactions. The plan should list contact information (names and current phone numbers with at least one person available any time (24 hours/day) and specific safe strategies the patient has used and/or can use to help reduce the emotional intensity of reexperiencing overwhelming trauma symptoms should they occur. Note: Let the patient know that they will be learning additional strategies in treatment and can add those if they are helpful later.

3) Introduce and practice deep-breathing relaxation (DBR), using the *DBR* handout, as a way of helping the patient tolerate negative emotions and reduce the urge to use substances.

4) Provide the DBR skills training. Make sure the patient practices and demonstrates initial proficiency. Elicit a commitment to a specific daily routine (e.g., twice daily for 10–15 deep breaths).

5) For more extensive relaxation training (with and without breath work), use Session 12 Using Mindfulness, Meditation, and Stepping Back, which includes many types of practices to generate a calm state of being to enhance wellness.

6) Distribute the *PTSD Fact Sheet* and explain that it is helpful when patients learn how HCPs understand the reactions to trauma and the current best forms of treatment for symptoms so the patient can help decide the best treatment plan.

Note to clinician: Express, when appropriate, that the patient's current trauma responses and coping strategies (including substance use, avoidance, or whatever they share) are not uncommon. Explain that research has found that while using substances or avoiding feelings for some patients has been beneficial in the short term, it is not helpful in the long run and is known to continue the trauma symptoms for longer than when other coping strategies are used.

7) In closing, summarize the session, reaffirm, and elicit a specific commitment to practice DBR daily. Assign the between-session challenge.

Session 16-3: Enhancing Self-awareness and Introducing Cognitive Restructuring

1) Welcome, build rapport, and review substance use and trauma symptoms and interactions. Review the between-session challenge (***DBR***).
2) Introduce the topic.
3) Provide session rationale.

📝 ***Note to clinician:*** Session 16–3 builds off ICBT Session 9. Refer to Session 11 for detailed descriptions of enhancing self-awareness and discovering new roads. See New Roads information previously mentioned. Whenever applicable, incorporate both trauma and substance use effects into the session's written protocol (use the Awareness Record).

4) Introduce and ask the patient to fill out the Awareness Record for the patient's trauma symptoms, substance use, and interactions of the two in the last month.
5) Ask the patient about at least three to five situations triggering trauma that affect their symptoms and/or substance use (functional analysis).
6) Discuss the situations to get a full understanding of the external and internal triggers, cues, and beliefs.
7) Scale the intensity of situations provoking trauma symptoms and substance use from minimal = 1 to overwhelming = 5, per instructions on ***Awareness Record***. Identify and prioritize skills and strategies to address the patient's trauma symptoms.
8) Conclude the session and discuss the between-session challenge. Elicit a specific daily commitment for patient to use the ***Awareness Record*** to monitor the external and internal triggers (intensity 1–5), behaviors, and consequences of any trauma-based cues and their responses.

ICBT Sessions 8 and 9

1) Introduce and deliver ICBT Session 8 (Working with Thoughts) and Session 9 (Working with Emotions), which focus on cognitive restructuring and coping strategies for reducing the effects of trauma.
2) For each session, integrate trauma-based reactions and substance misuse into the session outline and discussions. The Session 16 handouts provide a good example of the types of specific trauma-related additions needed to focus the ICBT intervention on reducing both trauma symptoms and substance misuse.
3) Generate a clearer, collaborative understanding of how the patient's inner and outer world leads to continued distress through the personalized reflective discussion. In Session 16, review situational analysis patterns for trauma-based reactions, substance misuse, triggers, thoughts, behaviors, and outcomes.
4) Once these triggering patterns are revealed in Session 16-3, follow Sessions 8 and 9 steps and handouts to work on reducing cognitive distortion and automatic thinking associated with trauma-based reactions and substance misuse.
5) Assign a between-session challenge associated with the session materials delivered. Include the daily use of both the ***Awareness Record*** and ***DBR*** between each session.

Session 16 Handouts: Using an MET/CBT Approach for Traumatic Stress and Substance Use

Clinician's Quick Reference to Session 16-1

1) Continue building rapport.
   - Check in on the past week.
   - Follow up on the between-session challenge.
   - Assess progress.
2) Orient the patient to the session agenda.
   - Personalized reflective discussion addressing trauma and substance use
3) Describe the model/approach for the trauma sessions.
   - Personalized reflective discussion addressing trauma and substance use
   - Safety planning
   - Learning a (stress-reducing) relaxation technique
   - Psychoeducation about trauma
   - Identifying, understanding, and monitoring for internal and external triggers
   - Developing skills for working with feelings and thoughts
4) Complete a PTSD screening, if indicated.
5) Review and summarize the results of the personalized reflective discussion about trauma and substance use. If completed, incorporate the results of the PTSD screen as part of the review discussion.
6) If indicated, seek further evaluation.
7) Summarize the session, and elicit a commitment to the between-session challenge.
8) Conclude session.

Clinician's Quick Reference to Session 16-2

1) Continue building rapport.
   - Check in on the past week.
   - Follow up on the between-session challenge.
   - Assess progress.
2) Orient the patient to the session agenda.
   - Safety planning
   - DBR
   - Psychoeducation on effects of trauma
   - Educate the patient on effects of trauma.
   - Elicit a personal discussion with the patient on trauma and substance use.
   - Ask the patient what they know about the effects of trauma experiences in general and how the trauma is affecting them (and others).
   - Ask how they believe the use of alcohol/drugs is affecting their feelings and behaviors.
   - Describe the ICBT session activities that can address those feelings and behaviors.
3) Introduce the *Safety Plan* and its rationale.
4) Screen for past suicidal history (*SBQ-R* handout).
5) Complete the *Safety Plan* handout.
6) Introduce, train, and practice *DBR*.
7) Distribute the *PTSD Fact Sheet*.
8) Conclude the session with the patient committing to the between-session challenge.

Clinician's Quick Reference to Session 16-3

1) Continue rapport building.
   - Check in on the past week.
   - Follow up on the between-session challenge.
   - Assess progress.
2) Orient the patient to session agenda.
   - Enhancing self-awareness.
   - Introducing cognitive restructuring (skills training).
3) Introduce and ask the patient to complete the ***Awareness Record*** handout.
4) Discuss and elicit three to five situations that trigger the patient's trauma symptoms and/or substance use.
5) Discuss situations for both clinician and patient to gain full understanding by using personalized reflective discussion.
6) Identify and prioritize skills and strategies to address trauma symptoms, incorporating a discussion of associated ICBT sessions/activities.
7) Individualize a patient plan by negotiating specific skills sessions and other indicated supports.
8) Summarize the session.
9) Assign a between-session challenge.
10) Conclude session.

PTSD Checklist, Civilian Version (PCL-C)

Patient's Name: _____

Instruction to patient: Below is a list of problems and complaints that veterans sometimes have in response to stressful life experiences. Please read each item carefully, and put an "X" in the box to indicate how much you have been bothered by that problem *in the last month*.

No.	Response	Not at all (1)	A little bit (2)	Moderately (3)	Quite a bit (4)	Extremely (5)
1.	Repeated, disturbing *memories, thoughts, or images* of a stressful experience from the past?					
2.	Repeated, disturbing *dreams* of a stressful experience from the past?					
3.	Suddenly *acting* or *feeling* as if a stressful experience *were happening* again (as if you were reliving it)?					
4.	Feeling *very upset* when *something reminded* you of a stressful experience from the past?					
5.	Having *physical reactions* (e.g., heart pounding, trouble breathing, or sweating) when *something reminded* you of a stressful experience from the past?					
6.	Avoid *thinking about* or *talking about* a stressful experience from the past or avoid *having feelings* related to it?					
7.	Avoid *activities* or *situations* because they *remind you* of a stressful experience from the past?					
8.	Trouble *remembering important parts* of a stressful experience from the past?					
9.	Loss of *interest in things that you used to enjoy*?					
10.	Feeling *distant* or *cut* off from other people?					
11.	Feeling *emotionally numb* or being unable to have loving feelings for those close to you?					
12.	Feeling as if your *future* will somehow be cut short?					
13.	Trouble *falling* or *staying asleep*?					

No.	Response	Not at all (1)	A little bit (2)	Moderately (3)	Quite a bit (4)	Extremely (5)
14.	Feeling *irritable* or having *angry outbursts*?					
15.	Having *difficulty concentrating*?					
16.	Being *"super alert"* or watchful on guard?					
17.	Feeling *jumpy* or easily startled?					

PTSD: National Center for PTSD. (2022). *PTSD checklist for DSM-5 (PCL-5)*. U.S. Department of Veterans Affairs. www.ptsd.va.gov/professional/assessment/adult-sr/ptsd-checklist.asp.

This is a government document in the public domain.

The PCL is a standardized, self-report, rating scale for PTSD composed of 20 items that correspond to the key symptoms of PTSD. Two versions of the PCL exist: (1) PCL-M is specific to PTSD caused by military experiences and (2) PCL-C is applied generally to any traumatic event.

The PCL can be easily modified to fit specific time frames or events. For example, instead of asking about "the past month," questions may ask about "the past week" or be modified to focus on events specific to a deployment.

How is the PCL completed?

- The PCL is self-administered.
- Respondents indicate how much they have been bothered by a symptom over the past month using a 5-point (1–5) scale, circling their responses. Responses range from 1 Not at All to 5 Extremely.

How is the PCL scored?

1) Add up all items for a total severity score.

   or

2) Treat response categories **3–5** (*Moderately* or above) as symptomatic and responses **1–2** (below *Moderately*) as non-symptomatic, then use the following DSM criteria for a diagnosis:
   - Symptomatic response to at least 1 "B" item (Questions 1–5)
   - Symptomatic response to at least 3 "C" items (Questions 6–12)
   - Symptomatic response to at least 2 "D" items (Questions 13–17)

Are the results valid and reliable?

- Two studies of both Vietnam and Persian Gulf theater veterans (Wilkins et al., 2011; Semage et al., 2013) show that the PCL is both valid and reliable.
- Additional references are available from the Psychological Health Center for Excellence.

PTSD Checklist, Military Version (PCL-M)

Name: _____

Unit: _____

Best contact number and/or email: _____

Deployed location: _____

Instructions: Below is a list of problems and complaints that veterans sometimes have in response to a stressful military experience. Please read each one carefully, put an "X" in the box.

No.	Response	Not at all (1)	A little bit (2)	Moderately (3)	Quite a bit (4)	Extremely (5)
1.	Repeated, disturbing *memories, thoughts, or images* of a stressful military experience?					
2.	Repeated, disturbing *dreams* of a stressful military experience?					
3.	Suddenly *acting* or *feeling* as if a stressful military experience *were happening again* (as if you were reliving it)?					
4.	Feeling *very upset* when *something reminded* you of a stressful military experience?					
5.	Having *physical reactions* (e.g., heart pounding, trouble breathing, or sweating) when *something reminded* you of a stressful military experience?					
6.	Avoid *thinking about* or *talking about* a stressful military experience or avoid *having feelings* related to it?					
7.	Avoid *activities* or *talking about* a stressful military experience or avoid *having feelings* related to it?					
8.	Trouble *remembering important parts* of a stressful military experience?					
9.	Loss of *interest* in things that you used to enjoy?					
10.	Feeling *distant* or *cut off* from other people?					
11.	Feeling *emotionally numb* or being unable to have loving feelings for those close to you?					

No.	Response	Not at all (1)	A little bit (2)	Moderately (3)	Quite a bit (4)	Extremely (5)
12.	Feeling as if your *future* will somehow be cut *short*?					
13.	Trouble *falling* or *staying asleep*?					
14.	Feeling *irritable* or having *angry outbursts*?					
15.	Having *difficulty concentrating*?					
16.	Being *"super alert"* or watchful on guard?					
17.	Feeling *jumpy* or easily startled?					

Has anyone indicated that you have changed since the stressful military experience? Yes ___ No ___

Primary Care PTSD Screen (PC-PTSD)

Description
The PC-PTSD is a 4-item screen that was designed for use in primary care and other medical settings and is currently used to screen for PTSD in veterans at the Veterans Administration. The screen includes an introductory sentence to cue respondents to traumatic events. The authors suggest that, in most circumstances, the results of the PC-PTSD should be considered "positive" if a patient answers "yes" to any three items. Those screening positive should then be assessed with a structured interview for PTSD. The screen does not include a list of potentially traumatic events.

In your life, have you ever had any experience that was so frightening, horrible, or upsetting that in the past month, you—

1) Had nightmares about it or thought about it when you did not want to?
   Yes/No
2) Tried hard not to think about it or went out of your way to avoid situations that reminded you of it?
   Yes/No
3) Were constantly on guard, watchful, or easily startled?
   Yes/No
4) Felt numb or detached from others, activities, or your surroundings?
   Yes/No

Prins et al. (2016).

Sample Safety Plan

Step 1: Warning signs (thoughts, images, mood, situation, behavior) that a crisis may be developing

1. _____
2. _____
3. _____

Step 2: Internal coping strategies: things I can do to take my mind off my problems without contacting another person (relaxation technique, physical activity)

1. _____
2. _____
3. _____

Step 3: People and social settings that provide distraction

1. Name _____ Phone _____
2. Name _____ Phone _____
3. Place _____ Phone _____

Step 4: People whom I can ask for help

1. Name _____ Phone _____
2. Name _____ Phone _____
3. Place _____ Phone _____

Step 5: Professionals or agencies I can contact during a crisis

1. Clinician Name _____ Phone _____
   Clinician Pager or Emergency Contact Number _____
2. Clinician Name _____ Phone _____
   Clinician Pager or Emergency Contact Number _____
3. Local Urgent Care Services _____
   Urgent Care Services Address _____
   Urgent Care Services Phone _____
4. 988 Suicide and Crisis Lifeline: 988

Step 6: Making the environment safe

1. _____

2. _____

The one thing that is most important to me and worth living for is:

_____

_____

Safety Plan Template © 2008 Barbara Stanley and Gregory K. Brown is reprinted with the express permission of the authors. No portion of the Safety Plan Template may be reproduced without their express, written permission. You can contact the authors at bhs2@columbia.edu or gregbrow@mail.med.upenn.edu

Deep-breathing Relaxation

Deep-breathing Relaxation	

Key Aspects	DBR is a well-known and widely used stress reduction technique. The essential elements include the following:
	a) Provide the rationale: relieves stress, can replace the need for substances, balances body chemistry, and helps calm and focus the mind. There are two parts:
	   1) Centering helps you reach a state of feeling present and stable.
	   2) The breathing technique helps you balance the breath for full inhalations and exhalations.
	b) After you have given the rationale, demonstrate centering and deep breathing, emphasizing the centering position and the enlarged abdomen, and then the chest expansion.
	c) Next, ask the patient to center themself. Have them get in a comfortable position, with both feet on the ground, and focus their mind on the core between the spine and belly button.
	d) Next, have the patient take a normal breath in through the nose and extend the exhalation out through the mouth.
	e) Coach the skill acquisition; repeat, "in through nose, longer out through mouth," 10–15 times.
	f) Talk with the patient about how it feels.
	g) Assign between-session challenge, suggesting the patient practice twice a day so the relaxation technique becomes automatic when needed.
	In the following scene, the clinician delivers the relaxation technique and coaches the attempts by the patient to adopt and practice the skill.

Relaxation Discussion	
Clinician	*You've told me you are most tempted to drink when there is a lot of stress, and alcohol almost immediately helps you stay calm.*
Patient	*Yes, but it has its downside. I do not get as much done so the pressures are actually worse.*
Clinician	*Other patients tell me that, too. May I suggest another way of dealing with your stress that other people have found particularly helpful?*
Patient	*Like taking some Xanax? It makes me groggy. I just fall asleep and still get nothing done.*
Clinician	*Actually, an even more effective way to relax is called deep-breathing relaxation. There are no negative side effects, and it can change and reduce your body's cortisol levels. Cortisol is one of the main stress hormones. If you want, we could take a moment now for you to learn and practice the technique.*
Patient	*Sure, why not.*
Clinician	*OK. First notice your breathing. Is it shallow? Is it quick?*
Patient	*Both shallow and quick.*

Deep-breathing Relaxation	
Clinician	*Watch as I demonstrate. [puts hands on stomach]. I breathe deeply through the nose and into my stomach, which gets larger; then to release the air, I simply let it flow out from my mouth.*
	To begin, I need you to begin to focus your mind and sit in a relaxing, but well-supported, position.
Patient	*Okay. I'll try.*
Clinician	*Try to sit with both feet firmly on the ground. Then, begin to breathe normally, focusing your mind on your core—the place between the belly button and spine. Let all your other thoughts go as you focus on your core.*
	Now just inhale through your nose, and, as you exhale, extend your breath out through your mouth.
Patient	*What should I think about?*
Clinician	*Just prior to breathing out, it helps to think of a calming word, such as "relax," or picture yourself in a relaxing Scene, like the beach or woods.*
Patient	*So, all I really need to do is just breathe air through my nose into my stomach. It expands, and then I release by slowly exhaling through my mouth. And do this 10–15 times.*
Clinician	*[Observing] Yes, that's right.*
Patient	*Okay, but it's weird to have you watch me breathe.*
Clinician	*Understandably, but I'll just get you started so you can do this on your own. Try to focus your mind on your core and relax. If you need to, place your hands on your stomach so you can make sure it expands when you breathe in and contracts when you breathe out.*
	Many people express it is harder at first but always worth the effort.
	It is best to practice twice a day for 10–15 breaths so it becomes more automatic when you begin to feel stress or experience a lot of pressure.
	What do you say you try this for the next few months, and we revisit this the next time you come in?
Patient	*This is bit stressful for me now, but I could see how it could help.*

Posttraumatic Stress Disorder Fact Sheet

What is posttraumatic stress disorder (PTSD)?
PTSD is a mental disorder that can develop after a person of any age directly experiences or witnesses a traumatic event (e.g., exposure to war, threatened or actual physical assault, threatened or actual sexual violence, violent crime or serious accident, natural disaster). Not everyone who experiences a traumatic event will develop PTSD. Among those who do, the traumatic event may cause mild symptoms in one person but prove devastating for someone else. The Diagnostic and Statistical Manual of Mental Disorders, Fifth Edition (DSM-5), classifies PTSD under Trauma- and Stressor-Related Disorders (American Psychiatric Association, 2013)

What are the risk factors for PTSD?
Risk factors include:

- Having direct exposure to a traumatic event, as a victim or witness
- Being seriously hurt during a traumatic event
- Experiencing trauma in childhood
- Having another mental health condition (e.g., depression, anxiety, substance abuse)
- Having a family member, such as a parent, with a mental health condition
- Exposure to combat or deployment to a war zone with or without exposure to combat
- Lacking social support from friends and family after a traumatic event

How often does PTSD occur?
Among the US population, 9% will have PTSD at some point in their lives. Approximately 10% of women and 4% of men develop PTSD at some point in their lives (American Psychiatric Association 2022). Approximately 8% of adolescents have met the criteria for PTSD in their lifetime.

What are the symptoms of PTSD?
Symptoms include:

- Flashbacks (reliving the traumatic event)
- Difficulty sleeping or bad dreams while sleeping
- Avoiding thoughts or feelings related to the traumatic event
- Being easily startled
- Angry outbursts
- Negative thoughts about oneself
- Distorted feelings like guilt or blame
- Trouble remembering key features of the traumatic event.[4]

How soon after the traumatic event do the symptoms appear?
Symptoms usually begin within three months of a traumatic event but may also show up years afterwards (American Psychiatric Association, 2022).

How long do the symptoms persist?
Symptoms generally last for at least one month. They may recur or intensify in response to reminders of the traumatic event, ongoing life stressors, or newly experienced traumatic events (American Psychiatric Association, 2022).

What treatment is available for PTSD? (U.S. Department of Veterans Affairs (VA), National Center for PTSD (NCPTSD), n.d.)

Treatment includes antidepressant medications, such as sertraline (Zoloft), paroxetine (Paxil), fluoxetine (Prozac), and venlafaxine (Effexor), and psychotherapy (e.g., prolonged exposure therapy, cognitive processing therapy, or cognitive behavioral therapy). Prolonged exposure therapy teaches a person how to gain control by facing their negative feelings. It involves talking about the traumatic event with a mental health or medical professional and doing some of the facing thoughts/memories the patient has avoided. Since the trauma. Cognitive processing therapy teaches a person to reframe negative thoughts about the trauma and involves talking with a mental health or medical professional about the negative thoughts and doing short writing assignments.

Psychotherapy usually lasts about 8–16 sessions. Medications can treat PTSD symptoms alone or with therapy, but only therapy treats the underlying cause of the symptoms. If the PTSD symptoms are treated only with medication, the person will need to keep taking it for it to keep working (U.S. Department of Veterans Affairs (VA), National Center for PTSD (NCPTSD), n.d.).

Which impairments co-occur with PTSD?

PTSD has high rates of co-occurrence, or comorbidity, with other mental disorders. Most commonly, comorbid diagnoses include major affective disorders, dysthymia, substance abuse disorders, anxiety disorders, or personality disorders (Friedman, n.d.). Dementia can also co-occur with PTSD. In one study of US veterans with and without PTSD, findings indicated that those with the diagnosis had almost double the risk of dementia, compared to those without it (Yaffe et al., 2021). While existing research has not been able to determine conclusively that PTSD causes poor health, some evidence indicates that PTSD is related to cardiovascular, gastrointestinal, and musculoskeletal disorders (Jankowski, 2013).

Which medical listings cover PTSD?

The Social Security Administration uses the following medical listings for adults (12.15; Social Security Administration (SSA), n.d.) and for children (112.15, Social Security Administration (SSA), n.d.), under the rubric *trauma- and stressor-related disorders*.

References

American Psychiatric Association. (2022). *Diagnostic and statistical manual of mental disorders* (5th ed., text rev.). https://doi.org/10.1176/appi.books.9780890425787

Friedman, M. J. (n.d.). *PTSD history and overview*. VA, NCPTSD.

Janowski, K. (n.d.). *PTSD and physical health*. U.S. Department of Veterans Affairs. National Center for PTSD. www.ptsd.va.gov/professional/treat/cooccurring/ptsd_physical_health.asp.

Merikangas, K. R., He, J. P., Burstein, M., Swanson, S. A., Avenevoli, S., Cui, L., ... & Swendsen, J. (2010). Lifetime prevalence of mental disorders in US adolescents: results from the National Comorbidity Survey Replication–Adolescent Supplement (NCS-A). *Journal of the American Academy of Child & Adolescent Psychiatry*, 49(10), 980–989. https://doi.org/10.1016/j.jaac.2010.05.017

National Institute of Mental Health. (2022). *Post-traumatic stress disorder*. https://www.nimh.nih.gov/health/topics/post-traumatic-stress-disorder-ptsd

Social Security Administration (SSA). (n.d.). *12.00 Mental disorders-adult*. https://www.ssa.gov/disability/professionals/bluebook/12.00-MentalDisorders-Adult.htm#12_15

SSA. (n.d.). *112.00 Mental disorders-childhood*. https://www.ssa.gov/disability/professionals/bluebook/112.00-MentalDisorders-Childhood.htm

Tortella-Feliu M, Fullana MA, Pérez-Vigil A, Torres X, Chamorro J, Littarelli SA, Solanes A, Ramella-Cravaro V, Vilar A, González-Parra JA, Andero R, Reichenberg A, Mataix-Cols D, Vieta E, Fusar-Poli P, Ioannidis JPA, Stein MB, Radua J, Fernández de la Cruz L. (2019). Risk factors for posttraumatic stress disorder: An umbrella review of systematic reviews and meta-analyses. *Neuroscience & Biobehavioral Reviews*, 107, 154–165. https://doi.org/10.1016/j.neubiorev.2019.09.013. (Epub 2019 Sep 11. PMID: 31520677).

U.S. Department of Veterans Affairs. National Center for PTSD. (n.d.). *Understanding PTSD treatment*. www.ptsd.va.gov/understand_tx/index.asp.

Yaffe, K., Vittinghoff, E., Lindquist, K., Barnes, D., Covinsky, K. E., Neylan, T., ... & Marmar, C. (2010). Posttraumatic stress disorder and risk of dementia among US veterans. *Archives of General Psychiatry*, 67(6), 608–613. https://doi.org/10.1001/archgenpsychiatry.2010.61.

The Suicide Behaviors Questionnaire-revised (SBQ-R) Overview

The SBQ-R has four items, each tapping a different dimension of suicidality

- Item 1 taps into lifetime ideation and/or suicide attempt.
- Item 2 assesses the frequency of suicidal ideation over the past 12 months.
- Item 3 assesses the threat of a suicide attempt.
- Item 4 evaluates self-reported likelihood of suicidal behavior in the future.

Clinical Utility

Due to the wording of the four SBQ-R items, a broad range of information is obtained in a very brief administration. Reponses can be used to identify at-risk individuals and specific risk behaviors.

Scoring

See scoring guideline on following page.

Psychometric Properties (Osman et al., 2021)[1]	Cutoff score	Sensitivity	Specificity
Adult General Population	≥7	90%	95%
Adult Psychiatric Inpatients	≥8	80%	91%

SBQ-R Scoring

Item 1: Taps into lifetime suicide ideation and/or suicide attempts			
Selected response 1	Non-suicidal subgroup	1 point	Total Points _____
Selected response 2	Suicide risk ideation subgroup	2 points	
Selected response 3a or 3b	Suicide plan subgroup	3 points	
Selected response 4a or 4b	Suicide attempt subgroup	4 points	

Item 2: Assesses the frequency of suicidal ideation over the past 12 months			
Selected Responses	Never	1 point	Total Points _____
	Rarely (1 time)	2 points	
	Sometimes (2 times)	3 points	
	Often (3–4 times)	4 points	
	Very Often (5 or more times)	5 points	

Item 3: Taps into the threat of suicide attempt		
Selected response 1	1 point	Total Points _____
Selected response 2a or 2b	2 points	
Selected response 3a or 3b	3 points	

Item 4: Evaluates self-reported likelihood of suicidal behavior in the future				
Selected Responses	Never	0 points	Total Points _____
	No chance at all	1 point	
	Rather unlikely	2 points	
	Unlikely	3 points	
	Likely	4 points	
	Rather likely	5 points	
	Very likely	6 points	
Sum all the scores circled/checked by the respondents. The total score should range from 3 to 18			Total Points _____

AUC = Area Under the Receiver Operating Characteristics Curve; the area measures discrimination, that is, the ability of the test to correctly classify those with and without the risk (0.90–1.0 = Excellent; 0.80–0.90 = Good; 0.70–0.80 = Fair, 0.60–0.70 = Poor).

	Sensitivity	Specificity	PPV	AUC
Item 1: A cutoff score of ≥2				
Validation Reference: Adult Inpatient	0.80	0.97	0.95	0.92
Validation Reference: Undergraduate College	1.00	1.00	1.00	1.00
Total SBQ-R: A cutoff score of ≥7				
Validation Reference: Undergraduate College	0.93	0.95	0.70	0.96
Total SBQ-R: A cutoff score of ≥8				
Validation Reference: Adult Inpatient	0.080	0.91	0.89	0.89

Permission has been provided by the developer. © Osman et al. (1999).

SBQ-R: The Suicide Behaviors Questionnaire, Revised

Patient Name Date of Visit _____

Instructions: Please check the number beside the statement or phrase that best applies to you.

1. Have you ever thought about or attempted to kill yourself? (Check one only)
   - ❏ 1. Never
   - ❏ 2. It was just a brief passing thought
   - ❏ 3a. I have had a plan at least once to kill myself but did not try to do it
   - ❏ 3b. I have had a plan at least once to kill myself and really wanted to die
   - ❏ 4a. I have attempted to kill myself but did not want to die
   - ❏ 4b. I have attempted to kill myself and really hoped to die

2. How often have you thought about killing yourself in the past year? (Check one only)
   - ❏ 1. Never
   - ❏ 2. Rarely (1 time)
   - ❏ 3. Sometimes (2 times)
   - ❏ 4. Often (3–4 times)
   - ❏ 5. Very often (5 or more times)

3. Have you ever told someone that you were going to commit suicide or that you might do it? (Check one only)
   - ❏ 1. No
   - ❏ 2a. Yes, at one time but did not really want to die
   - ❏ 2b. Yes, at one time and really wanted to die
   - ❏ 4a. Yes, more than once but did not want to do it
   - ❏ 4b. Yes, more than once and really wanted to do it

4. How likely is it that you will attempt suicide some day? (Check one only)
   - ❏ 0. Never
   - ❏ 1. No chance at all
   - ❏ 2. Rather unlikely
   - ❏ 3. Unlikely
   - ❏ 4. Likely
   - ❏ 5. Rather likely
   - ❏ 6. Very likely

Permission has been provided by the developer. © Osman et al. (1999).

Section 3

Techniques and Tools Supporting Fidelity of Implementation and Clinical Supervision

Introduction

Adopting and implementing any new clinical intervention in an existing community practice can be a daunting and challenging task. This section offers clinicians research-proven methods to reduce the burden on agency administration and clinical staff, while increasing enthusiasm and motivation for the new treatment. In addition to a list of acronyms the guide uses throughout, it provides basic information on fidelity, presenting a "best-practice" training model, describing essential clinical skills, and introducing a structured clinical supervision model. To ease implementation burdens and to enhance adherence to the essential elements of ICBT, the tools include a ***Clinical Supervision Agenda***, ***Clinician Session Review Checklist***, and ***Adherence and Competency Checklist***.

The science of implementation and dissemination is evolving rapidly. Research findings across large-scale clinical trials demonstrate that the quality with which an EBP is delivered can significantly affect patient outcomes. Quality in providing manual- or guide-based interventions is primarily associated with the term "fidelity," or faithful delivery of the model, which is defined by two components (Schillinger, 2010):

1) **Adherence:** the extent to which the intervention procedures are delivered as prescribed in the manual or guide.
2) **Competence:** the qualitative measure of skillfulness with which the primary intervention components are delivered.

Many clinical researchers have summarized findings on evidence-based methods for medical practices, SUD, COD, mental health, and juvenile justice systems, with the conclusion that fidelity is a primary factor in determining an intervention's effectiveness (Schoenwald et al., 2004, 2009; Wilson & Lipsey, 2005; Webb et al., 2010; Carroll et al., 2007). Contemporary investigations build on this earlier work that began nearly 20 years ago (Wiltsey Stirman, 2022; Kimber et al., 2019).

Like most effective manualized interventions, this ICBT guide contains essential elements in each session that must be delivered. Clinicians should prepare themselves by reading and understanding basic concepts related to structured, integrated interventions (i.e., MI, MET, and CBT) and by practicing the delivery of each session activity. The MET component of ICBT focuses on enhancing patient readiness, willingness, and confidence to change unhealthy behaviors. The

Integrated Motivational Interviewing and Cognitive Behavioral Therapy (ICBT): A Practitioners Guide,
First Edition. Joseph Hyde, Maria Torres, Win Turner, and R. Lyle Cooper.
© 2024 John Wiley & Sons, Inc. Published 2024 by John Wiley & Sons, Inc.

skills-based CBT components focus on building self-awareness in the patient, along with healthy avoidance, coping, and replacement skills.

Based on research on effective methods to learn clinical interventions (Martino, 2010), the recommended method of learning to use this model is as follows:

- Two-day exposure training, emphasizing session skills practice with feedback from an expert clinical trainer.
- Practice delivering each session, using checklists and session handouts (with colleagues and with patients).
- Continued feedback from an expert supervisor, based on session notes, checklists, and (preferably) digital or video recordings.

To deliver ICBT with fidelity, clinicians need to develop competence in primary clinical skills, including how to:

- Engage patients, build rapport, and increase readiness with MI techniques
- Choose, coach, and deliver needed CBT skills activities
- Provide the rationale for each session activity chosen
- Teach, model, and effectively transfer skills to the patient using session handouts
- Coach and motivate during the in-session practice of relevant skills
- Elicit commitment from the patient to practice the skills between sessions and in the future

To guide the delivery of the model, sessions are typically broken into three parts, following the "law of thirds" and 20/20/20 rule: (1) building rapport and review, (2) main session activities, and (3) summary and between-session challenge and commitments (Carroll, 1998). Session handouts are included for each, and session checklists help clinicians adhere to the essentials of the main parts. There are proven clinical reasons to deliver the MET sessions prior to the skills-based CBT sessions. However, the clinician may choose the primary framework of the intervention (i.e., number of sessions, session length, and session skill topics), depending on patient readiness and need.

Acronyms

AA	Alcoholics Anonymous
AUD	Alcohol use disorder
CAMS	Collaborative Assessment and Management of Suicidality
CBT	Cognitive behavioral therapy
CFI	Clinical Formulation Interview
COD	Co-occurring disorders
CSAT	Center for Substance Abuse Treatment
DBR	Deep-breathing relaxation
DEA	Drug Enforcement Administration
DSM-5	Diagnostic and Statistical Manual of Mental Disorders, 5th Edition
EBP	Evidence-based practice
EDARS	Express Empathy, Develop Discrepancy, Assist in Awareness of Ambivalence, Roll With Sustain Talk/Discord, and Support Self-Efficacy
FDA	Food and Drug Administration
GAD-7	Generalized Anxiety Disorder 7-item Scale
HCP	Health care provider

ICBT	Integrated cognitive behavior therapy
MAOIs	Monoamine oxidase inhibitors
MET	Motivational enhancement therapy
MI	Motivational interviewing
NA	Narcotics Anonymous
OARS	Open-Ended Questions, Affirmations, Reflections, and Summary
OCD	Obsessive-compulsive disorder
OTP	Opioid treatment program
OUD	Opioid use disorder
PCL-C/M	PTSD Checklist for civilians/for military
PC-PTSD	Primary Care PTSD
PDH-CPG	Post-Deployment Health Clinical Practice Guideline
PHQ-2/-9	Patient Health Questionnaire-2/-9
PRS	Personal reflective summary
SBQ-R	Suicide Behaviors Questionnaire
SDOH	Social determinants of health
SNRI	Serotonin-norepinephrine reuptake inhibitor
SSRIs	Selective serotonin reuptake inhibitors
SUD	Substance use disorder

Adherence Tools and Techniques: Checklists

It is recommended that clinicians review and use the session agendas, handouts, and checklists prior to meeting with the patient. The **ICBT Clinician Checklist** facilitates a general review of the session and helps staff keep track of progress. As an added convenience, this checklist can be easily transformed into the session clinical (and billing) record by changing the focus of Section 7. This is simply accomplished by incorporating session notes about the patient's engagement, progress, and other clinical markers of treatment success and by removing notes on the clinician's experience of the session.

The **Adherence and Competence Checklists** were developed by taking the Session Protocol and Steps at the beginning of each session and grading the delivery of each step on a 3-point Likert scale (from insufficient, through sufficient, to exemplary). For greater adherence to the model, clinicians are encouraged to use the agenda in combination with the **Adherence and Competence Checklists** to cross off each essential element while delivering the intervention. Supervisors are encouraged to review the checklists and note examples from the session discussion and activities while providing feedback.

To reinforce fidelity, clinical supervisors would be expected to model and show available videos portraying the MI-, MET-, and CBT-specific session techniques needed. To further increase competence, it is recommended that the clinician deliver 80% of the session's essential activities with a sufficient or exemplary status. To produce the most accurate assessment of clinical competency, structured interventions typically use objective information (e.g., digital, audiotaped, or videotaped sessions). Supervisors then listen to the recordings within weekly or biweekly individual or group supervision. This method ensures all staff are involved in building a learning community based on clinical skills and techniques, rather than on administrative details or other clinical material.

Clinical Supervision Techniques to Improve Adherence

Agencies adopting and implementing manual-based interventions like this one are presented with an exciting opportunity for changing the format of clinical supervision to include an emphasis on skill development, as well as on other clinical (e.g., when necessary, administrative) needs. This shift will also highlight the parallel process with the ICBT intervention, focusing energy on motivating change and on skill learning, even for clinicians. There is an added benefit when the supervisor and the clinician further understand the challenges of changing "routines and typical habits," which we are asking of the patient in session. We find having a framework for clinical supervision to also be helpful, as is the framework for delivering CBT sessions. The acronym BASIC and its essential components for the framework follow:

- Build Rapport
- Assess Readiness
- Select Strategy
- Instruction on strategy
- Commitment to use strategy

The BASIC framework provides an easily remembered pneumonic and fits in both individual and group supervision sessions. As illustrated in the more detailed agenda below, to pick a specific clinical strategy or skill, supervisors could review staff *ICBT Clinician* and *Adherence and Competence Checklists*, noting areas of strengths and needed improvement. Then, they can select from the MET and CBT skills list.

The detailed supervision agenda below also integrates the use of new training technologies or short video clinical skills vignettes. There are many video resources available on the web for illustrating MET and CBT clinical skills. This type of structured approach to clinical supervision clearly highlights the focus on learning, practicing, and monitoring competency in essential clinical strategies to improve outcomes.

Structured Supervision Model

① Step One	1) Build rapport; find out how things are going 2) Check-in on patients, general 3) Is there a case the staff wants to talk about because of concerns? 4) Is there a need for feedback and improvement?
② Step Two	Assess patient and staff readiness by reviewing the *ICBT Clinician* and *Adherence and Competence Checklists* Talk about specifics of the clinical session work What strategies have been delivered by staff? What strategies will now be helpful to the patients?
③ Step Three	Choose from the list of strategies below MI and MET • Building rapport • Collaboration • Increasing change talk • Working with resistance/unwillingness • Providing feedback (e.g., severity, problems, reasons for quitting, and motivation)

	• Goal setting • Generating commitment CBT Skills Development • Monitoring urges/cravings • Awareness training • Replacement activities • Mindfulness • Assertiveness • Emotions • Managing thoughts • Social support • Problem solving • Medication • Self-help
④ **Step Four**	1) State, "Let us watch a video that applies to that patient's needs" 2) Watch clinical skills video vignettes (one or two) 3) Discuss the strategy or strategies, and answer any questions 4) Role play clinical skills 5) Discuss how staff will deliver the skills for the patient next week 6) State, "Let us discuss how to use this skill in the next week with this patient"
⑤ **Step Five**	1) Elicit a commitment to practice and deliver using clinical skills in the next week 2) Staff commits to a specific date, time, and patient session

Continuing Structured Supervision

- Review the practice of skills in an upcoming supervision.
- Repeat steps one through five.
- Try another video and skill.

To summarize, while more studies are needed across all populations and types of disorders, it is evident that factors affecting implementation and dissemination in delivering ICBT and any EBP require attention from clinicians and supervisors. All developers of EBPs fear the pressures of "real-world" demands, including workforce factors (e.g., education, attitude, experience, and turnover), organizational factors (e.g., increasing caseloads, billing mandates, and record keeping), and the like will override the importance of fidelity.

The word "drift" is used to describe the difference between the intended delivery of techniques and tools in a guide or manual and the actual delivery. The ICBT tools and techniques offered in this section, along with the technical assistance available (web-based and onsite training), should provide sufficient user-friendly resources to thwart drift and to facilitate implementation and dissemination. As with any guide or manual, the feedback from clinicians and supervisors in individual or group supervision will be critical to ICBT's ultimate success in helping treatment to become a routine practice to enhance the quality of patient care.

ICBT Clinician Checklist Protocol

ICBT clinicians are encouraged to complete a brief checklist following each ICBT session. This checklist focuses on aspects of the session from the clinician's perspective. It can be used both to self-monitor the quality of delivery of ICBT and as a tool in supervision.

How to Complete the Clinician Checklist

1) **Patient Identification (ID).** This ID consists of the initials for your site and a number corresponding to the patient referred to you. Assign the number based on with which patient you are working. Please keep track of this number/ID in your records by keeping a sheet that lists the name of the patient and this ID.
2) **Clinician ID.** Insert first initial and last name (e.g., GWASHINGTON).
3) **Date of Session.** Use the following format for recording the date: MM/DD/YYYY.
4) **Approximate Length of Session.** Record the number of minutes you met with the patient.
5) **Session Conducted.** Please check (P) the session that was conducted with the patient. If you planned to conduct a particular session (e.g., Session 1) but needed to respond to an urgent situation or crisis, indicate this by checking the "other" space, and then describe.
6) **Please indicate which elements were used in your session.** Check (P) the strategies or elements you used during the session with the patient.
7) **Please indicate your experience during the session with patient.** Circle the number that corresponds most closely with your experience.
8) For these items, use the Likert scale (from 1 to 5) to describe your experience with the patient during the session. Each item asks about an aspect that clinicians are often able to describe regarding a session with a patient. We are interested in (1) how engaged you felt with the patient during the session, (2) how well you felt you and the patient were working together, (3) how smoothly you felt the session went, (4) your subjective sense about whether the patient benefited from the work during the session, and (5) your sense of ease with incorporating the behavioral therapy material with the patient during the session.
9) Finally, if you have any other comments to add about the session, please describe them in the space provided.

ICBT Clinician Checklist (Based on Today's Session)

1. Patient ID: _____ 2. Clinician ID: _____

3. Date of Session: _____ 4. Approximate Length _____ Minutes

5. Please check ("P") which session you conducted today:

☐ MET1, Life Movie	☐ MET2, Awareness Record	☐ MET3, Social Support
☐ CBT, Awareness	☐ CBT, Just Thoughts	☐ CBT Problem-Solving
☐ CBT, Urges/Cravings	☐ CBT, Assertiveness	☐ CBT, Emotions
☐ CBT, Mindfulness	☐ CBT, Wellness Planning	☐ CBT, Replacement Activities
☐ Self-help	☐ Medication	
☐ Other, describe:_____		

ICBT Clinician Checklist Protocol | 285

6. Please check ("P") any of the following that were elements of your session with this patient.

☐ Life Movie	☐ Awareness Record
☐ Supporter/Family member	☐ Emotions
☐ Mindfulness or meditation	☐ Reviewed information on cravings/coping
☐ Thoughts/Cognitive distortions	☐ Problem solving
☐ Assertiveness	☐ Plan for handling a high-risk situation
☐ Plan for coping with a lapse or slip	☐ Gave between-session challenge
☐ Discussed termination issues	☐ Provided referral information
☐ Addressed a crisis with the patient	☐ Thoughts about alcohol/Substance use

7. Indicate your experience of the session with the patient (circle number that best fits)

I felt engaged in session with patient.				I felt somewhat removed.
1	2	3	4	5

Patient and I seemed to be working well.				Patient and I had difficulty connecting.
1	2	3	4	5

Session went smoothly.				Session felt fragmented.
1	2	3	4	5

Patient seemed to benefit from session.				I'm not sure whether patient benefited.
1	2	3	4	5

It was relatively easy to incorporate ICBT material.				It was difficult to incorporate ICBT material.
1	2	3	4	5

8. Comments

Adherence and Competence Checklist Protocol

This checklist provides a succinct method for evaluating the extent to which the clinician delivers the essential elements of each session. Both clinical supervisors and clinicians will find it a useful tool in helping to provide specific direction for how the session should be delivered to avoid drift. Many clinicians print these checklists prior to delivering the session and use them as agendas to check as they go through each activity. Clinical supervisors are advised to complete the ***Adherence and Competence Checklist*** following a review of any session recorded. As the ***Supervision Agenda*** above illustrates, the tool can also be used for ongoing supervision/training in both individual and group formats. The following recommendations may help supervisors discuss and review competency:

1) Focus first on the clinician's strengths in delivering the session.
2) Discuss the therapeutic alliance and patient factors (e.g., engagement, readiness, and motivation).
3) Next, describe the overall quality in delivering the basic structure of the session including the law of thirds or 20/20/20 rule, providing rationales, teaching/transferring main skill, skill demonstration and practice, eliciting commitment to practice between sessions, etc.
4) Use the competency ratings for each specific element (checklist row) to provide feedback on how to further refine the technique.
5) Teach through written examples, video examples, and role plays.
6) Elicit a commitment to incorporate feedback in upcoming sessions.

Adherence and Competence Checklists

ICBT Session 1: Eliciting the Life Movie Adherence and Competence Checklist

Client ID _____   Date _____

To what extent did you demonstrate the following:	Extensively	Sufficiently	Missed Opportunity
1) Build rapport between clinician and patient	☐	☐	☐
2) Review Treatment Information Sheet and discuss expectations	☐	☐	☐
3) Orient patient to session agenda and rationale for session activity	☐	☐	☐
4) Facilitate the "Eliciting the Life Movie" discussion, exploring multiple domains of the patient's life	☐	☐	☐
5) Explore patient attitudes about change, including ambivalent attitudes	☐	☐	☐
6) Affirm readiness for change and change strategies	☐	☐	☐
7) Summarize the "Life Movie" discussion, emphasizing change talk and patient values that support change	☐	☐	☐
8) Negotiate between-session challenge focused on having patient complete the "Change Plan" handout and/or commit to using or engaging 1–2 coping strategies	☐	☐	☐
9) Summarize motivation, review, and conclude session	☐	☐	☐

MI Skills and Strategies Practiced

To what extent did you demonstrate the following:	Extensively	Sufficiently	Missed Opportunity
1) MI Spirit (evocation, collaboration, compassion, autonomy)	☐	☐	☐
2) OARS (including complex reflections)	☐	☐	☐
3) Change Talk strategies (i.e., used one or more of pros and cons, readiness-to-change rulers, looking forward/backward, and going to extremes)	☐	☐	☐
4) Ratio of clinician-to-patient talk	30/70	50/50	70/30

Comments _____

Name _____

Reviewer _____ Date _____

ICBT Sessions 2–16: Fidelity Monitoring Form

Client ID _____   Date _____

To what extent did you demonstrate the following:	Extensively	Sufficiently	Missed Opportunity
1) Strengthen rapport	☐	☐	☐
2) Review progress	☐	☐	☐
3) Review between-session challenge	☐	☐	☐
4) Provide rationale	☐	☐	☐
5) Teach session skill	☐	☐	☐
6) Lead demonstration/Role play	☐	☐	☐
7) Facilitate patient-led practice (assess skills transfer)	☐	☐	☐
8) Identify real-world application	☐	☐	☐
9) Negotiate and prepare between-session challenge	☐	☐	☐
10) Elicit commitment	☐	☐	☐
11) Summarize and conclude the session	☐	☐	☐

MI Skills and Strategies Practiced
As a reminder, consider to what degree you demonstrated the following:

- MI spirit (evocation, collaboration, compassion, and autonomy)
- OARS (including complex reflections)
- Change talk strategies (i.e., used one or more of pros and cons, readiness-to-change rulers, looking forward/backward, and going to extremes)
- Ratio of clinician-to-patient talk: Goal 30/70

Comments _____

Name _____

Reviewer _____   Date _____

References

Addis, M. E., & Mahalik, J. R. (2003). Men, masculinity, and the contexts of help seeking. *American Psychologist*, *58*(1), 5–14. https://doi.org/10.1037/0003-066X.58.1.5

Agostinelli, G., Brown, J. M., & Miller, W. R. (1995). Effects of normative feedback on consumption among heavy drinking college students. *Journal of Drug Education*, *25*(1), 31–40. https://doi.org/10.2190/XD56-D6WR-7195-EAL3

Alegria, M., Atkins, M., Farmer, E., Slaton, E., & Stelk, W. (2010). One size does not fit all: Taking diversity, culture and context seriously. *Administration and Policy in Mental Health and Mental Health Services Research*, *37*(1), 48–60. https://doi.org/10.1007/s10488-010-0283-2

Alegria, M., Chatterji, P., Wells, K., Cao, Z., Chen, C. N., Takeuchi, D., Jackson, J., & Meng, X. L. (2008). Disparity in depression treatment among racial and ethnic minority populations in the United States. *Psychiatric Services*, *59*(11), 1264–1272. https://doi.org/10.1176/ps.2008.59.11.1264

Alegria, M., Nakash, O., Johnson, K., Ault-Brutus, A., Carson, N., Fillbrunn, M., Wang, Y., Cheng, A., Harris, T., & Polo, A. (2018). Effectiveness of the decide interventions on shared decision making and perceived quality of care in behavioral health with multicultural patients: A randomized clinical trial. *JAMA Psychiatry*, *75*(4), 325–335. https://doi.org/10.1001/jamapsychiatry.2017.4585

Allen, L. B., McHugh, R. K., & Barlow, D. H. (2008). Emotional disorders: A unified protocol. In D. H. Barlow (Ed.), *Clinical handbook of psychological disorders: A step-by-step treatment manual* (pp. 216–249). The Guilford Press.

American Psychiatric Association. (2013). *Diagnostic and statistical manual of mental disorders* 5th ed.

American Psychiatric Association. (2022). *Diagnostic and statistical manual of mental disorders*, 5th ed., text rev., https://doi.org/10.1176/appi.books.9780890425787

Atkins Jr., R. G., & Hawdon, J. E. (2007). Religiosity and participation in mutual-aid support groups for addiction. *Journal of Substance Abuse Treatment*, *33*(3), 321–331.

Barlow, D., (2008). *Clinical handbook of psychological disorders: A step-by-step treatment manual*, 4th ed. Guilford Press.

Benjet, C., Bromet, E., Karam, E. G., Kessler, R. C., McLaughlin, K. A., Ruscio, A. M., ... & Koenen, K. C. (2016). The epidemiology of traumatic event exposure worldwide: Results from the World Mental Health Survey Consortium. *Psychological Medicine*, *46*(2), 327–343. https://doi.org/10.1017/S0033291715001981

Betancourt, J. R. (2003). Cross-cultural medical education: Conceptual approaches and frameworks for evaluation. *Academic Medicine, 78*(6), 560–569. https://doi.org/10.1097/00001888-200306000-00004

Blum, D. (2022 April 22). A private war: Why PTSD is still overlooked. *The New York Times.* https://www.nytimes.com/2022/04/04/well/mind/ptsd-trauma-symptoms.html.

Brady, K. T., Back, S. E., & Coffey, S. F. (2004). Substance abuse and posttraumatic stress disorder. *Current Directions in Psychological Science, 13*(5), 206–209. https://doi.org/10.1111/j.0963-7214.2004.00309.x

Brady, K. T., Killeen, T. K., Brewerton, T., & Lucerini, S. (2000). Comorbidity of psychiatric disorders and posttraumatic stress disorder. *Journal of Clinical Psychiatry, 61,* 22–32. https://www.psychiatrist.com/read-pdf/3403

Buber, M. (1971). *I and thou.* (W. Kaufman, Trans.). Scribner's.

Carroll, C., Patterson, M., Wood, S., Booth, A., Rick, J., & Balain, S. (2007). A conceptual framework for implementation fidelity. *Implementation Science, 2,* 1–9. https://doi.org/10.1186/1748-5908-2-40

Carroll, K. M. (1996). Relapse prevention as a psychosocial treatment: A review of controlled clinical trials. *Experimental and Clinical Psychopharmacology, 4*(1), 46–54.

Carroll, K. M. (1998). A cognitive-behavioral approach: Treating cocaine addiction. *Manual 1: Therapy Manuals for Drug Addiction Series.* NIH Publication No. 94-4308. U.S. Department of Health and Human Services, National Institute on Drug Abuse. https://archives.drugabuse.gov/sites/default/files/cbt.pdf

Center for Substance Abuse Treatment. (1999). *Brief interventions and brief therapies for substance abuse.* Treatment Improvement Protocol (TIP) Series 34. HHS Publication No. (SMA). Substance Abuse and Mental Health Services Administration (SAMHSA). https://store.samhsa.gov/product/TIP-34-Brief-Interventions-and-Brief-Therapies-for-Substance-Abuse/SMA12-3952

Center for Substance Abuse Treatment (1999). *Brief interventions and brief therapies for substance abuse.* Rockville, MD: Substance Abuse and Mental Health Services Administration (US). Report No.: (SMA) 99-3353. PMID: 22514840.

Centers for Disease Control and Prevention. (2022). *Facts about suicide.* https://www.cdc.gov/suicide/facts/index.html

Chiles, J. A., Strosahl, K. D., & Roberts, L. W. (2018). *Clinical manual for assessment and treatment of suicidal patients,* 2nd ed. American Psychiatric Association.

Chorpita, B. F., Daleiden, E., & Weisz, J. R. (2005). Identifying and selecting the common elements of evidence-based interventions: A distillation and matching model. *Mental Health Services Research, 7,* 5–20. https://doi.org/10.1007/s11020-005-1962-6

Chorpita, B. F., & Regan, J. (2009). Dissemination of effective mental health treatment procedures: Maximizing the return on a significant investment. *Behaviour Research and Therapy, 47,* 990–993. https://doi.org/10.1016/j.brat.2009.07.002

Colby, S. L., & Ortman, J. M. (2015). Projections of the size and composition of the U.S. population: 2014 to 2060. Population estimates and projections. *Current Population Reports.* P25-1143. U.S. Census Bureau. https://www.census.gov/content/dam/Census/library/publications/2015/demo/p25-1143.pdf

Cooke, R. A., & Szumal, J. L. (1993). Measuring normative beliefs and shared behavioral expectations in organizations: The reliability and validity of the Organizational Culture Inventory. *Psychological Reports, 72*(3_suppl), 1299–1330. https://doi.org/10.2466/pr0.1993.72.3c.1299

Crosby, A. E., Han, B., Ortega, L. A., Parks, S. E., Gfroerer, J., & Centers for Disease Control and Prevention (CDC). (2011). Suicidal thoughts and behaviors among adults aged ≥18 years—United States, 2008–2009. *MMWR Surveillance Summaries, 60*(13), 1–22. PMID: 22012169.

Davis, T. M., Baer, J. S., Saxon, A. J., & Kivlahan, D. R. (2003). Brief motivational feedback improves post-incarceration treatment contact among veterans with substance use disorders. *Drug and Alcohol Dependence, 69,* 197–203. https://doi.org/10.1016/S0376-8716(02)00317-4

Donovan, D. M., Ingalsbe, M. H., Benbow, J., & Daley, D. C. (2013). 12-Step interventions and mutual support programs for substance use disorders: An overview. *Social Work in Public Health, 28*(3–4), 313–332. https://doi.org/10.1080/19371918.2013.774663

D'Zurilla, T. J., & Goldfried, M. R. (1971). Problem solving and behavior modification. *Journal of Abnormal Psychology, 78*(1), 107–26. https://doi.org/10.1037/h0031360

Emery, G. (1981). Cognitive therapy with the elderly. In G. Emery, S. D. Hollon, & R. C. Bedrosian (Eds.). *New directions in cognitive therapy: A casebook* (pp. 84–98). Guilford Press.

Friedman, M. J. (2013) Finalizing PTSD in DSM-5: getting here from there and where to go next. *J Trauma Stress., 26*(5), 548–56. doi: 10.1002/jts.21840. PMID: 24151001.

Fredrickson, B. L. (2000). Cultivating positive emotions for optimizing health and well-being. *Prevention and Treatment, 3*(1), 1. https://doi.org/10.1037/1522-3736.3.1.31a

Freedman, D. A. (1999). Ecological inference and the ecological fallacy. *International Encyclopedia of the Social & Behavioral Sciences, 6*(4027–4030), 1–7. https://www.stat.berkeley.edu/users/census/549.pdf

Fromm, E. (2007). *Art of loving*. Joanna Cotler Books.

Gainsbury, S. M. (2017). Cultural competence in the treatment of addictions: Theory, practice and evidence. *Clinical Psychology & Psychotherapy, 24*(4), 987–1001. https://doi.org/10.1002/cpp.2062

Gielen, N., Havermans, R., Tekelenburg, M., & Jansen, A. (2012). Prevalence of post-traumatic stress disorder among patients with substance use disorder: It is higher than clinicians think it is. *European Journal of Psychotraumatology, 3*(1), 17734. https://doi.org/10.3402/ejpt.v3i0.17734

Goleman, D. (Ed.). (2003). *Healing emotions: Conversations with the Dalai Lama on mindfulness, emotions, and health*. Shambhala Publishing.

Hamblen, J. L., Norman, S. B., Sonis, J. H., Phelps, A. J., Bisson, J. I., Nunes, V. D., Megnin-Viggars, O., Forbes, D., Riggs, D. S., & Schnurr, P. P. (2019). A guide to guidelines for the treatment of posttraumatic stress disorder in adults: An update. *Psychotherapy (Chic.), 56*(3), 359–373. https://doi.org/10.1037/pst0000231. PMID: 31282712

Harris, R. (2009). *ACT Made Simple: An Easy-To-Read Primer on Acceptance and Commitment Therapy*. New Harbinger Publications.

Harris, R. (2021). *Trauma-focused ACT: A practitioner's guide to working with mind, body, and emotion using acceptance and commitment therapy*. New Harbinger Publications.

Hayes, S. C., & Hofmann, S. G. (Eds.) (2018). *Process-based CBT: The science and core clinical competencies of cognitive behavioral therapy*. New Harbinger Publications.

Hayes, S. C., Levin, M. E., Plumb-Vilardaga, J., Villatte, J. L., & Pistorello, J. (2013). Acceptance and commitment therapy and contextual behavioral science: Examining the progress of a distinctive model of behavioral and cognitive therapy. *Behavior Therapy, 44*(2), 180–198. https://doi.org/10.1016/j.beth.2009.08.002

Hayes, S. C., Strosahl, K. D., & Wilson, K. G. (2012). *Acceptance and commitment therapy: The process and practice of mindful change*. 2nd ed. Guilford Press.

Huey Jr., S. J., Tilley, J. L., Jones, E. O., & Smith, C. A. (2014). The contribution of cultural competence to evidence-based care for ethnically diverse populations. *Annual Review of Clinical Psychology, 10*, 305–338. https://doi.org/10.1146/annurev-clinpsy-032813-153729

Jankowski, K. (2013). *PTSD and physical health*. U.S. Department of Veterans Affairs, National Center for PTSD. www.ptsd.va.gov/professional/pages/ptsd-physical-health.asp

Jankowski, M. K., Schifferdecker, K. E., Butcher, R. L., Foster-Johnson, L., & Barnett, E. R. (2019). Effectiveness of a trauma-informed care initiative in a state child welfare system: a randomized study. *Child Maltreatment, 24*(1), 86–97. https://doi.org/10.1177/1077559518796336

Javanbakht, A. (2022 March 11). Psychological wounds from Russian invasion. *Scientific American*. https://www.scientificamerican.com/article/

ukrainians-face-lasting-psychological-wounds-from-russian-invasion1/#:~:text=Another%20 study%20in%202019%20foundChildren%20are%20specifically%20vulnerable

Jimenez, D. E., Cook, B., Bartels, S. J., & Alegría, M. (2013). Disparities in mental health service use of racial and ethnic minority elderly adults. *Journal of the American Geriatrics Society*, 61(1), 18–25. https://doi.org/10.1111/jgs.12063

Juarez, P., Walters, S. T., Daugherty, M., & Radi, C. (2006). A randomized trial of motivational interviewing and feedback with heavy drinking college students. *Journal of Drug Education*, 36(3), 233–246. https://doi.org/10.2190/753N-8242-727T-G63L

Kadden, R. M., Litt, M. D., & Cooney, N. L. (1994). Matching alcoholics to coping skills or interactional therapies: Role of intervening variables. *Annals of the New York Academy of Sciences*, 708(1), 218–29. https://doi.org/10.1111/j.1749-6632.1994.tb24715.x

Kaiser Family Foundation (KFF). (n.d.). *Adults reporting symptoms of anxiety or depressive disorder during the COVID-19 pandemic by sex*. Phase 3.5: 6/1/2022–6/13/2022. KFF analysis of the U.S. Census Bureau Household Pulse Survey, 2020–2022. https://www.kff.org/other/state-indicator/adults-reporting-symptoms-of-anxiety-or-depressive-disorder-during-the-covid-19-pandemic-by-sex/?currentTimeframe=0&sortModel=%7B%22colId%22:%22Location%22%22sort%22:%22asc%22%7D

Kelly, J. F., & Yeterian, J. D. (2011). The role of mutual-help groups in extending the framework of treatment. *Alcohol Research and Health*, 33(4), 350–355. https://www.researchgate.net/profile/John-Kelly-67/publication/236196522_The_Role_of_Mutual-Help_Groups_in_Extending_the_Framework_of_Treatment/links/0deec53443fa6a665f000000/The-Role-of-Mutual-Help-Groups-in-Extending-the-Framework-of-Treatment.pdf

Kimber, M., Barac, R., & Barwick, M. (2019). Monitoring fidelity to an evidence-based treatment: Practitioner perspectives. *Clinical Social Work Journal*, 47(2), 207–221. https://doi.org/10.1007/s10615-017-0639-0

Kimerling, R., Weitlauf, J. C., & Street, A. E. (2021). Gender issues in PTSD. In M. J. Friedman, P. P. Schnurr, & T. M. Keane (Eds.), *Handbook of PTSD: Science and practice* (pp. 229–245). The Guilford Press.

Koenen, K. C., Ratanatharathorn, A., Ng, L., McLaughlin, K. A., Bromet, E. J., Stein, D. J., ... & Kessler, R. (2017). Posttraumatic stress disorder in the world mental health surveys. *Psychological Medicine*, 47(13), 2260–2274. https://doi.org/10.1017/s0033291717000708

Larsen, J. T., Berntson, G. G., Poehlmann, K. M., Ito, T. A., & Cacioppo, J. T. (2008). The psychophysiology of emotion. In M. Lewis, J. M. Haviland-Jones, & L. F. Barrett (Eds.), *Handbook of emotions* (pp. 180–195). The Guilford Press.

Leahy, R. (1996). *Cognitive therapy: Basic principles and applications*. Jason Aronson.

Leake, G. J., & King, A. S. (1977). Effect of counselor expectations on alcoholic recovery. *Alcohol Health & Research World*, 1(3), 16–22. https://findings.org.uk/PHP/dl.php?f=Leake_GJ_1.txt

Lecrubier, Y. (2004). Posttraumatic stress disorder in primary care: A hidden diagnosis. *Journal of Clinical Psychiatry*, 65(Suppl. 1), 49–54. https://www.psychiatrist.com/wp-content/uploads/2021/02/16152_posttraumatic-stress-disorder-primary-care-hidden.pdf

Linehan, M. M., Schmidt, H., Dimeff, L. A., Craft, J. C., Kanter, J., & Comtois, K. A. (1999). Dialectical behavior therapy for patients with borderline personality disorder and drug-dependence. *American Journal on Addictions*, 8(4), 279–292. https://static1.squarespace.com/static/52b2081ae4b09f7904df9d89/t/5d80eda5279c20351eb3efd2/1568730533215/Linehan_et_al-1999-The_American_Journal_on_Addictions.pdf

Livingston, N. A., Berke, D., Scholl, J., Ruben, M., & Shipherd, J. C. (2020). Addressing diversity in PTSD treatment: Clinical considerations and guidance for the treatment of PTSD in LGBTQ populations. *Current Treatment Options in Psychiatry*, 7, 53–69. https://doi.org/10.1007/s40501-020-00204-0

Longabaugh, R., Zweben, A., LoCastro, J. S., & Miller, W. (2005). Origins, issues and options in the development of the combined behavioral intervention. *Journal of Studies on Alcohol (Suppl. 15)*, 179-187. https://doi.org/10.15288/jsas.2005.s15.179

López, S. R., & Guarnaccia, P. J. (2005). Cultural dimensions of psychopathology: The social world's impact on mental illness. In J. E. Maddux & B. A. Winstead (Eds.), *Psychopathology: Foundations for a contemporary understanding* (pp. 19-37). Lawrence Erlbaum Associates Publishers.

Magill, M., & Ray, L. A. (2009). Cognitive-behavioral treatment with adult alcohol and illicit drug users: A meta-analysis of randomized controlled trials. *Journal of Studies on Alcohol and Drugs*, 70(4), 516-527. https://doi.org/10.15288/jsad.2009.70.516

María-Ríos, C. E., & Morrow, J. D. (2020). Mechanisms of shared vulnerability to post-traumatic stress disorder and substance use disorders. *Frontiers in Behavioral Neuroscience*, 14, 6. https://doi.org/10.3389/fnbeh.2020.00006

Marlatt, G. A. (1996). Taxonomy of high-risk situations for alcohol relapse: Evolution and development of a cognitive-behavioral model. *Addiction*, 91(12s1), 37-49. https://doi.org/10.1046/j.1360-0443.91.12s1.15.x

Marlatt, G. A., & Gordon, J. R. (1985). *Relapse prevention: Maintenance strategies in the treatment of addictive behaviors*. Guilford Press.

Marmot, M., & Wilkinson, R. (2005). *Social determinants of health*. OUP Oxford.

Martino, S. (2010). Strategies for training counselors in evidence-based treatments. *Addiction Science and Clinical Practice*, 5(2), 30-39. https://www.ncbi.nlm.nih.gov/pmc/articles/PMC3120122

Meichenbaum, D. (2007). Stress inoculation training: A preventative and treatment approach. In P. M. Lehrer, R. L. Woolfolk, & W. E. Sime (Eds.), *Principles and practice of stress management*, 3rd ed. pp. 497-516). Guilford Press.

Michaels, T. I., Stone, E., Singal, S., Novakovic, V., Barkin, R. L., & Barkin, S. (2021). Brain reward circuitry: The overlapping neurobiology of trauma and substance use disorders. *World Journal of Psychiatry*, 11(6), 222-231. https://doi.org/10.5498/wjp.v11.i6.222. PMID: 34168969; PMCID: PMC8209534

Miller, G. A. (2003). The cognitive revolution: A historical perspective. *Trends in Cognitive Sciences* 7(3), 141-144. https://doi.org/10.1016/s1364-6613(03)00029-9. PMID: 12639696

Miller, W. R., Benefield, R. G., & Tonigan, J. S. (1993). Enhancing motivation for change in problem drinking: A controlled comparison of two therapist styles. *Journal of Consulting and Clinical Psychology*, 61(3), 455-461. https://doi.org/10.1037/0022-006X.61.3.455

Miller, W. R., & Carroll, K. M. (Eds.) (2006). *Rethinking substance abuse: What the science shows, and what we should do about it*. Guilford Press.

Miller, W. R., Forcehimes, A. A., & Zweben, A. (2011). *Treating addiction: A guide for professionals* (2nd ed.) The Guilford Press.

Miller, W. R., & Rollnick, S. (2012). *Motivational interviewing: Helping people change*, 3rd ed. Guilford Press.

Miller, W. R., Yahne, C., Moyers, T., Martinez, J., & Pirritano, M. (2004). A randomized trial of methods to help clinicians learn motivational interviewing. *Journal of Consulting and Clinical Psychology*, 72(6), 1050-1062. https://doi.org/10.1037/0022-006X.72.6.1050

Monti, P. M., Abrams, D. B., Kadden, R. M., & Cooney, N. L. (1989). *Treating alcohol dependence: A coping skills training guide*. Guilford Press.

Monti, P. M., Kaden, R., Rohsenow, D. J., Cooney, N., & Abrams, D. (2002). *Treating alcohol dependence: A coping skills training guide*, 2nd ed. Guilford Press.

Moyers, T. B., & Huck, J. (2011). Combining motivational interviewing with cognitive-behavioral treatments for substance abuse: Lessons from the COMBINE Research Project. *Cognitive and Behavioral Practice*, 18(1), 38-45. https://doi.org/10.1016/j.cbpra.2009.09.005

Nakash, O., & Saguy, T. (2015). Social identities of clients and therapists during the mental health intake predict diagnostic accuracy. *Social Psychological and Personality Science*, *6*(6), 710–717. https://doi.org/10.1177/1948550615576003

O'Farrell, T. J., & Fals-Stewart, W. (2006). *Behavioral couples therapy for alcoholism and drug abuse*. Guilford Press.

Oliffe, J. L., Rossnagel, E., Seidler, Z. E., Kealy, D., Ogrodniczuk, J. S., & Rice, S. M. (2019). Men's depression and suicide. *Current Psychiatry Reports*, *21*(10), 103. https://doi.org/10.1007/s11920-019-1088-y

Pohar, R., & Argáez, C. (2017). *Acceptance and commitment therapy for post-traumatic stress disorder, anxiety, and depression: A review of clinical effectiveness*. Canadian Agency for Drugs and Technologies in Health.

Prins, A., Bovin, M. J., Smolenski, D. J., Marx, B. P., Kimerling, R., Jenkins-Guarnieri, M. A., Kaloupek, D. G., Schnurr, P. P., Kaiser, A. P., Leyva, Y. E., & Tiet, Q. Q. (2016). The primary care PTSD screen for DSM-5 (PC-PTSD-5): Development and evaluation within a veteran primary care sample. *Journal of General Internal Medicine*, *31*(10), 1206–1211. https://doi.org/10.1007/s11606-016-3703-5. Epub 2016 May 11. PMID: 27170304; PMCID: PMC5023594

Prochaska, J., & DiClemente, C. (1998). Toward a comprehensive, transtheoretical model of change. In W. Miller & N. Heather (Eds.). *Treating addictive behaviors* (pp. 3–24). Plenum Press.

Regier, D. A., Farmer, M. E., Rae, D. S., Locke, B. Z., Keith, S. J., Judd, L. L., & Goodwin, F. K. (1990). Comorbidity of mental disorders with alcohol and other drug abuse: Results from the Epidemiologic Catchment Area (ECA) Study. *JAMA 264*(19), 2511–2518. https://doi.org/10.1001/jama.1990.03450190043026

Rosenfield, L. (2020). Unraveling cultural countertransference: The experience of Caucasian therapists working with Asian-American adults. *Psychoanalytic Social Work*, *27*(1), 61–82. https://doi.org/10.1080/15228878.2020.1712660

Sampl, S., & Kadden, R., (2001). Motivational enhancement therapy and cognitive behavioral therapy for adolescent cannabis users: Five sessions. *Cannabis youth treatment series. Vol. 1*. Substance Abuse and Mental Health Services Administration. https://eric.ed.gov/?id=ED478681

Schein, J., Houle, C., Urganus, A., Cloutier, M., Patterson-Lomba, O., Wang, Y., ... & Davis, L. L. (2021). Prevalence of post-traumatic stress disorder in the United States: A systematic literature review. *Current Medical Research and Opinion*, *37*(12), 2151–2161. https://doi.org/10.1080/03007995.2021.1978417

Schillinger, D. (2010). *An introduction to effectiveness, dissemination, and implementation research. A resource manual for community engaged research*. Clinical Translational Science Institute, Community Engagement Program, University of California San Francisco. https://citeseerx.ist.psu.edu/document?repid=rep1&type=pdf&doi=0d86bb17660bf0500d459bc279c2c9c8d706b8fa

Schoenwald, S. K., Chapman, J. E., Sheidow, A. J., & Carter, R. E. (2009). Long-term youth criminal outcomes in MST transport: The impact of therapist adherence and organizational climate and structure. *Journal of Clinical Child Adolescent Psychology*, *38*(1), 91–105. https://doi.org/10.1080/15374410802575388

Schoenwald, S., Sheidow, A., & Letourneau, E. (2004). Toward effective quality assurance in evidence-based practice: Links between expert consultation, therapist fidelity, and child outcomes. *Journal of Child and Adolescent Psychology*, *33*, 94–104. https://doi.org/10.1207/S15374424JCCP3301_10

Seedat, M., Van Niekerk, A., Jewkes, R., Suffla, S., & Ratele, K. (2009). Violence and injuries in South Africa: Prioritising an agenda for prevention. *The Lancet*, *374*(9694), 1011–1022. https://doi.org/10.1016/S0140-6736(09)60948-X

Semage, S., Sivayogan, S., Forbes, D., O'Donnell, M., Monaragala, R. M., Lockwood, E., & Dunt, D. (2013). Cross-cultural and factorial validity of PTSD check list—Military version (PCL-M) in Sinhalese language. *European Journal of Psychotraumatology*, *4*(1), 19707. https://doi.org/10.3402/ejpt.v4i0.19707

Shalev, A. Y., Gevonden, M., Ratanatharathorn, A., Laska, E., Van Der Mei, W. F., & Qi, W. (2019). Estimating the risk of PTSD in recent trauma survivors: Results of the International Consortium to Predict PTSD (ICPP). *World Psychiatry, 18*(1), 77–87. https://doi.org/10.1002/wps.20608

Sue, D. W., Arredondo, P., & McDavis, R. J. (1992). Multicultural counseling competencies and standards: A call to the profession. *Journal of Counseling & Development, 70*(4), 477–486. https://doi.org/10.1002/j.1556-6676.1992.tb01642.x

Tyndal, T., Zhang, I., & Jobes, D. A. (2022). The Collaborative Assessment and Management of Suicidality (CAMS) stabilization plan for working with patients with suicide risk. *Psychotherapy, 59*(2), 143–149. https://doi.org/10.1037/pst0000378

U.S. Department of Health and Human Services (HHS), National Institute of Mental Health (NIMH). (1999). *Mental health: A report of the Surgeon General.* https://profiles.nlm.nih.gov/spotlight/nn/catalog/nlm:nlmuid-101584932X120-doc

U.S. Department of Veterans Affairs (VA), National Center for PTSD (NCPTSD). (n.d.). *How common is PTSD in adults?* www.ptsd.va.gov/understand/common/common_adults.asp#:~:text=About%205%20out%20of%20everysome%20point%20in%20their%20life

VA, NCPTSD. (n.d.). *How common is PTSD in veterans?* www.ptsd.va.gov/understand/common/common_veterans.asp

VA, NCPTSD. (2021). Posttraumatic stress disorder and racial trauma. *PTSD Research Quarterly, 32*(1). www.ptsd.va.gov/publications/rq_docs/V32N1.pdf

Valentine, S. E., Livingston, N. A., Salomaa, A. C., & Shiperd, J. C. (n.d.). *Trauma, discrimination and PTSD among LGBTQ+ people.* VA, NCPTSD. www.ptsd.va.gov/professional/treat/specific/trauma_discrimination_lgbtq.asp

Webb, C., DeRubeis, R., & Barber, J. (2010). Therapist adherence/competence and treatment outcome: A meta-analytic review. *Journal of Consulting and Clinical Psychology, 78*(2), 200–211. https://doi.org/10.1037/a0018912

Wilkins, K. C., Lang, A. J., & Norman, S. B. (2011). Synthesis of the psychometric properties of the PTSD Checklist (PCL) military, civilian, and specific versions. *Depression and Anxiety, 28*(7), 596–606. https://doi.org/10.1002/da.20837

Williams, M. T., Printz, D., Ching, T., & Wetterneck, C. T. (2018). Assessing PTSD in ethnic and racial minorities: Trauma and racial trauma. *Directions in Psychiatry, 38*(3), 179–196. https://www.researchgate.net/publication/328056753_Assessing_PTSD_in_ethnic_and_racial_minorities_Trauma_and_racial_trauma

Wilson, S. J., & Lipsey, M. W. (2005). *The effectiveness of school-based violence prevention programs for reducing disruptive and aggressive behavior.* https://www.ojp.gov/pdffiles1/nij/grants/211376.pdf

Wiltsey Stirman, S. (2022). Implementing evidence-based mental-health treatments: Attending to training, fidelity, adaptation, and context. *Current Directions in Psychological Science, 31*(5), 436–442. https://doi.org/10.1177/09637214221109601

Witkiewitz, K., Marlatt, G. A., & Walker, D. (2005). Mindfulness-based relapse prevention for alcohol and substance use disorders. *Journal of Cognitive Psychotherapy, 19*(3), 211–228. https://doi.org/10.1891/jcop.2005.19.3.211

Witkiewitz, K., Marlatt, G. A., & Walker, D. (2005). Mindfulness-based relapse prevention for alcohol and substance use disorders. *Journal of Cognitive Psychotherapy, 19*(3), 211–228. https://doi.org/10.1891/jcop.2005.19.3.211

Yaffe, K., Vittinghoff, E., Dublin, S., et al. (2024) Effect of Personalized Risk-Reduction Strategies on Cognition and Dementia Risk Profile Among Older Adults: The SMART Randomized Clinical Trial. *JAMA Intern Med., 184*(1), 54–62. doi:10.1001/jamainternmed.2023.6279

Index

Note: Page numbers in *italic* and **bold** refers to figures and tables, respectively.

20/20/20 rule   29, 280, 286

a

acamprosate   238
"action steps"   45
adherence   279
   clinical supervision techniques   282
   structured supervision model   **283–283**
   tools and techniques   281
Adherence and Competence Checklist Protocol   281, 282, 286, **288**
Adult Children of Alcoholics   250
affiliative activities   154
affirmations   8, 30, 36
aggressive communication   75, **81**
agitation   243
Alcoholics Anonymous (AA)   20, 250
   12 steps of   251
   12 traditions of   251
   meeting   250
alcohol use disorder (AUD)   18, 238–240
alprazolam   241
ambivalence of patients   5, 6, 10, 173
   about behavior change   10, 11
   resolving   7–10, 60, 234
   toward change   6
amplified reflection   9
anger   17, 47, 54, 107, 144, 165, 209
Antabuse. *See* disulfiram

antianxiety medications   241
antidepressants   241
   medications   274
   side effects   242
   types of   242
   work on neurotransmitters   243
anxiety   25, 47, 53, 99, 127, 155
   beta blockers control physical symptoms of anxiety   241
   CBT interventions triggering   15
   clinical interventions   **19**
   CODs   230
   COVID pandemic impact   18
   GAD-7 screen for   230
   interpersonal skills training for people with   17
   medications to treat   241–242
   meditation for people with   214–215
   MET for   4
   practice of mindfulness for people with   208
   self-awareness to people with   55
   skills-building approach for   16
   skills deficits associated with   15
   social support for people with   18
   SUDs in people with   18
approach emotions. *See* positive emotions
assertive communication   30, 71, 75–78, 82, 85
Ativan. *See* lorazepam

Integrated Motivational Interviewing and Cognitive Behavioral Therapy (ICBT): A Practitioners Guide,
First Edition. Joseph Hyde, Maria Torres, Win Turner, and R. Lyle Cooper.
© 2024 John Wiley & Sons, Inc. Published 2024 by John Wiley & Sons, Inc.

a

automatic thoughts   120, 126, 139, 145, 160, 162, 195
autonomy of patients   7, 10, 229, 247
avoidance   131
awareness raising   13, 31, 55, 60, 62–63
Awareness Record   55, 57–58, 61, 172, 203–205, 259
  in between-session challenge   200
  in between-session practice   73
  components   62
  in exploring high-risk situations and triggers   196–197
  form   66
  and review progress   125
  substance use and mood examples   67

b

BASIC framework   282
behavior(al)   62, 128, 129, 154. See also cognitive behavioral therapy (CBT)
  addictive behavior   16
  change talk and   4
  cognitive fusion and   161
  coping   113, 136
  health issues   4, 12
  mood-dependent   89, 99
  nonverbal   60
  responses   62
beliefs   10, 62, 130, 172
  about acceptability and effectiveness   232
  into conscious awareness   55
  elicit examples of   193, 202
  self-limiting   111
  about substances   195
  White supremacist   22
benzodiazepines   241
benzodiazepines, side effects for   242
"best-practice" training model   279
beta blockers   241–242
beta blockers, side effects of   242
between-session challenge   33
  negotiation   31–32, 34, 45–46, 63, 78
  preparation   31–32, 63, 78
broaden-and-build model of emotions   154
buprenorphine   234, 237
bupropion   241, 242
Buspar. See buspirone
buspirone   241
buspirone, side effects of   242

c

care management for suicidal patient   221
catastrophizing   **168**
Center for Substance Abuse Treatment (CSAT)   16, 107
Centers for Disease Control and Prevention   220
change:
  elements   5
  through learning and practicing new skills   16
  MI and cognitive behavioral skills building to elicit   3–4
  mindfulness for   209
  patient commitment to   14
  patient experiencing ambivalence toward   6
  patient's readiness to   44–45
  process of   5–6
  stage of   60
Change Plan   45–48, 52, 59–60, 63
change talk   4, 10–14, 55, 178
citalopram   241, 242
Clinical Formulation Interview (CFI)   25
clinical sessions   2, 32, 35
Clinician-Administered PTSD Scale   252
clinicians   14
  expectations   5
  research-proven methods   279
clomipramine   241
Clonazepam   241
Cocaine Anonymous   250
Co-Dependents Anonymous   250
cognitive behavioral therapy (CBT)   1, 3, 14–15, 274. See also integrated cognitive behavioral therapy (ICBT)
  behavioral health issues   4
  emotions in   139
  experience of negative emotional states   155
  functional analysis   55
  practice elements   34
  process skills   34–35
  skills   16–18
  skills-based components   280
cognitive coping   113, 136, 255
cognitive dissonance   10
cognitive fusion   161–162, **168**
Cognitive Fusion That Dampens One's Mood and Restricts Behavior   161, 162, **168**
cognitive processing therapy   254, 274

cognitive restructuring 259
collaboration 7, 11, 13, 36, 42
Collaborative Assessment and Management of Suicidality model (CAMS model) 221
Columbia-Suicide Severity Rating Scale 222, **227**
commitment 32
  strengthening 10–14
  talk 11
  to treatment 49
communication:
  skills 69
  styles 74–76, 81–82
compassion 4, 7
competence 279–281
complex reflections 8–9
confidence, building 10–14
connect session 30
contextual factors of suicide 221
continuing structured supervision 283
conversations with patients 9, 10, 42, 121, 172, 229
  engagement 14, 24, 247
  functional analysis 13
  Life Movie 36, 45, 51
  MI 50–51, 232
  nonjudgmental 37, 173
  uncomfortable 34
co-occurring disorders:
  clinical interventions addressing mental disorders 19
  treament 18–19
coping strategies 197, 200
cravings 47, 54
  automatic thoughts 120
  between-session challenge 125
  clinician preparation 122
  commitment 134
  coping with 136
  demonstration/role play 133
  external situations 130
  internal states 130
  negotiate and prepare between-session challenge 134
  outline and overview 123–124
  patient-led practice/assess skills transfer 133
  protocol with scripts 125–134
  real-world application 133–134

  review progress 125
  session goals 120
  session rationale 125–127
  session skill 127–130
  strategies for coping with triggers 130–133
  strengthen rapport 125
cultural/culture 22
  competency 23
  identity 25–27
  perceptions of cause 25
cultural relevance in clinical practice 22–27
  importance of 22–23
  strategies to improving 23

d

DEA-licensed HCP 237
Decisional Balance 60
Decision-Making Guide 175, 177–178, 181, 187–190
deep-breathing relaxation (DBR) 257–258, **271–272**
demonstration/role play 31, 62
depression 47, 61, 127, 155, 242
  clinical interventions **19**
  CODs 230
  COVID pandemic impact 18
  identifying negative feelings 161
  interpersonal skills training for people with 17
  managing negative moods and 169
  medications to treat 242–243
  meditation for people with 214–215
  MET for 4
  PHQ-9 to screen for 230
  practice of mindfulness for people with 208
  self-awareness to people with 55
  skills-building approach for 16
  skills deficits associated with 15
  social support for people with 18
  SUDs in people with 18
desire to change, ability to change, reasons to change, need for change, commitment, activation, taking steps (DARN-CAT) 10–11
Diagnostic and Statistical Manual of Mental Disorders 5th Edition (DSM-5) 25, 252–253, 273
directing style 4
disappointment 144

discomfort:
  automatic thoughts   120
  between-session challenge   125
  clinician preparation   122
  commitment   134
  coping with   136
  demonstration/role play   133
  external situations   130
  internal states   130
  negotiate and prepare between-session challenge   134
  outline and overview   123–124
  patient-led practice/assess skills transfer   133
  protocol with scripts   125–134
  real-world application   133–134
  review progress   125
  session goals   120
  session rationale   125–127
  session skill   127–130
  strategies for coping with triggers   130–133
  strengthen rapport   125
discord, reducing   7
discrepancy development   7
distraction   54, 131, 215, 219
disulfiram   239–240
double-sided reflection   9
dropping anchor   120–121
Drug Enforcement Administration (DEA)   237
duloxetine   242

e

ecological fallacies   23
ecological inferences   23
embarrassment   144
emotions   154
  clinician preparation   **156**
  clinician's quick reference   164
  cognitive fusion   161–162, **168**
  concept of   159
  in day-to-day life   158
  focus on   165–167
  GAD-7   171
  managing negative moods and depression   169
  negative. *See* negative emotions
  outline and overview   157
  patient's experience of   155
  PHQ-9   170
  pleasant activities   167
  positive. *See* positive emotions
  protocol   158–162
  review   162
  and substance use   165–166
empathy   4, 37
empathy, expressing   7, 43, 59
empowerment of patient   7, 20, 195
engagement conversations   14, 24, 247
engagement with patient   7–10, 30
escape   131
  from negative states   155
  from reality   199
  from situations   144
  suicide and   220
escitalopram   241, 242
evidence-based practices (EBPs)   2, 279
eye movement desensitization and reprocessing   254

f

failure   144, 172
fatigue   47, 54
fear   17, 107, 127, 144, 165, 209
feelings   15–17, 55, 62, 203, 219
  of confidence or efficacy   12
  distressing   127
  elicit examples of   193, 202
  negative   144, 158, 160, 161
  physical   130
  positive   154, 155, 165, 195
  unpleasant   107
fidelity   279
  ICBT with   280
  monitoring form   **289**
  tools   2
fluoxetine   241, 242, 274
following style   4
Food and Drug Administration (FDA)   237, 238
frustration   17, 47, 54
functional analysis   1, 15, 28, 172, 191, 209
  conversations   13
  to raise awareness, identify treatment priorities, and individualize treatment   *14*
  for situational awareness   55

g

Gamblers Anonymous 250
Generalized Anxiety Disorder 7-item Scale (GAD-7) 7, 12, 171, 230
generalized anxiety disorders (GAD) 241
giving advice 9–10
grief 165, 209
guiding style 4
guilt 107

h

handouts 28, 34, 36. *See also* Change Plan; Life Movie
health care provider (HCP) 237
healthy replacement activities 85
   between-session challenge 111
   between-session commitment 101
   clinician preparation 98, 108
   commitment 102, 115
   demonstration/role play 114–115
   negotiate and prepare between-session challenge 115
   outline and overview 99, 109–110
   patient-led practice/assess skills transfer 115
   pleasant activities 105
   problem solving 119
   protocol with scripts 100–102, 111–116
   rationale 97
   real-world application 100–101, 115
   replacement activities 106
   review of progress and between-session challenges 104, 118
   review progress 111
   session goals 97
   session rationale 100, 111–112
   session skill 112–114
   strengthen rapport 111
   supporting recovery through 97
helping interactions, types of 4
higher-order coping strategies 107
hope, loss of 220
humiliation 144
hurt 144

i

identify the problem, state the problem, options, look at the consequences of the choices, vote on the most promising approach, evaluate effectiveness (I-SOLVE) 107, 112–113, 119

imipramine 241
Inderal. *See* Propranolol
individual factors of suicide 221
initial engagement 24
   addressing culture and exploring experiences of discrimination 24
   cultural identity 25–27
   cultural perceptions of cause 25
   differences in understanding or defining problem 25
   domains and sample questions from cultural formulation interview **26**
insomnia 47, 54
integrated cognitive behavioral therapy (ICBT) 13. *See also* cognitive behavioral therapy (CBT)
   CBT process skills 34–35
   Clinician Checklist 281, 283–286
   focus on cognitive restructuring and coping strategies 259
   law of thirds 29–32
   patient activation within context of 20
interpersonal conflict 47, 54
interpersonal skills training 15, 17
irritability 47, 54, 155
isocarboxazid 241

j

joy 26, 97, 127, 165

k

Kaiser Family Foundation (KFF) 18, 220
kindness 4
Klonopin. *See* Clonazepam

l

law of thirds *29*, 29–32, 280
learning assertiveness 69
   between-session challenge 73, 83–84
   clinician preparation 70
   commitment 78
   communication styles 74–76, 81–82
   demonstration/role play 77
   negotiate and prepare between-session practice 78
   outline and overview 71–72
   patient-led practice/assess skills transfer 77
   protocol with scripts 73–78
   real-world application 77

learning assertiveness (cont'd)
   review of progress and between-session challenges 80
   review progress 73
   session goals 69
   session rationale 73–74
   session skill 74
   skill guidelines 76–77
   strengthen rapport 73
Learning New Coping Strategies 46, 53, 178
   first actions 53
   mood and anxiety 53
   new activities 53
   new thoughts 54
   social interactions and environment 54
   specific suggestions for some common, high-risk situations 54
   substance use reduction 53
life decisions:
   clinician preparation **174**
   clinician's quick reference 181
   Decision-Making Guide 187–190
   focuses on 172–173
   MI skills and strategies **182**
   outline and overview 175–176
   patient's experience 173
   protocol 177–179
   Readiness-to-Change Ruler explanation 183
   values exploration 184–185, *186*
Life Movie 12–13, 36, 44
   Change Plan 52
   clinician preparation 38
   contextual understanding for treatment 36
   conversations 36, 45, 51
   domains 43
   MI conversation 50–51
   negotiate between-session challenge 45–46
   outline and overview 39–40
   patient's readiness to change 44
   protocol with scripts 41–47
   rapport 41
   rationale 42
   review progress 41
   review treatment information handout 42
   session goals 36–37
   specific suggestions for addressing common high-risk situations 47
   treatment information sheet 49

lorazepam 241
low energy 47, 54, 161

m

magnifying **168**
male suicide 220–221
Managing Negative Moods and Depression 162
manual-based interventions 282
medication 20
   agonist and partial agonist 234
   clinician preparation **230**
   clinician's quick reference 236
   outline and overview 231
   patient's experience 229
   protocol 232–234
   in support of treatment and recovery 229
   to treat alcohol use disorder 238–240
   to treat anxiety disorders and depression 241–243
   to treat opioid use disorder 237
meditation 17, 208
   clinician preparation 210
   clinician's quick reference 217
   exercise 214, 219
   involving breath 215
   mindfulness meditation instructions 218
   outline and overview 211
   patient's experience 209
   protocol 212
   session and description of 212–213
meetings, structure of 49
mental disorders 161
methadone 234, 237
mindfulness 1, 17, 21, 208
   clinician preparation 210
   clinician's quick reference 217
   exercise 214
   increasing for change 209
   mindfulness meditation instructions 218
   outline and overview 211
   patient's experience 209
   protocol 212
   session and description of 212–213
mindreading **168**
minimizing **168**
"momentary thought-action" repertoire 154
monoamine oxidase inhibitors (MAOIs) 241
mood 53, 100

motivation   5–6
  approaches   3
  building   7–10
  to skills development   16
motivational enhancement therapy (MET)   1, 3–4
motivational interviewing (MI)   1, 3–4, 34
  conversations   50–51, 232
  helping interactions   4
  phases   6–14
  and process of change   5–6
  skills and strategies   **288, 289**
  strategies   8–9, 197

n

naltrexone   237
  injectable   239, 250
  oral   238–239
Narcotics Anonymous (NA)   244
National Center for PTSD (NCPTSD)   252, 253, 274
negative emotions   47, 54, 154, 158
  focus on reducing negative and constricting emotions   161
  link of negative moods and substance use   160
  managing negative moods and depression   169
  reduction of   155
  role of   165–166
nervousness   47, 54
nonjudgmental conversations   37, 173

o

obsessive-compulsive disorder (OCD)   241
open-ended questions   8
opioid treatment programs (OTPs)   237
opioid use disorder (OUD)   237
oral naltrexone   238–239
organizational factors   283
Overeaters Anonymous   250
overgeneralizing   **168**

p

panic disorder   241
paroxetine   241, 242, 274
passive-aggressive communication   75
passive communication   74

patient empowerment through self-knowledge   195–197
Patient Health Questionnaire-2 (PHQ-2)   222
Patient Health Questionnaire-3 (PHQ-3)   222
Patient Health Questionnaire-9 (PHQ-9)   12, 161, 170, 222, **228**, 230
patient(s)
  activation within context of ICBT   20
  expectations   5
  identification   284
  patient-led practice/assess skills transfer   62
  practices   31
  readiness   177–179
personalized reflective discussion (PRD)   11–14, *13*
personalized reflective summary (PRS)   3
personalized session rationale   31
personalizing   **168**
phenelzine   241
pleasant activities   159–160, 167, **167**
positive emotions   154–155, 158
  pleasant activities and developing plan   159–160
  rationale for fostering   159
  role of   165–166
posttraumatic stress disorder (PTSD)   241, 252, 272–274, 273
  clinician preparation   256
  clinician's quick reference   261–263
  combat exposure   254
  deep-breathing relaxation   **271–272**
  diagnosis and symptoms   252–253
  enhancing self-awareness and cognitive restructuring   259
  impairments co-occur with   274
  medical listings cover   274
  patient's experience   254–255
  PC-PTSD   268
  PCL-C   264–265
  PCL-M   266–267
  personalized reflective discussion addressing trauma and substance use   257
  prevalence and types of trauma   253–254
  safety planning, deep breathing relaxation, and psychoeducation   257–258
  sample safety plan   269–270
  SBQ-R   276–278
  treatment types and efficacy   254

practice exercises 49
present-centeredness 21, 208
Primary Care PTSD (PC-PTSD) 252, 268
problem solving 107, 119
prolonged exposure therapy 254, 274
Propranolol 241
psychoeducation 257–258
psychological dependence on substances 199
psychotherapy 274
PTSD Checklist (PCL) 252
PTSD Checklist, Civilian Version (PCL-C) 264–265
PTSD checklist for DSM-5 (PCL-5) 265
PTSD Checklist, Military Version (PCL-M) 265, 266–267

q

Qudexy XR. *See* topiramate
quitting 46

r

Race-Based Traumatic Stress Symptoms Scale 253
racial trauma 253
rapport:
   establishing and strengthening 30
   rapport-building strategies 177
readiness 5, 37
Readiness-to-Change Ruler 177–178, 181, 183, 247
real-world application 31
reason giving 146–147
recovery supports 15, 20
reflections 8, 10
   amplified 9
   complex 8–9
   double-sided 9
   simple 8–9
reframing 9
reinforcement, negative 197
reinforcement, positive 197
rejection 144
relaxation practice exercise 207
replacement therapies 234
resistance 7, 10, 234
   engendered 11
   from patients 9
   rolling with 10, 43
   to treatment 5

ReVia. *See* oral naltrexone
review between-session challenge 30
review progress 30, 33
rolling with resistance 10, 43

s

sadness 107, 127, 144, 209
safety planning 257–258
sample safety plan 269–270
sampling sobriety 46
sampling sobriety period 39, 181
Screening, Brief Intervention, referral to treatment (SBIRT) 222, 254
selective serotonin reuptake inhibitors (SSRIs) 241–243
self-awareness 259
self-awareness of substance use:
   awareness record 203–205
   clinician preparation 192
   clinician's quick reference 202
   enhancing 201
   future self letter 206
   new roads worksheet *198*, 199–200
   outline and overview 193
   patient's experience 191
   protocol 194–200
   relaxation practice exercise 207
self-blame **168**
self-change advice 14
self-comparison **168**
self-efficacy 16, 17, 20, 29, 155, 194, 212
self-help 20
   AA meeting 250–251
   clinician preparation 245
   clinician's quick reference 248
   outline and overview 246
   patient's experience 244
   protocol 247
   twelve-step programs 244
self-image 47, 54
self-talk 54, 132–133
serotonin-norepinephrine reuptake inhibitor (SNRI) 241, 242, 243
sertraline 241, 242, 274
session activities 18–19, 78, 280
session rationale 31, 39, 57, 60–61, 71, 73–74, 87–90, 99, 100, 109, 111–112, 123

session skill(s)   31, 39, 57, 61–62, 71, 74, 109, 112, 123–127
Sex Addicts Anonymous   250
shame   107, 111, 233
simple reflections   8–9
situational awareness   55
  Awareness Record   66–67
  between-session challenge   59–60
  clinician preparation   56
  commitment   63
  lead demonstration/role play   62
  negotiate and prepare between-session challenge   63
  outline and overview   57–58
  patient-led practice/assess skills transfer   62
  planning to feel good   68
  protocol with scripts   59–63
  real-world application   62–63
  review of progress and between-session challenges   65
  review progress   59
  session goals   55
  session rationale   60
  session skill   61–62
  strengthen rapport   59
skills:
  deficits   14, 15
  interpersonal skills training   17
  intrapersonal skills training   17
  motivation to skills development   16
  skills-building approach   16–17
  skills-based CBT   280
  social support   18
skills training   2, 20, 144
  DBR   258
  interpersonal   15, 17
  intrapersonal   15, 17
social atom   95, 95
social determinants of health framework (SDOH framework)   23
social factors of suicide   221
social learning model   16
social phobia   241–242
social pressure   47, 54
Social Security Administration (SSA)   274
social supports   18, 23, 34
  between-session challenge   89
  clinician preparation   86
  commitment   91
  outline and overview   87–88
  patient-led practice/assess skills transfer   91
  protocol with scripts   89–91
  real-world application and negotiate and prepare between-session challenge   91
  review of progress and between-session challenges   93
  review progress   89
  seeking support   96
  session goals   85
  session rationale   89–90
  social atom   95
  social support   94
  strengthen rapport   89
  supporting recovery through enhanced   85, 94
spirit of MI   4, 7, 21, 30, 182, 222, 223, 289
spirituality   20–22, 51
"stages of change" model   5
stress inoculation   154
structured supervision model   **282–283**
Suboxone   238, 239
substance abuse/use   49, 60–61, 155
  clinical interventions   **19**
  emotion and substance use   165–166
  link of negative moods and substance use   160
  using MET/CBT approach for   260–274
  using MI/CBT approach for   252–259
  personalized reflective discussion addressing trauma and   257
  practice of mindfulness for people with   208
  reduction   53
  self-awareness to people with   55
  social support for people with   18
substance use disorder (SUD)   2, 100, 193, 194–195
suicidal behavior   220, 277
suicidal ideation. *See* suicidality
suicidality   220, 222
  addressing   226
  clinical objectives for addressing   222–223
  clinician preparation   224
  Columbia Suicide Severity Rating Scale   **227**
  PHQ-9   **228**
  protocol   225

suicide 220
　care management for suicidal patient 221
　common predictors and levels of suicide risk **222**
　factors for formulating risk stratification 221
　identification and early intervention matters 222
　male 220–221
　patient's experience 220
　PHQ-3 innovation 222
　recommended elements of suicide safety plan 225
　redefining understanding of 221
Suicide Behaviors Questionnaire-revised (SBQ-R) 276–278
summaries 9, 30, 32, 57
sustain talk 4, 10–11

t

tension relief 47, 54
therapy process 49
thoughts 15, 17, 54, 62, 128–129, 139
　about drinking or drug use 130
　automatic 120, 126
　between-session practice 147–148
　clinician preparation 140
　clinician's quick reference 150
　conceptual difficulties 144–145
　distressing 127
　fusion with thoughts 142–144
　gaining distance and perspective on troubling thoughts 153
　naming the brain 146
　outline and overview 141
　patient's experience 139
　problems and values 152
　protocol 142–148
　rapport and review 142
　reason giving 146–147
　skills for thought defusion 145–146
　substance use 151
　thought-stopping 54
timeout 47, 54
Topamax®. *See* topiramate
topiramate 240
tranylcypromine 241

trauma:
　gender and sexual identification/orientation 253–254
　personalized reflective discussion addressing 257
　prevalence and types of 253
　racial 253
　skills-building approach for 16
　social support for people with 18
Trauma Symptoms of Discrimination Scale 253
traumatic stress:
　clinical interventions **19**
　COVID pandemic causes 18
　using MET/CBT approach for 260–274
　using MI/CBT approach for 252–259
Treatment Information Handout 42
treatment information sheet 36, 39, 49
tricyclic antidepressants 241, 243
tricyclics 241, 243
triggers 15, 62, 85, 130, 197, *198*
　exploration 195
　identification 129, 197
　internal or external 71, 109, 114, 125, 255, 259
　personal 196
　for relapse 127
　relationship with effects 199
　strategies for coping with 130–131, 136
Trokendi XR®. *See* topiramate
tyramine 243

u

urges 47, 54, 120
　automatic thoughts 120
　between-session challenge 125
　clinician preparation 122
　commitment 134
　daily record 137
　demonstration/role play 133
　external situations 130
　internal states 130
　negotiate and prepare between-session challenge 134
　outline and overview 123–124
　patient-led practice/assess skills transfer 133
　protocol with scripts 125–134

real-world application   133–134
review progress   125
session goals   120
session rationale   125–127
session skill   127–130
sitting with   131–132
strategies for coping with triggers   130–133
strengthen rapport   125
surfing   120, 138
U.S. Department of Health and Human Services (HHS)   22
U.S. Department of Veterans Affairs (VA)   253, 254, 274

V

values   4, 21, 172, *186*
 exploration   184–185
 values-based clinical practices   1
venlafaxine   241, 242, 274
Vivitrol. *See* naltrexone—injectable

W

withdrawal emotions. *See* negative emotions
workforce factors   283
worksheets   2, 34

X

Xanax. *See* alprazolam